LAND RECLAMATION, SOIL QUALITY AND AGRICULTURE

ENV BOOKS SERIES

LAND RECLAMATION SOIL QUALITY AND AGRICULTURE

Editors

Dr. Pawan Kumar 'Bharti'

Society for Environment, Health, Awareness of Nutrition & Toxicology (SEHAT)
1775, Sohan Ganj, Near Clock Tower
Delhi - 110 007 (India)
E-mail: gurupawanbharti@rediffmail.com

&

Dr. Alka Chauhan

Society for Environment, Health, Awareness of Nutrition & Toxicology (SEHAT)
1775, Sohan Ganj, Near Clock Tower
Delhi - 110 007 (India)

DPH

DISCOVERY PUBLISHING HOUSE PVT. LTD.
INDIA

Published by:
Namit Wasan
DISCOVERY PUBLISHING HOUSE PVT. LTD.
4383/4B, Ansari Road, Darya Ganj
New Delhi-110 002 (India)
Phone : +91-11-23279245, 43596064-65
Fax : +91-11-23253475
E-mail : discoverypublishinghouse@gmail.com
namitwasan9@gmail.com
sales@discoverypublishinggroup.com
web : www.discoverypublishinggroup.com

***First Edition:* 2017**

ISBN: 978-93-5056-882-8

Land Reclamation, Soil Quality and Agriculture

Printed at:
Infinity Imaging Systems
Delhi

ENV Books Series, India

Calls descriptive and error free chapters for upcoming volumes of books on various environmental issues. Send your manuscripts to envbooks@gmail.com

Founding Editor (Editor-in-Chief)

Dr. Pawan Kumar 'Bharti'

Society for Environment, Health, Awareness of Nutrition & Toxicology (SEHAT-India)
1775, Sohanganj, Near Clock Tower, Delhi-7, (India)
E-mail:*gurupawanbharti@rediffmail.com*

Other Important Titles by Editor-in-Chief:

1. **Advances in Biotechnology and Ecological Sciences**
   Bharti, P.K., Chauhan, A. and Ray, J. (eds.)
   (ISBN: 978-93-5056-358-8).
2. **Advances in Agriculture and Ecology**
   Bharti, P.K.; Chauhan, A. and Ezeaku Peter Ikemefuna (eds.)
   (ISBN: 978-93-5056-362-5).
3. **Agriculture and Environmental Biotechnology**
   Bharti, P.K. and Chauhan, A. (eds.)
   (ISBN: 978-93-5056-479-0).
4. **Agriculture Crops and Food Security**
   Bharti, P.K. and Chauhan, Alka (eds.)
   (ISBN: 978-93-5056-881-1).
5. **Agriculture Development and Sustainable Environment**
   Ray, J. and Bharti, P.K. (eds.)
   (ISBN: 978-93-5056-759-3).
6. **Agriculture Ecology and Environment**
   Bharti, P.K. and Olubukola O. Babalola (eds.)
   (ISBN: 978-93-5056-480-6).
7. **Agriculture Ecology, Sustainable Development and Agribusiness Management**
   Mehta Piyush; Sharma Pankaj; and 'Bharti' P.K. (eds.)
   (ISBN: 978-93-5056-851-4).
8. **Agriculture, Environment and Nano-science**
   Bharti, Pawan K. (ed.)
   (ISBN: 978-93-5056-760-5).

9. **Agricultural Practices and Crop Disease Control**
Chauhan Alka and Sharma Anubhuti (eds.)
(ISBN: 978-93-5056-859-0).

10. **Agro-biodiversity: *Conservation and Sustainable Development***
Sharma, Pankaj; Singh, Narayan; and Bharti, P.K. (eds.)
(ISBN: 978-93-505-782-1).

11. **Agro-forestry and Climate Change**
Bharti, Pawan K. and Singh, Narayan (eds.)
(ISBN: 978-93-5056-514-8).

12. **Agro-forestry and Sustainable Agriculture**
Sharma, Pankaj; Bharti, P.K. (eds.)
(ISBN: 978-93-5056-786-9).

13. **Air Pollution and Ecosystem Health**
Swami Abhishek and Bharti, P.K. (eds.)
(ISBN: 978-93-5056-877-4).

14. **Aquaculture and Fisheries Environment**
Gupta, S.K. and Pawan K. Bharti (eds.)
(ISBN: 978-93-5056-408-0).

15. **Aquatic Biodiversity and Pollution**
Bharti, P.K.; Chauhan, A. and Kaoud, H.A.H. (eds.)
(ISBN: 978-93-5056-359-5).

16. **Aquatic Ecology and Biotechnology**
Bharti, P.K. and Zaki, M.S.A. (eds.)
(ISBN: 978-93-5056-451-6).

17. **Aquatic Environment and Toxicology**
Bharti, Pawan K. (ed.)
(ISBN: 978-93-5056-236-9).

18. **Biodiversity, Biotechnology and Environmental Conservation**
Bharti, P.K. and Bhandari, G. (eds.)
(ISBN: 978-93-5056-750-0).

19. **Biodiversity, Biotechnology and Pollution Control**
Bharti, P.K. and Chauhan, Alka (eds.)
(ISBN: 978-93-5056-887-3).

20. **Biodiversity of Aquatic Ecosystem: *Significance, Threat and Conservation* (2013)**
Bharti, P.K. and Kaoud, H.A.H. (eds.)
(ISBN: 978-93-5056-297-0).

21. **Biological Diversity and Ecology**
Arya, M.K.; Bharti, P.K. and Ritesh Joshi (eds.)
(ISBN: 978-93-5056-785-2).

22. **Bioremediation and Microbial Biotechnology**
Gupta, Sandeep; and Bharti, P.K. (eds.)
(ISBN: 978-93-5056-783-8).

23. **Biotechnological Approaches and Water Ecosystem**
Zaki, M.S.A.; and Bharti, P.K. (eds.)
(ISBN: 978-93-5056-779-1).

24. **Biotechnology, Agro-ecology and Environment**
Chauhan, Avnish and Bharti, P.K. (eds.)
(ISBN: 978-93-5056-757-9).

25. **Biotechnology and Environmental Management**
Arya Arun; Maheswari Raaz K., & Bharti, P.K (eds.)
(ISBN: 978-93-5056-862-0).

26. **Clean Technologies and Environmental Protection**
Chauhan, A.; Sharma, S. and Bharti, P.K. (eds.)
(ISBN: 978-93-5056-731-9).

27. **Climate Change and Agriculture**
Bharti, P.K. and Chauhan, Avnish (eds.)
(ISBN: 978-93-5056-148-5).

28. **Climate Change and Biodiversity**
Bharti, P.K. and Chauhan, Avnish (eds.)
(ISBN: 978-93-5056-360-1).

29. **Climate Change, Disaster Management and Environment**
Chauhan, Alka; Bharti, P.K. (eds.)
(ISBN: 978-93-5056-784-5).

30. **Conservation and Cultivation of Medicinal Plants**
Bharti, P.K. and Singh Narayan (eds.)
(ISBN: 978-93-5056-740-1).

31. **Crop Productivity and Plant Disease Management**
Chauhan, Alka; Bharti, P.K. and Sadana, Deepti (eds.)
(ISBN: 978-93-5056-791-3).

32. **Eco-toxicology and Eco-technology**
Bharti, P.K. and Zaki, M. (eds.)
(ISBN: 978-93-5056-313-7).

33. **Environmental Biotechnology and Application**
Bharti, P.K. and Chauhan, Avnish (eds.)
(ISBN: 978-93-5056-262-8).

34. **Environmental Conservation and Biotechnology**
Chauhan, A. and P.K. Bharti (eds.)
(ISBN: 978-93-5056-512-4).

35. **Environmental Health and Problems**
Bharti, P.K. and Gajananda, Kh. (eds.)
(ISBN: 978-93-5056-263-5).

36. **Environmental Pollution and Biodiversity**
Bharti, P.K.; Chauhan, Avnish and Kumar, P. (eds.)
(ISBN: 978-93-5056-149-2).

37. **E-Waste and Environmental Issues**
Bhalla, Resham and Bharti, P.K. (eds.)
(ISBN: 978-93-5056-886-6).

38. **Farming Techniques and Crop Production**
Chauhan Alka; Sharma Anubhuti; Ray Jaswant and 'Bharti' P.K. (eds.)
(ISBN: 978-93-5056-855-2).

39. **Fisheries and Toxicology**
Zaki, M.S.A.; Bharti, P.K. and Chauhan, A. (eds.)
(ISBN: 978-93-5056-452-3).

40. **Fish Habitat and Aquaculture**
Bharti, P.K.; Gupta Kr. Sanjay (eds.)
(ISBN: 978-93-5056-744-9).

41. **Forest and Biodiversity Conservation**
Chauhan Alka; Bharti, P.K. (eds.)
(ISBN: 978-93-5056-873-6).

42. **Food Processing, Management and Nanotechnology**
Chauhan, Avnish; Bharti, P.K. (eds.)
(ISBN: 978-93-5056-796-8).

43. **Freshwater Ecosystem and Xenobiotics**
Bharti, P.K.; Zaki, M. and Chauhan, A. (eds.)
(ISBN: 978-93-5056-299-4).

44. **Geospatial Technology and Water Management**
Chauhan, Alka; Bharti, P.K. (eds.)
(ISBN: 978-93-5056-885-9).

45. **Heavy Metals and Metalloids in Biosphere:** ***Impacts & Assessment***
Chauhan, Avnish, Gupta, Sandeep; and Bharti, P.K. (eds.)
(ISBN: 978-93-5056-860-6).

46. **Limnology and Aquatic Science**
Sharma, S., and Bharti, P.K. (eds.)
(ISBN: 978-93-5056-735-7).

47. **Medicinal and Nutritional Values of Plants**
Chauhan, Alka; Bharti, P.K. (eds.)
(ISBN: 978-93-5056-883-5).

48. **Medicinal Plants:** ***Distribution, Utilization and Significance***
Sharma, P.; Bharti, P.K. and Narayan Singh (eds.)
(ISBN: 978-93-5056-734-0).

49. **Microbial Applications and Environment**
Bharti, Pawan K. (ed.)
(ISBN: 978-93-5056-515-5).

50. **Microbial Ecology and Habitat**
Bharti, Pawan K. (ed.)
(ISBN: 978-93-5056-514-8).

51. **Microbial Environment and Bioremediation**
Chauhan Alka; K. Rathoure Ashok; and K Maheshwari Raaz (eds.)
(ISBN: 978-93-5056-856-9).

52. **Microbiological and Pharmacological Aspects of Biodiversity**
Sharma Pankaj; Sharma Gautam Neha and Sharma Pankaj (eds.)
(ISBN: 978-93-5056-878-1).

53. **Natural Ecosystem and Climate Change**
Bharti, P.K., and Kh. Gajananda (ed.)
(ISBN: 978-93-5056-745-6).

54. **Pest Management and Agro-Techniques**
Biswas, Asim; Bharti, P.K., Chauhan, Avnish (eds.)
(ISBN: 978-93-5056-794-4).

55. **Plant Biotechnology and Industrial Applications**
Chauhan, Alka; Bharti, P.K. (eds.)
(ISBN: 978-93-5056-884-2).

56. **Prakriti me Aushadhi (*in Hindi*)**
Singh, J.R.; Bharti, P.K. and Bharti, B.
(ISBN: 978-93-5056-200-0).

57. **Seed Technology, Plant Growth and Cropping System**
Tyagi, P.K. and Bharti, P.K. (eds.)
(ISBN: 978-93-5056-738-8).

58. **Seed Treatment, Plant Heath and Agro-technology**
Chauhan, A. and Bharti, P.K. (eds.)
(ISBN: 978-93-5056-810-1).

59. **Soil Characteristics and Agro-ecology**
Avnish Chauhan and Bharti, P.K. (eds.)
(ISBN: 978-93-5056-758-6).

60. **Soil Contamination and Conservation**
Ezeaku, P.I. and Bharti, P.K. (eds.)
(ISBN: 978-93-5056-737-1).

61. **Soil Quality and Contamination**
Bharti, P.K. and Chauhan, Avnish (eds.)
(ISBN: 978-93-5056-361-8).

62. **Sustainable Aquaculture Management**
Gupta, S.K.; Bharti, P.K (eds.)
(ISBN: 978-93-5056-797-5).

63. **Waste Disposal and Management**
Bharti, P.K.; Tabassum, B. and Bajaj, P. (eds.)
(ISBN: 978-93-5056-729-6).

64. **Waste Generation and Utilization**
Bajaj Priya; Tabassum, B., and Bharti, P.K. (eds.)
(ISBN: 978-93-5056-792-0).

65. **Waste Management and Environmental Health**
Tabassum, B., Bajaj Priya, and Bharti, P.K. (eds.)
(ISBN: 978-93-5056-777-7).

66. **Water Resources:** ***Mapping Monitoring and Management***
Tyagi, P.K., Chauhan, Avnish and Bharti, P.K. (eds.)
(ISBN: 978-93-5056-861-3).

67. **Water Resources and Agriculture**
Bharti, P.K. and Ezeaku Peter Ikemefuna (eds.)
(ISBN: 978-93-5056-481-3).

68. **Waste Resources Management:** ***Monitoring and Assessment***
Gupta, Sandeep and Bharti, P.K. (eds.)
(ISBN: 978-93-5056-799-9).

Preface

Reclamation of lands with adverse physical properties is aimed at improving soil aeration, as well as increasing its porosity and permeability. To this effect, proper crop rotation practice is introduced, sand is applied to muddy soil and mole drainage is performed which contributes to air and water permeability of deep soil layers.

Reclamation of lands with adverse chemical properties consists in removing harmful salts by leaching, lowering soil acidity by applying lime, raising soil nutrient-supplying power by distributing fertilizers and introduction of proper crop rotation with higher ratio of grass.

Reclamation of lands liable to water and wind erosion generally includes the measures aimed at reducing the quantity and lowering the rate of running down surface water, raising soil resistivity to erosion and dispersion. These measures based on using a wide set of re-afforesting, agro-technical, and hydro-technical means.

Under current conditions, in the majority of the areas subject to reclamation works, usually not one but several of the above-considered reclamation types are carried out depending on a combination of natural and economic conditions.

The present book updates the subject content of land reclamation, soil quality degradation and improvement, wasteland restoration and different problems in agriculture soils.

Thanks are due to publisher and contributors from various institutions and universities. The book will be helpful for the researchers, academia working in the field of land reclamation, soil quality degradation and improvement, wasteland restoration and different problems in agriculture soils.

Editors
(envbooks@gmail.com)

Contents

Introduction

Land reclamation, usually known as reclamation, and also known as land fill (not to be confused with a landfill), is the process of creating new land from ocean, riverbeds, or lake beds. The land reclaimed is known as reclamation ground or land fill.

Land reclamation is a specific technologic way to maintain favorable conditions of lands, natural resource that is critical for agriculture.

Land reclamation implies radical change of lands in the result of set of measures. Among various land reclamation forms, irrigation and drainage are the most common.

Land clearance operations (brushwood clearing, leveling of mole hills, etc.), chemical reclamation (liming and gypsuming of soils), silvicultural reclamation, stabilization of loose sands, water and wind erosion control, etc.

Land reclamation contributes to the maintenance and improvement of soil fertility, growth of crop capacity, rise of farming sustainability, mitigation of the effect of climate and weather fluctuations on production capacity. The scale of land reclamation expands; however, at the current stage the main focus is on enhancing its efficiency.

Three key land reclamation objectives are discerned as follows:

- Improvement of the lands that are under adverse water regime conditions manifested in either excess moisture or its shortage as compared to the quantity that is deemed sufficient for efficient use of the area for economic purposes;
- Improvement of the lands that are under adverse physical and chemical properties of soil (heavy clay and muddy soils, saline, with higher acidity, etc.);
- Improvement of the lands that are liable to damaging physical impacts, i.e. water and wind erosion consisting in the formation of ravines, development of landslides, soil scattering and so on.

Depending on a concrete purpose, different types of reclamation are employed.The reclamation oriented to remove excessive moisture from an area is called drainage reclamation. It is used, in addition to agriculture, in public utility, industrial, and road construction, peat extraction, when carrying out curative measures on swamp areas, and other land development activities.

The reclamation intended to eliminate water shortage in the soil of agricultural fields is referred to as irrigation.

Reclamation of lands with adverse physical properties is aimed at improving soil aeration, as well as increasing its porosity and permeability. To this effect, proper crop rotation practice is introduced, sand is applied to muddy soil, and mole drainage is performed which contributes to air and water permeability of deep soil layers.

Reclamation of lands with adverse chemical properties consists in removing harmful salts by leaching, lowering soil acidity by applying lime, raising soil nutrient-supplying power by distributing fertilizers, and introduction of proper crop rotation with higher ratio of grass.

Reclamation of lands liable to water and wind erosion generally includes the measures aimed at reducing the quantity and lowering the rate of running down surface water, raising soil resistivity to erosion and dispersion. These measures based on using a wide set of reafforesting, agrotechnical, and hydrotechnical means.

Under current conditions, in the majority of the areas subject to reclamation works, usually not one but several of the above-considered reclamation types are carried out depending on a combination of natural and economic conditions.

For example, forest belts are planted, crop rotation is introduced on irrigated fields, fertilizers are applied, and leaching of saline land plots, etc. is carried out simultaneously with irrigation of the territory. All this, especially at large scale of reclamation construction in our country, makes land reclamation one of the major anthropogenic factors of transformation of nature as a whole and hydrological regime in particular.

Land reclamation is performed with the view of improving soil productivity and keeping viable farming, as well as ensuring guaranteed agricultural production based on maintaining and improving land fertility, as well as creating necessary conditions for drawing of unused and low-yield lands into agricultural production, formation of rational pattern of lands, integrated forest management and conservation, reproduction, and efficient use of natural resources.

Land reclamation measures make the soil, hydrologic, and other natural conditions of vast regions more suitable for human economic activity. They help create the water, air, temperature, and nutrient conditions in the soil and the moisture, temperature, and air circulation conditions in the bottom layer of the atmosphere that are favorable to useful flora and fauna. Land reclamation promotes healthful conditions and improves the environment.

Because it gives greater stability to gross harvests and to agriculture in general, land reclamation is very important to this branch of the national economy. It makes it possible to use land resources more productively. Like mechanization and the introduction of chemicals, it is an important factor in increasing agricultural production and promoting scientific and technological progress in agriculture. It opens broad opportunities for increasing yields, establishing a stable feed base for animal husbandry, and bringing desert and swampy lands into use. The technical level of land reclamation is determined by the character of production relations, the level of development of the country's productive forces, the zonal conditions of different territories, and economic goals.

Classification of lands and types of reclamation. The most common type of land reclamation involves land with unfavorable water conditions. In swamps and excessively wet lands reclamation is aimed at increasing aeration of the soil, improving its temperature, and stimulating the aerobic decay of organic matter. These goals are achieved by draining the land—that is, by removing excess water from the soil cover by means of ditches or pipes that run into streams or other bodies of water. In arid farming regions where there is little precipitation and the rate of evaporation is high, reserves of soil moisture are supplemented by water brought to the fields by artificial means (irrigation ditches or pipes). In deserts, semideserts, and steppes where animal husbandry has developed, pastures are flooded. In many cases this technique is combined with selective oasis irrigation (in deserts, for example). Where there is little water, management of water resources is improved by seasonal and long-term regulation of river flows, which may be accomplished by building a reservoir, by changing the flow within a basin, or by excavating a new channel. In places where rivers have insufficient carrying capacity their channels are regulated. Low-lying areas are improved by siltation. The set of measures designed to improve the unfavorable water conditions of a region is referred to as hydromechanical land reclamation.

Land with unfavorable chemical and physical characteristics is improved by agricultural technology and chemical reclamation measures. In steppe and desert regions saline soils and solonetzes containing an excess of salts, which are harmful to most agricultural crops, are improved by leaching, by applying gypsum, and by deep tillage. Chemical reclamation agents such as gypsum, calcium chloride, iron sulfate and sulfuric acid help remove soda, the salt most toxic to agricultural plants, from the soil. Liming increases the fertility of acid soils. On sandy soils large quantities of organic fertilizers are applied, legumes are planted, and clay is spread. Sand is applied to heavy soils. The plowing horizon is made deeper on compacted soils. Uneven surfaces are graded.

The reclamation of lands subject to the harmful mechanical action of wind or water entails preventing the erosion of soils by surface water and wind and combating moving sands, landslides, and gullies. On eroded land, reclamation measures aim at reducing the amount and the speed of surface runoff, increasing the soil's resistance to movement and to water and wind erosion, and establishing obstacles to soil movement and the action of water and wind. Hydraulic engineering methods are applied to achieve these ends. Man-made terraces, water retention ridges, and ditches are built to eliminate soil erosion on slopes, diversion canals are dug along the edges of gullies, hydraulic engineering structures are built to regulate flow and prevent gullying, and shelterbelts are planted.

Characteristics of land reclamation. The duration of its effect distinguishes land reclamation from other measures for improving the land and increasing soil fertility. Consequently, unlike procedures such as autumn tillage, harrowing, and continuous grading of fields, which must be repeated every year, land reclamation is referred to as "fundamental," "long-term," or "major" work. For example, drainage systems ensure the long-term removal of excess water from an area. Irrigation systems are long-term structures that supply the fields with the necessary volume of water and make it possible to water agricultural crops whenever necessary. Agricultural technology and shelterbelts also have a positive effect on the soil and on the natural conditions of the land for a long time.

Land reclamation is most effective when different methods are combined and their use is closely linked with the preparation of virgin lands for agricultural use, the improvement of natural pastures, and farming methods. Taken together, all of these activities constitute an integral set of measures to improve the natural conditions of the land. On land requiring drainage, optimal soil moisture conditions are best ensured by two-way regulation—that is, by systems that remove water during the heavy spring rains and supply water during the dry season, thus providing both drainage and irrigation. Where irrigation is necessary, a collection and drainage network is usually built at the same time as the irrigation network, in order to prevent an excessive rise of the water table and possible salinization of the soil. Drained acid soils are limed. Land reclamation must be combined with the correct development and agricultural use of the land (crop rotation, selection of crops and varieties, and cultivation technology, for example).

Especially in arid regions, the climate may be improved by land reclamation. Owing to the evaporation of moisture from the soil and vegetation, irrigation increases the humidity of the layer of air near the ground. This, in turn, reduces the temperature and mitigates the effect of droughts.

Currently, most reclamation projects encompass tens and hundreds of thousands of hectares (ha). When vast areas such as these are involved, it becomes more important to make a scientifically sound choice of reclamation measures that will not have negative effects on nature and natural resources. For example, if an area's irrigation system is incorrectly designed, the soil may be salinized or eroded, and marshes may develop. Improper drainage may make the land under forests, meadows and other agricultural lands too dry. The creation of reservoirs without regard for groundwater conditions may cause the water table to rise and may result in the development of marshy lands and the deterioration of sanitary conditions. Where the rules of land reclamation are not followed, rivers and bodies of water become polluted, fish die and fishing becomes less profitable. Before a land reclamation plan is drawn up, the area is surveyed. Topo-graphicgeodetic, geological, hydrogeological, soil, geobotanical, climatologic, and other studies are included in the survey. Theories on the biosphere, biological communities, and conservation are of enormous practical importance in planning land reclamation.

Land reclamation requires significant capital expenditures. However, these are repaid in a few years by the increase in the economic fertility of the improved lands—that is, by the rise in their productivity. In the USSR, for example, the yield of cereal crops on irrigated lands is 1.5–2 or more times higher than on nonirrigated lands and the alfalfa yield, 4 5 times greater. Liming increases the yield of grain by an average of 3–4 quintals per ha, potatoes by 15 quintals, and sugar beets by 60. Land reclamation has a favorable effect on the efficiency of agricultural production. The productivity and profitability of agriculture rise, as do output and income per unit of labor input and per ha, owing to intensive crops, increased yield, and repeated plantings. The income from farming irrigated and drained lands is significantly higher than the income from farming unimproved lands.

There is a natural balance within a healthy soil - a balance between the micro-organisms and animals living in the soil, and in the nutrient and water cycles where the soil connects to the wider world, and in the physical structure and chemical makeup of the soil. A soil in balance works as a 'system' with many parts. However soil and land can become damaged environmentally by a number of means. Previous industrial, mining and land-fill activities can damage and pollute the soil - hugely affecting the physical and chemical make-up of the soil. Poor agricultural practices can also reduce the quality of the soil. Once damaged, the 'soil system' cannot work properly and the delicate balance between all the parts that make up the healthy soil become disrupted. One implication could be that animal life in the soil becomes impossible and the complex web of interactions in the soil cease. Imagine a complex motor engine with all its many parts driving forward, damaged by some means and prevented from working. In such cases, the soil system, its habitat and the landscape must be managed to coax the soil motor back into life. This is the role of Land Reclamation and Restoration - literally restoring the functions of soil back into working order.

Habitat restoration is now an important part of nature conservation. Government planning regulations try to encourage restoration by a number of means, such as by making money available to fund restoration of existing damaged sites. It is important that those who undertake such projects understand the way that the soil system works, so that their plans can have the biggest positive effect. For instance when restoring a site, understanding the soil and ecological conditions in nearby surrounding landscapes can help guide the correct course of action. One example could be in choosing which plant types to encourage to enhance biodiversity. Another example could be in developing links between habitats in the landscape, allowing animals to travel between locations.

Together with climate and the influence of other living things, such as animals and particularly humankind, soil conditions can both limit as well as support plant growth and the development of plant communities. For any habitat restoration project to be successful, it is important to understand the existing soil conditions and the kinds of vegetation and habitats these can sustain. Restoration projects should use the existing properties and distribution of soils to guide opportunities for habitat restoration. These properties are the result of centuries, if not millennia, of change caused by forest removal, grazing, cultivation, climate change and environmental pollution.

Land reclamation refers to the process of repairing or restoring disturbed land to a useful state. Land reclamation is an important part of the construction, mining, forestry and agricultural industries, as those industries generally disturb the soil with the use of heavy earthmoving machinery. When land is disturbed, it is sometimes necessary for it to undergo reclamation, not only to help the environment flourish, but so it can be of use once again to these industries.

Land is used for many reasons:

- For the extraction of natural resources, such as in mining
- For the extraction of fruits, vegetables and grains
- For raising livestock
- To build structures and buildings
- To raise animals and grow food
- To harvest trees and plant new ones

Reclamation has been practiced for centuries. Farmers reclaimed land by irrigating regions neglected by rainfall or by draining marshes and wetlands. By the 20th century, several irrigation projects were carried out in the U.S., Pakistan, and the Soviet Union, when it became evident how much damage to the environment could occur if reclamation projects were not initiated.

Types

Land reclamation is important to the health and sustainability of the environment and wildlife. When large regions of land are damaged by machinery or other elements, it results in the inability of vegetation and the wildlife that depends on it, to flourish.

There are various other reasons for land reclamation to occur. In some instances, beaches are in need of restoration. Wind and water erosion can have a dire effect on beach sediment, sometimes requiring alternatives to be sought out to maintain the area.

Land reclamation is also important to the agricultural industry. Farmers often restore wetlands and marshes by draining them. This process converts once-unusable land into farmland that can be used for growing fruits, vegetables and grains and for raising livestock.

In the construction of a series of man-made islands in Dubai, the United Arab Emirates, including the World Islands and the Palm Islands, dredgers were used to pump sand from the seabed in order to formulate more beaches. The project was one of the biggest land reclamation projects in the world.

Similarly, desert land can also be reclaimed and involves providing provisions for water and soil stabilization.

Process

In order to reclaim land, studies must be conducted to understand what soil was like in its original state, including any characteristics it might have, its vegetation and how it has been altered.

Depending on the damage to the soil, it may be necessary to employ irrigation or drainage in order to restore soil that has been damaged through mining, erosion, or earthmoving processes.

One of the biggest contributors to disturbed land is surface mining, which accounts for half of the total land area classified as damaged in the U.S. In surface mining, the top layer of rock, known as overburden, is removed and the lower layers of soil and rock are exposed. The removal of overburden drastically alters the chemical and physical properties that are returned to soil. These properties react badly for seed germination and can kill or prevent plant growth. Without soil cover and vegetation, wind and water erosion can pollute nearby streams with sediment.

Similarly, strip mining for coal also significantly impacts the quality of soil. Because of this, contractors are required to restore the land as per U.S. Surface Mining Control and the Reclamation Act of 1977. This process involves filling in excavations that were made in order to obtain the coal; grading the land to prevent deep slopes; and placing the original topsoil on the graded surface. Some vegetation is planted as well in order to encourage growth. Unfortunately, even when topsoil is replaced, vegetation doesn't always flourish due to sediments having coarse texture and containing fragmented rock. The result is sometimes land that has low fertility.

Other methods of restoring land include the use of fertilizers to change the texture and mineral content of the soil, irrigation, drainage and flood control.

Soil health is the foundation of productive farming practices. Fertile soil provides essential nutrients to plants. Important physical characteristics of soil-like structures and aggregation allow water and air to infiltrate, roots to explore and biota to thrive. Diverse and active biological communities help soil resist physical degradation and cycle nutrients at rates to meet plant needs. Soil health and soil quality are terms used interchangeably to describe soils that are not only fertile but also possess adequate physical and biological properties to "sustain productivity, maintain environmental quality and promote plant and animal health" (Doron 1994).

According to the (USDA) Natural Resource Conservation Service, "Soil quality is how well soil does what we want it to do." In order to grow our crops, we want the soil to hold water and nutrients like a sponge where they are readily available for plant roots to take them up, suppress pests and weeds that may attack our plants, sequester carbon from the atmosphere, and clean the water that flows through it into rivers, lakes and aquifers.

Healthy, high-quality soil has:

- Good soil tilth
- Sufficient depth
- Sufficient, but not excessive, nutrient supply
- Small population of plant pathogens and insect pests
- Good soil drainage
- Large population of beneficial organisms
- Low weed pressure
- No chemicals or toxins that may harm the crop
- Resilience to degradation and unfavorable conditions

As soil managers we can help build soil aggregates by growing green manure cover crops or adding animal manure. Also think about your tillage regime. Over the long term, repeated soil tillage can reduce soil tilth and break down stable soil aggregates. Such soils can be so degraded that they become addicted to tillage and crop establishment requires a soil-loosening operation. If you can reduce your tillage operations, you may reduce the disturbance to the soil biota that are essential for building aggregation. Feeding the soil food web with cover crops or other organic materials also increases the numbers of these organisms. Then bacteria and fungi work to help make aggregation happen.

References

https://www.epa.gov/climate-impacts/climate-impacts-agriculture-and-food-supply

http://www.cawater-info.net/bk/4_e.htm

https://en.wikipedia.org/wiki/Land_reclamation

http://encyclopedia2.thefreedictionary.com/Land+Reclamation

Rozov, L. P. Meliorativnoe pochvovedenie, 2nd ed. Moscow, 1956.

Cherkasov, A. A. Melioratsiia i seVskokhoziaistvennoe vodosnabzhenie, 4th ed. Moscow, 1958.

Kostiakov, A. N. Osnovy melioratsii, 6th ed. Moscow, 1960.

Shumakov, B. A. Oroshenie v zasushlivoi zone Evropeiskoi chasti SSSR. Moscow, 1969.

Shubladze, K. K. Melioratsiia zemel'. Moscow, 1970.

http://www.soil-net.com/dev/page.cfm?pageid=secondary_functions_reclamation & loginas=anon_secondary

http://www.ritchiewiki.com/wiki/index.php/Land_Reclamation#ixzz4MsE6BnLT

http://www.ritchiewiki.com/wiki/index.php/Land_Reclamation

http://extension.psu.edu/business/start-farming/soils-and-soil-management/soil-quality

Land Reclamation, Soil Quality and Agriculture
Edited by: Dr. Pawan Kumar 'Bharti' and Alka Chauhan
ISBN: 978-93-5056-882-8
Edition: 2017
Published by: Discovery Publishing House Pvt. Ltd., New Delhi (India)

1 Degrdation of Total Petroleum Hydrocarbons by Combined Photocatalytic TiO_2 and Biodegradation in Crude Oil Contaminated Soil

[1]Tiwi Aminati and [2]Agus Jatnika Effendi

ABSTRACT

One of continuous environmental problems is hydrocarbon contaminations caused by the activity of petroleum and its products, especially in oil and gas industries. Although many contaminated sites were successfully cleaned up by bioremediation treatments, a number of field reports indicated that biological treatments may sometimes be very slow or incomplete. The lack of bioavailability has been identified as the prominent factors that may inhibit a fast and complete contaminant degradation. The enhancement of chemicals biodegradability and solubility during chemical oxidation gives a presumption to investigate the ability of combinedphotocatalytic TiO_2 under sunlight illumination and biodegradation to overcome the limitation of hydrocarbon bioavailability to indigenous microorganisms and to enhance the rates of hydrocarbon degradation in bioremediation of crude oil contaminated soil using landfarming technique. The experiments used three sandy soils (soil-1, soil-2, and soil-3) with different uniformity coefficient (5.6, 2.6, 3.1) and initial TPH concentration (3.3, 5.2, 2.7%) and were conducted in a 25 cm x 15 cm × 10 cm glass pans microcosms by varying TiO_2 concentration from 0.5, 1, 2, to 3% wt. and two controlreactors: biostimulation and natural attenuation. During the 12-month study, several parameters were analyzed, including the main paramaters: TPH gravimetric, heterotrophic bacteria, petrophilic bacteria, and other parameters, such as pH, temperature, moisture content, organic carbon, total nitrogen, and UV intensity. The results showed that the addition of photocatalyst TiO_2 were adequately significant in enhancing TPH removal rates compared to the addition of nutrient solely in biostimulation. However, the increasing concentration of TiO_2 added to the reactors did not always show proportionality to the increasing of TPH degradation rates. TPH degradation rates were influenced by indigenous

[1] Environmental Engineering Department Faculty of Civil and Environmental Engineering, Institut Teknologi Bandung, Jl Ganesha 10 Bandung 40132

[2] Corresponding address: Jalan Pisangan Baru No. 29 RT.005 RW.013, Kelurahan Pisangan Baru, Kecamatan Matraman, Jakarta, Indonesia 13110

petrophilic bacteria activities and energy derived from UV light, but was not affected bysoil uniformity coefficient. The highest TPH degradation rates in soil-1, soil-2, and soil-3 were given by TiO_2 concentration of 0.5%, 1%, and 2%, respectively.

Keywords: biodegradation, bioremediation, landfarming, photocatalytic TiO_2, TPH

INTRODUCTION

One of continuous environmental problems is hydrocarbon contaminations caused by the activity of petroleum and its products, especially in oil and gas industries. Introduction of hydrocarbon contaminants into the environment may be naturally occurring, as in natural oil seeps, or anthropogenic, as in the case of accidental spills and leakages (Bossert & Compeau, 1995). Both naturally and accidentally occurring oil spills have potentials to contaminate soil. The potentials are likely high in Indonesia due to crude oil exploitations in several areas.

Crude oil contaminated soil affects the environment negatively since hydrocarbon is classified as persistent organic pollutants(POPs) and is able to degrade soils, its ecosystems, and biodiversities. One of biological treatments to clean up the polluted soils is bioremediation, which is widely used for the last several decades (Maletiæ *et al.*, 2013; Fritsche and Hofrichter, 2000; Eweis *et al.*, 1998; Bossert and Compeau, 1995; Crawford & Crawford, 1995). In Indonesia, the application of bioremediation must be done in accordance with *KeputusanMenteri Negara LingkunganHidup No. 128 Tahun 2003*.

Although many contaminated sites were successfully cleaned up by bioremediation treatments, a number of field reports indicated that biological treatments may sometimes be very slow or incomplete. The lack of bioavailability has been identified as the prominent factors that may inhibit a fast and complete contaminant degradation.

Implementation of oxidation technologies in conjunction with biodegradation to destroy contaminants in crude oil contaminated soils has not been widely studied. The enhancement of biodegradability and solubility during chemical oxidation gives a presumption to investigate the ability of combined photocatalytic TiO_2 and biodegradation to overcome the limitation of hydrocarbon bioavailability to indigenous microbes and to enhance TPH removal rates in crude oil contaminated soil bioremediation using landfarming technique.

MATERIALS AND METHODS

A. Soil Sample

The present study used three crude oil contaminated soil samples which had the same sandy texture based on USDA classification.

B. Titanium Dioxide Catalyst

The titanium dioxide catalyst (TiO_2) used was a technical grade powder produced by PT. Brataco. TiO_2 had fulfilled USP NF 19 requirement with 99.76% purity.

C. Soil Amendment

Chemicals were added as soil amendment to increase nutrient concntrations and adjust pH to maintain it in neutral level. The nutrients used were urea (46% N) and TSP fertilizers (21.52% P) while the pH adjustment used lime($Ca(OH)_2$) and dolomite ($CaMg(CO_3)_2$).

D. Experimental Designs in Soil Microcosms

Before experiments started, initial soil characterization for physical, chemical, and biological paramteres and soil preparation were conducted. Soil preparation was initiated by air-drying the soil without subjected it directly to sunlight exposure for several days. The aggregated soils were crushed to improve the drying. The disturbing materials, such as wood branch, stone, and leaves were removed. After being dried, the soils were passed to 2-mm sieves. The retained soils were crushed more and sieved again. Then, the soils were homogenized by mixing them until hydrocarbons were spread evenly within the soils. For each of the three soils, 1000 g were placed into a 25 cm × 15 cm × 10 cm glass pan as landfarming batch reactor. Soil microcosms in the pans were covered to prevent volatilization and contamination, and were kept in room temperature.

To evaluate the efficiency of TPH degradation, three treatments were carried out. The water content was maintained at 40-80% water holding capacity(Sihag *et al.*, 2014). The treatments were as followed:

1. *Natural attenuation*: utilized natural ability of soil to degrade contaminant. There was no nutrient and catalyst applied, but tilling once a week and water adding. This treatment was control reactor.
2. *Biostimulation:* nutrients were added to enhance natural biodegradation. C:N ratio were maintained at optimum condition of 100-300:10(Eweis *et al.*, 1998) during the study. The soils were tilled twice a week to supply oxygen and initial pH were adjusted to optimum range 6-8. This reactor also served as control.
3. *Combined biodegradation and photocatalytic TiO_2:* at the beginning of experiments (T_0), nutrients and varying TiO_2 content from 0, 5, 1, 2, and 3 % wt. were added to each pan. The soils were illuminated under sunlight in sunny days to activate the catalyst. After that, each reactor was covered so that there was no other light penetrated to the pans. The soils were aerated by tilling them two to three times a week to maximize the activation process and contaminants oxidation. Levels of pH and nutrients were also maintained during the experiments.

D. Bioremediation Monitoring

Monitoring throughout the study was conducted to ensure bioremediation performance. The analytical and instrumental methods used are shown in table 1.1. Soil sample was collected compositely in five different points (random sampling) using spatula to reach the bottom part of each reactor.

Tabel 1.1: Analytical and Instrumental Methods for Parameters Monitored

Sl.No.	Parameter	Analytical / Instrumental Methods
1.	Temperature	Termometer
2.	pH	EPA Method 9045D: soil dan waste pH
3.	Water content	SNI 03-1965-1990
4.	Total nitrogen: NO_2–N + NO_3–N + NTK	
	NO_2-N	EPA Method 354.1: Diazotasi Reaction Method – Spektrophotometry
	NO_3-N	EPA Method 352.1: Brusin Method – Spektrophotometry
	Total Nitrogen Kjeldahl = N-organic + NH_3	APHA Method 4500-N_{org}: Macro-Kjeldahl Method
5.	Total phosphorus (P)	APHA Method 4500-P: Stannous Chloride Method
6.	C-organic	Walkley & Black Method
7.	Total Petroleum Hydrocarbon (TPH) - Gravimetric	EPA SW-846 Method 9071B; followed by APHA Method 5520: Hydrocarbon
8.	Heterotrophic bacteria	EPA *Standard Method* 9215B: *Heterotrophic Plate Count* (HPC) or *Total Plate Count* (TPC)
9.	Petrophilic bacteria	Modified EPA *Standard Method* 9215D
10.	UV intensity	UVX Radiometer
11.	TCLP: Pb, As, Ba, Cd, Cr, Cu, Hg, Se, Zn (based on *Kepmen LH 128/2003*)	EPA SW-846 Method 1311: *Toxicity Characteristic Leaching Procedure*
12.	Heavy metals: Pb, As, Ba, Cd, Cr, Cu, Hg, Se, Zn	AAS (*Atomic Absorption Spectrometry*)
13.	Particle size distribution	Sieve analysis
14.	Water-holding capacity (WHC)	Water was added to saturate soil sampels and left for 24 hours until drained. The remained water was measured as WHC

RESULTS AND DISCUSSION

A. Soil Characterization

The hydrocarbon contaminated soils used in the study had initial character as presented in table 1.2. The populations of indigenous heterotrophic and petrophilic bacteria which were less than 10^4 CFU/gram indicated that the consortium were stressed since the environment condition was not favourable for growth and TPH biodegradation. The slightly acidic pH, low water content, and low concentrations of N and P are three possible explanations.

According to table 1.2, it is observed that TPH concentration of soil-2 > soil-1 > soil-3. This indicated that the weathering and ageing process in soil-3 lasted the longest, and followed by soil-1 and soil-2. Other parameter which distinguish the three soils is the value of uniformity coefficient (C_U). Although all the three soils are poorly-graded (Cu < 6), it can be seen that permeability is the highest in soil-2, and followed by soil-3 and soil-1, consecutively, based on its Cu (Onur, 2014). Permeability refers to the ease of water to flow in porous media. The higher the permeability of soil, it can be expected that the higher amount of water will be retained. Therefore, the water-holding capacity of soil decreases.

Table 1.2: Initial Soil Characters

Parameter	Tanah 1	Tanah 2	Tanah 3
Particle size distribution	*Gravel* 3%, *sand* 94%, *silt* 4%	*Sand* 99%, *silt* 1%	*Sand* 95%, *silt* 5%
Uniformity coefficient, Cu	5.567	2.623	3.080
pH	5.37	5.96	4.93
Temperature, °C	26	26.1	25.9
Water holding capacity(%)	26	46	30
Water content (%)	0.64	1.16	1.76
C-organic (mg/kg)	24084.21	31200	34494.02
Total N (mg/kg)	903.83	1042.04	995.36
Total P (mg/kg)	6,62	7,11	5,14
C:N:P ratio	3638:137:1	4388:147:1	6711:194:1
TPH gravimetric (mg/kg)	32529.02	52212.86	2669.95
Heterotrophic bacteria (CFU/g)	36×10^1	13×10^2	45×10^2
Petrophilic bacteria (CFU/g)	49×10^1	11×10^2	95×10^1

B. TPH Degradation in Soil Microcosms

The combination of biodegradation and phocatalytic TiO_2 were applied to degrade hydrocarbons for 12 weeks. The TPH removal for all treatments in soil-1, soil-2, and soil-3 are shown in figure 1.1, figure 1.2, and figure 1.3, consecutively.

The TPH degradation was accomplished primarily during the first week (67% and 59% removal efficiency) in soil-1 with TiO_2 content of 0.5% and 2%. This phenomena indicated that photocatalysis occurred and was continued by TPH utilization. However, weathering and aging had decreased hydrocarbon bioavailability. Therefore, TPH degradation tend to follow flat pattern for other treatments. In soil-2 and soil-3, TPH removal was fluctuated. The possible explanations were uneven contaminant distribution within the soils and ineffective tilling. Another reason might be due to sorption-desorption process in soil matrices which mobilized soils from inaccessible pores to bioaccessible regions, and thus could be extracted and analyzed, and vice versa.

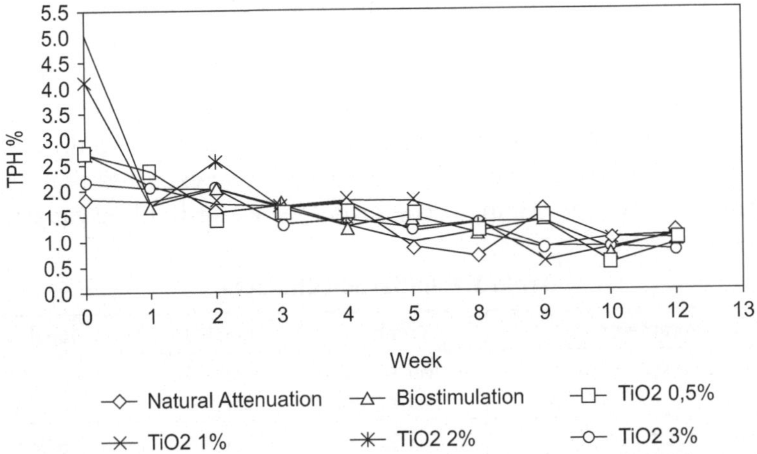

Fig. 1.1: TPH degradation pattern in soil-1

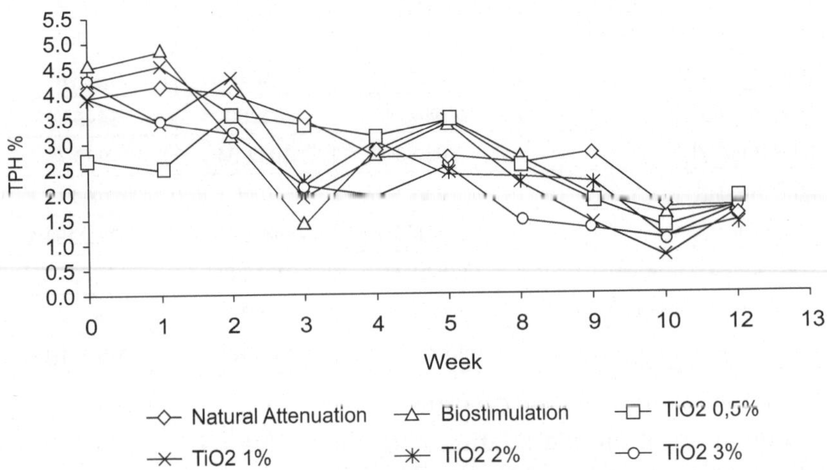

Fig. 1.2: TPH degraddation pattern in soil-2

The final TPH removal efficiencies were 51-77% for soil-1, 45-75% for soil-2, and 40-63% for soil-3. In other words, the TPH removal in soil-1 > soil-2 > soil-3. However, these results did not agree with Sandra (2011). It was stated that hydrocarbon degradation rates in sandy soils increased as the uniformity coefficient decreased.

TPH degradation profiles for the three soils showed photocatalytic reaction occurred during the first few weeks in the study, but the rates slowed down, and then further degradation were dominated by biodegradation by indigenous microbes. The decreasing photoctalytic rates were influenced by relative humidity in which water molecule may compete with contaminant particles to be absorbed to photocatalys surface when the water content is excessive. Another way is the water molecule will form thin film which prevents contaminant to reach TiO_2 surface.

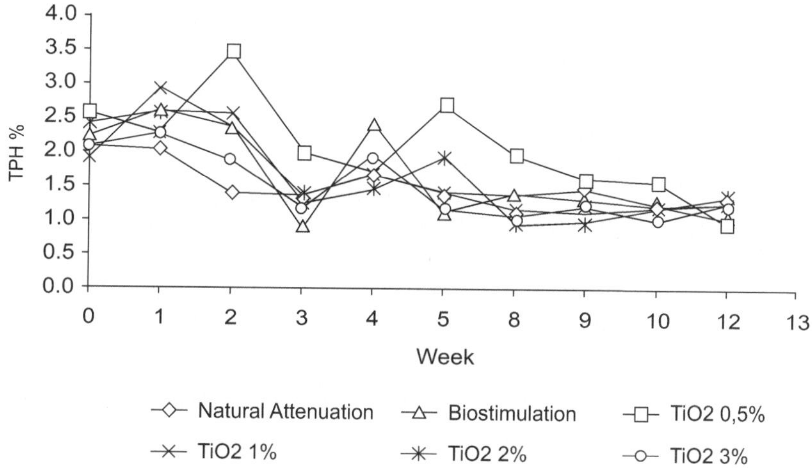

Fig. 1.3: TPH degradation pattern in soil-3

C. Effects of Photocatalyst Concentration

Kinetic modelling was performed to estimate the rates of photocatalysis and biodegradation in the studied systems. The present study showed the experimental results followed pseudo first-order kinetics as also described by other authors (Eweis *et al.*, 1998; Haque *et al.*, 2012; Maletiæ *et al.*, 2013; Ohtani, 2016; Suja, *et al.*, 2014). TPH removal rates *r*, half-life $t_{1/2}$ and R^2 were shown in Table 1.3. The TPH degradation rates, *r* (%.week^{-1}), were 0,06-0,167 (soil-1); 0,052-0,145 (soil-2); and 0,052-0,102 (soil-3). Based on TPH degradation rates, TiO_2 concentration which were more favourable and gave high removal in soil-1, soil-2, and soil-3, were 0,5%, 1%, and 2%, respectively.

Tabel 1.3: The Value ofr (% week^{-1}), R^2, and $t_{1/2}$ (week) of Soil Microcosms

Variasi Perlakuan	Soil-1			Soil-2			Soil-3		
	r	R^2	$t_{1/2}$	*r*	R^2	$t_{1/2}$	*r*	R^2	$t_{1/2}$
Natural attenuation	0,060	0,817	11,6	0,052	0,814	13,3	0,052	0,958	13,3
Biostimulation	0,078	0,832	8,9	0,062	0,818	11,2	0,061	0,819	11,4
Nutrien + TiO_2 0,5 %	0,167	0,817	4,2	0,095	0,913	7,3	0,081	0,848	8,6
Nutrien + TiO_2 1 %	0,084	0,876	8,3	0,145	0,925	4,8	0,096	0,839	7,2
Nutrien + TiO_2 2 %	0,141	0,820	4,9	0,1	0,842	6,9	0,102	0,855	6,8
Nutrien + TiO_2 3 %	0,095	0,873	7,3	0,115	0.927	6,0	0,079	0,872	8,8

From table 1.3, it can be seen that the addition of nutrients solely in biostimulation did not significantly enhance the removal rates of TPH compared to natural attenuation. In the meanwhile, the addition of photocatalyst in all soils for various TiO_2 concentrations were able to enhance TPH removal rates adequately significant and reached as twice as the rates in biostimulation.

It was interesting that the variation of TiO_2 concentration from 0,5 to 3% wt. did not always show proportionality to TPH degradation rates. This fact was not in agreement with Chien *et al.,* (2011). It was found that photocatalytic degradation of organic contaminants were improved as TiO_2 concentration increased, which was likely due to the increasing of active sites for photocatalysis. However, Zhang *et al.,* (2008) showed the same results with the present study. According to Haque *et al.,* (2012), in the beginning, photocatalysis rate was proportional to photocatalyst concentration, yet at a certain level of concentration the rates would decline and became independent of the concentration. The same situation also occurred in soil-3, in which the degradation rates increased until certain TiO_2 concentrations, then dropped.

The possible explanations for insignificant effect of variation TiO_2 concentrations are followed. Low load TiO_2 concentration might had provided enough catalyst surface area to promote TPH degradation, meanwhile at higher loading rates, UV light scattering by catalyst particles attenuated light absorption inside the soil medium. On the other hand, the higher catalyst concentration, the higher its possibilities to form aggregates, especially after watering and tilling. Therefore, in this study, the proportionality of TiO_2 concentration to TPH degradation rate was only valid until particular concentration and might slowed down in higher concentration (Zhang *et al.,* 2008; Osborn, 2010; Hamerski *et al.,* 1999).

D. Correlation of Microbial Populations and TPH Degradation

One parameter which can indicate if biodegradation occurs is the growing soil microbes. The microbial growth shows that the microbes are able to utilize hydrocarbon as energy source and carbon source. Figure 1.4, figure 1.5, and figure 1.6 showed correlation between TPH and microorganisms in soil microcosms at the optimum removal.

In soil-1 and soil-2, bacterial growth increased from week 0 to week 10, and then came down. Meanwhile, in soil-3, bacteria reached its peak in week 8. The growth pattern of petrophilic bacteria in all soils demonstrated the same pattern. The phase lag occurred very rapidly, continued by exponential phase, stationer phase (which also took place very quickly), and followed by death phase. Nutrients adding in the beginning of experiments and routine tilling and water spiking had stimulated the microbial growth. However, the increasing microbial populations should not be directly translated as significant decrease in TPH concentrations. The decreasing of microbial populations during the study were affected by environmental factors, such as pH, nutrient limiting, or the presence of toxic metabolite products which inhibit the growth.

As explained above, the treatment 0,5% TiO_2 in soil-1 gave high TPH removal in the first week despite the fact that petrophilic bacteria just started growing from 10^4 to 10^6 CFU/g. This showed that photocatalysis reactions occurred prominently. As time went by, the catalyst surface became saturated, both by water and contaminant particles. Therefore, the degradation rates were dominated by the ability of bacteria petrophilic consortium. It can be seen from figure 1.4 that there was negative correlation between bacteria populations and TPH.

It was interesting to note that when bacteria population reached its peak in week 12, TPH reduction was not significant. This was due to the lack of contaminant bioavailability and the toxic residues of contaminants after previous degradation were less preferred by bacteria. There was also possibility of cometabolism where bacteria consumed other source of carbon presented in the soils.

The lack of bioavailability might be affected by the weathered soils and, therefore, influences sorption-desorption process. Contaminants molecule might become smaller than bacteria sizes after being attacked by photocatalyst, and thus, were absorbed to inaccessible regions. (Fritsche & Hofrichter, 2000). Finally, the death phase took place since the bacteria could no longer utilize TPH as carbon and energy source.

TPH concentration in soil-2 with 1% TiO_2 was fluctuated, which might be caused by less homogenized tilling process so that sample collecting was less accurate. TPH decreased until week-3 as the bacteria grew. The removal kept continuing from week 5. The graph indicated that TPH could be degraded biologically. The same phenomena as soil-1 also occurred, that was the maximum bacterial growth did not give the highest TPH degradation.

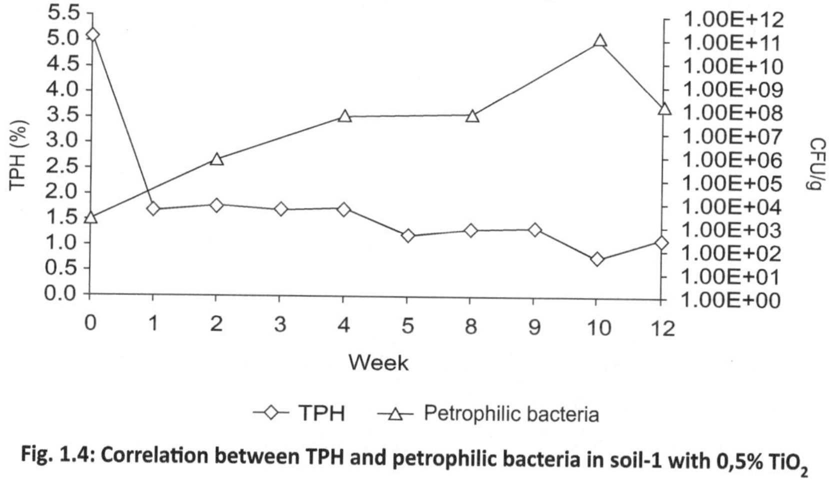

Fig. 1.4: Correlation between TPH and petrophilic bacteria in soil-1 with 0,5% TiO_2

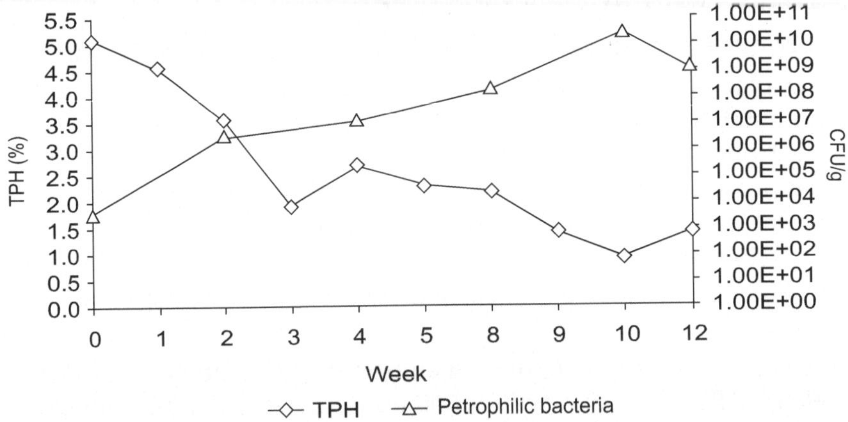

Fig. 1.5: Correlation between TPH and petrophilic bacteria in soil-2 with 1% TiO_2

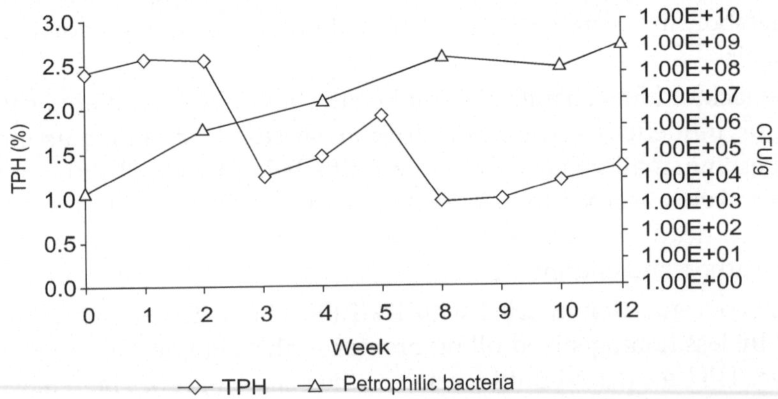

Fig. 1.6: Correlation between TPH and petrophilic bacteria in soil-3 with 2% TiO_2

Fluctuated TPH concentration could also be seen in soil-3 with 2% TiO_2. According to figure 1.5, TPH removal happened twice: started from week 3 and week 8. The first removal was highly likely contributed by combined photocatalytic reaction and biodegradation while the latter was dominated by biodegradation as the petrophilic bacteria reached its peak (~ 10^8 CFU/g).

In general, the results demonstrated the ability of consortium indigenous petrophilic bacteria to degrade TPH (in conjunction with photocatalysis) as indicated by their presence and growth in soil microcosms. Bacteria would form substrate preferential to choose degradation pathways of hydrocarbon.

E. Profile of Soil pH

As a semiconductor, TiO_2 has amphoteric properties. It can be protonated (becomes positively charged) in acidic pH < 6,8 and deprotonated (becomes negatively charged) in alkaline pH > 6,8 (Zhang *et al.*, 2008; Haque *et al.*, 2012). For this reason, pH is one essential parameter which contributes to surface-charge in photocatalysis and can determine reaction occurred in the surface of semiconductor particles (Zhang *et al.*, 1998 dalamZhang *et al.*, 2008). In the combined system, the essence of pH is because it supports the indigenous bacterial growth. The change of pH level during the experiments are shown in figure 1.7.

Soil-1, soil-2, and soil-3 had pH level of 6,5-9,3; 6,5-7,9; and 6,8-8,7, sequencely, for all treatments, except the control reactors. The pH level of each soil is able to support both bacterial growth and degradation, though several treatments have pH more than maximum of optimal range 5,5-8,8 for growth and 6,5-8 for hydrocarbon biodegradation (Sihag *et al.*, 2014). The control reactors had lower pH level (more acidic) since the pH level were not adjusted at the beginning of the experiments.

The change of pH monitored tend to decrease until week 4 or 5, became quite stable, and slightly increase in week 12. Overall, it showed the decreasing pattern. The decreasing pH level during the study indicated the occurring biodegradation by producing carboxylic acid (Bossert & Compeau, 1995) while the increasing pH shoed the slow down biodegradation rates as carboxylic acid were produced less.

The high or low degradation rates in acidic or alkaline pH level can be attributed to the orientation of molecular structure which is more preferable to be attacked by photocatalyst. Based on figure 1.7, the preferential pH level of photocatalytic process of hydrocarbon in the treatments which gave high TPH degradation rates and removal is alkaline (pH > 6,8):

- Soil-1, nutrient + 0,5% TiO_2 treatment: 6,7-8,4;
- Soil-2, nutrient + 0,1% TiO_2 treatment: 6,6-7,9;
- Soil-3, nutrient + 2% TiO_2 treatment: 6,9-8,3.

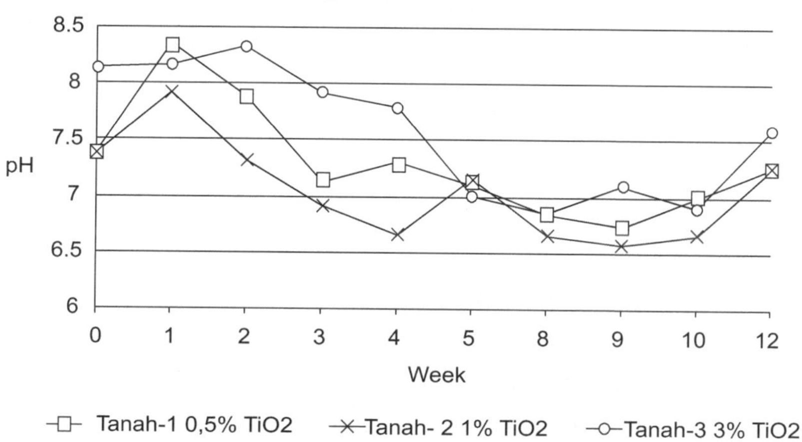

Fig. 1.7: The change of pH level during the experiments

F. Effects of Sunlight Irradiation

In this study, sunlight was used as UV source to activate TiO_2. It was based on the fact that sunlight produces UV-A and UV-B which can reach the earth atmosphere and have λ 400-320 nm and 320-290 nm, consecutively. The effect of UV intensity on TPH removal efficiency is shown in figure 1.8 in which the best concentration of TiO_2 is chosen based on the largest degradation rates, r. The reactors are 0.5% TiO_2 (soil-1), 1% TiO_2 (soil-2), and 2% TiO_2 (soil-3).

It is stated that TiO_2 is activated by the energy of 3.2 eV or at the wavelength < 387 nm with minimal intensity of ~ 1 μW/cm² (Fujishima *et al.*, 2000). Therefore, the sunlight irradiation which had occurred for 12 weeks (24 sunny days) with a total of 72 hours exposure with the average intensity of 109 μW/cm² at λ = 365 nmwas able to activate the titania and it indicated the ocurrance of photocatalytic reaction in soil microcosm.

From figure 1.8, it can be seen that the highest intensity happened in week two, that was 273 μW/cm². The TPH profiles which showed decrement as the UV light was exposed indicated that UV light played important role in activating TiO_2 and thus, enhanced TPH removal. However, UV intensity level at certain wavelength measured did not significantly affect TPH removal because TiO_2 can be activated to produce hydroxyl radical by several photons with enough energy (Jacoby *et al.*, 1996 in Osborn, 2010).

During the experiment, the soil depth might reach around 8 cm. Hamerski *et al.*, (1999) stated that systematic tilling and humidification could distribute the photocatalyst evenly in soil. However, the photocatalytic only took place in the soil surface due to the inability of sunlight to penetrate further to soil depth. Osborn (2010) also added that correlation between UV intensity and degradation rate depend on pollutant chemicals.

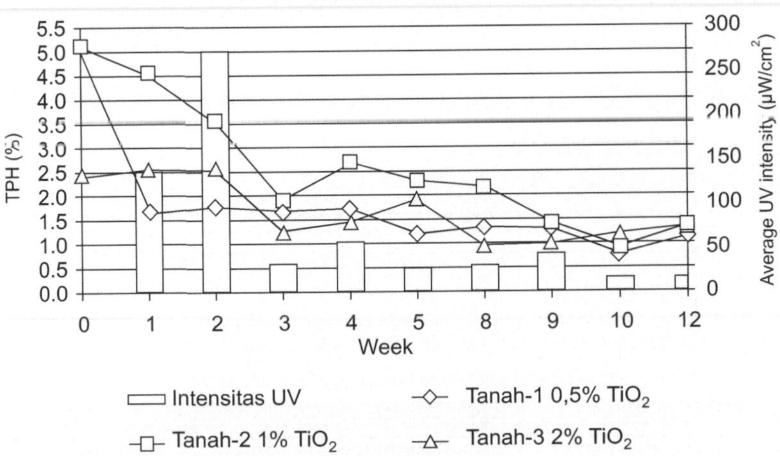

Fig. 1.8: Profile of UV intensity and TPH removal in soil microcosms

CONCLUSION

The present study investigated showed a possibility of combining chemical oxidation (photocatalytic TiO_2 under sunlight irradiation) and biodegradation to improve TPH degradation in crude oil contaminated soil bioremediation using landfarming technique. The results indicated that the addition of photocatalys were able to enhance TPH removal rates compared to biostimulation solely. However, the increasing rates were not always proportional to the increasing variation of TiO_2 concentration from 0.5% to 3% wt. The degradation processes were influenced by the indigenous microbial activity and energy derived from UV light, but was not affected by soil uniformity coefficient. The highest TPH degradation rates in soil-1, soil-2, and soil-3 were given by TiO_2 concentration of 0.5%, 1%, and 2%, respectively.

Based on the research conducted, the application of combined photocatalytic TiO_2 and biodegradation shall pay attention to the soil depth which still be able to be penetrated by sunlight irradiation. Also, for contaminated soil with very low TPH concentrations, it might be necessary to add exogenous bacteria to improve TPH removal.

REFERENCES

Bossert, I. D., & Compeau, G. C. (1995). Cleanup of Petroleum Hydrocarbon Contamination in Soil. In L. Y. Young & C. E. Cerniglia, *Microbial Transformation and Degradation of Toxic Organic Chemicals* (pp. 77-125). New York: Wiley-Liss, Inc.

Chien, S. W., Chang, C. H., Chen, S. H., Wang, M. C., Rao, M. M., & Veni, S. S. (2011). Effect of Sunlight Irradiation on Photocatalytic Pyrene Degradation in Contaminated Soils by Micro-nano Size TiO_2. *Science of the Total Environment*, 4101-4108.

Crawford, D. L., & Crawford, R. L. (1995). *Bioremediation: Principles and Applications.* Cambridge University Press.

Eweis, J. B., Ergas, S. J., Chang, D. P., & Schroeder, E. D. (1998). *Bioremediation Principles* (International Editions ed.). Malaysia: McGraw-Hill Companies, Inc.

Fritsche, W., & Hofrichter, M. (2000). Aerobic Degradation by Microorganisms. In H. -J. Rehm, G. Reed, A. Puhler, & P. Stadler (Eds.), *Biotechnology Environmental Processes II* (Vol. 11b, pp. 146-164). Weinheim: WILEY-VCH.

Hamerski, M., Crzechulska, J., & Morawski, A. W. (1999). Photocatalytic Purification of Soil Contaminated with Oil Using Modified TiO_2 Powders. *Solar Energy*, 395-399.

Haque, M. H., Bahnemann, D., & Muneer, M. (2012). Photocatalytic Degradation of Organic Pollutants: Mechanisms and Kinetics. In T. Puzyn (Ed.), *Organic Pollutants Ten Years After the Stockholm Convention - Environmental and Analytical Update.* InTech.

Maletiæ, S., Dalmacija, B., & Ronèeviæ, S. (2013). Petroleum Hydrocarbon Biodegradability in Soil — Implications for Bioremediation. In V. Kucherov, & A. Kolesnikov (Eds.), *Hydrocarbon.* InTech.

Ohtani, B. (2016). *Photocatalysis A to Z - What We Know and What We Don't Know in A Scientific Sense.* Hokkaido University, Sapporo.

Osborn, D. J. (2010). *Quantification of NOx Reduction via Nitrate Accumulation on A TiO_2 Photocatalytic Concrete Pavement.* Louisiana: Louisiana State University.

Sandra, A. C. (2011). *Effects of Particle Sizes on Bioremediation of Crude Oil Polluted Pusi Soils.* Nsukka: University of Nigeria.

Sihag, S., Pathak, H., & Jaroli, D. P. (2014). Factors Affecting the Rate of Biodegradation of Polyaromatic Hydrocarbons. *International Journal of Pure and Applied Bioscience,* 185-202.

Suja, F., Rahim, F., Taha, M. R., Hambali, N., Razali, M. R., Khalid, A., *et al.,* (2014). Effects of Local Microbial Bioaugmentation and Biostimulation on the Bioremediation of Total Petroleum Hydrocarbon (TPH) in Crude Oil Contaminated Soil Based on Laboratory and Field Observations. *International Biodeterioration & Biodegradation,* 115-122.

Zhang, L., Li, P., Gong, Z., & Li, X. (2008). Photocatalytic Degradation of Polycyclic Aromatic Hydrocarbons on Soil Surfaces using TiO_2 under UV Light. *Journal of Hazardous Materials,* 478-484.

Land Reclamation, Soil Quality and Agriculture
Edited by: Dr. Pawan Kumar 'Bharti' and Alka Chauhan
ISBN: 978-93-5056-882-8
Edition: 2017
Published by: Discovery Publishing House Pvt. Ltd., New Delhi (India)

2 Soil Solarization Technique As a Weed Management Tool

[1]M. Pavithra, [2]Ashoka Reddy Yerva and [3]K. Brindha

INTRODUCTION

Weeds are plants that are objectionable or interfere with the activities or welfare of human. About 30,000 plant species are identified as weeds in the world infesting crop lands, water bodies, wood lands, gardens, orchards, airfield and utility areas. About 300 plants are trouble-some and universally called as weeds. Weeds compete with crop plants for nutrients, moisture, space and sunlight and considerably reduce the yield. Of the total annual loss of agricultural produce from various pests in India, weeds account for 45 per cent, insects 30 per cent, diseases 20 per cent and other pests 5 per cent. Yield losses due to weeds are estimated as 69% in rice, 34% in wheat, 40-50% in pulses, 72% in sugarcane and 80-90% in vegetables. The world food loss due to weeds is estimated to be 287 million tones accounting for 11.5% of the total food production. Also, estimates show that weeds in India cause monetary loss of about Rs. 30,000 crores per annum.

Weed menace in agricultural field is ever increasing in spite of constant efforts to get rid of it. Weeds by their manifold harmful effects on the growing crop plants and interference with land uses, ranked prime enemies in crop production. Dormancy and longevity of weed seeds are natural mechanisms for the perpetuation of weed species on account of which it is impossible to deplete the soil weed seeds completely. There is a tendency to regard weeds as an unavoidable problem in the farming.

Weed control by mechanical and cultural means have some limitations as they are laborious, time consuming and expensive. Besides, these methods are employed only after the crop attained certain stage of growth, by this time the weed would have also grown sufficiently to cause damage to the crop plants by depriving them of nutrients, moisture and space. Chemical weed control although is one of the effective methods, there has been a growing apprehension

[1] Ph.D Scholar (Agronomy), TNAU, Coimbatore, Tamil Nadu, India
[2] Ph.D Scholar (Agronomy), TNAU, Coimbatore, Tamil Nadu, India
[3] Ph.D Scholar (Agronomy), TNAU, Coimbatore, Tamil Nadu, India

among ecologists about the use of chemicals which have plagued with problems such as pollution of environment, development of weed resistance and above all is depend on fossil fuel. Hence, there is a need for developing eco-friendly alternate methods of weed control. Consequently, researchers in their search for new methods also took interest in some of the traditional practices with a hope of evolving a much efficient tool of weed management. The time demands that the new method besides, being efficient, economically viable, ecologically sound and acceptable to the users and environmental friendly. In this direction soil disinfection through soil solarization offers greater potentialities.

The possible mechanisms of weed control by soil solarization are direct killing of weed seeds by solar heat, indirect microbial killing of weed seeds weakened by sublethal heating, killing of seeds stimulated to germinate in the moist mulched soil and killing of germinating seeds whose dormancy is broken. Basically, all these are caused due to raising of soil temperature to lethal levels. Different terms are used to describe the method of solarization like solar heating, plastic or polyethylene tarping, plastic or polyethylene mulching and solar pasteurization.

'Soil Solarization' is a hydrothermal process that occurs in moist soil which is covered by a transparent plastic film and exposed to sunlight during the warm summer months. This method is nonhazardous to the user and the environment can be kept cleaner as it is dependent on renewable Source of energy.

Principle

During solarization, soil temperatures are achieved which are lethal to many plant pathogens, weed sand pests. The process changes physical, chemical and biological properties of soil that improve the growth and development of plants.

History

Soil solarization is a rather recently developed technique, which has shown promise for the control of several soil borne pathogens and weeds in warm areas. First extensive scientific detail was described in Israel by Katan *et al.*, in 1976, presenting the results of a series of studies performed under field conditions, initiated in 1973, for controlling soilborne pathogens and weeds, mostly as a preplanting soil treatment. Soil is mulched and then covered with transparent polyethylene during the hot season, thereby heating it and killing the pests. Later, attempts to control nematodes by soil solarization were also made in Australia, USA, Italy and South Africa.

I. Effect of Soil Solarization on Weed Management

A. Solarization material

Transparent polyethylene films are more efficient in trapping solar radiation and residual weed control than colour or black films. Besides, clear transparent polyethylene sheets costs less and has high strength and allows maximum transmittances of solar radiation. Thinner films are more effective for solar heating than thicker films and are proportionately less expensive.

B. Solarization technique

Soil solarization is recommended to be done for 4-6 weeks during warm months of the year. The soil to be solarized must be worked up to good seed- bed condition by cultivating the soil until it is loose and friable with no large clods or other debris in the soil surface as they create air pockets, which, reduces heating of the soil and keep the tarp from fitting tightly over the soil surface. A clean, flat surface will also prevent the accidental puncturing of the thin plastic mulch by debris. Adequate moisture level (up to field capacity) for working the soil before laying the plastic tarp is essential. If the soil is dry, irrigating the areas to be solarized is required before covering the sheet, since most weeds are more sensitive to high temperatures in wet soil than in dry soil.

Results of the experiment conducted at UAS, Bangalore indicated that soil moisture upto FC was essential for achieving higher soil temperature and reduced weed infestation followed by irrigation upto 50% FC. Then dig a shallow trenches all around the bed or plot at 6-8 inches deep. When the soil bed is ready for tarping two edges of polyethylene sheets of thickness 100-200 gauge or 0.025 - 0.05 mm should be inserted into the furrows and covered and tarped air tightly by maintaining minimum gap between polyethylene sheet and the soil surface. Soil solarization in nursery beds can be done manually. In the fields, soil solarization can be done either manually or by using improved machinery. Any damage to polyethylene sheets should be sealed at the earliest. Entry into plots covered with polyethylene sheet should be avoided to the extent possible. If entry is necessary, such as for sealing leaks, bare feet or smooth-soled shoes are preferable.

C. Months of soil solarization

It is clearly understood that the success of soil solarization largely depends on the availability of intense radiation. Summer months with bright sunshine at least for one or two months are essential for effective soil solarization. In India, March - May in Southern parts and May - June in northern parts experiences the intense radiation and are best suited for solarization. Systematic experimentation at UAS, Bangalore revealed that higher soil temperature, WCE with lower weed count with soil solarization during March & April attributing to the bright intense radiation.

D. Duration of soil solarization

Effectiveness of soil solarization depends actually on the cumulative heat accumulation which, in turn on the duration of solarization. The annual weeds are susceptible even at slightly lower cumulative heating but the perennials needs longer periods as they have several mechanism of escape. Solarization for a period of 10 weeks effectively control perennials.

E. Extent of Increase in soil temperature

The basic phenomenon helping weed control upon soil solarization is build up of lethally high temperature. Maximum temperature in upper soil layers under ideal condition are achieved in 3-4 days after solarization begins. The soil temperature goes up to 50-55 °C at 5 cm and 46-47 °C at 10 cm depth of soil where most of the dormant and viable seeds are present. The increase in soil temperature is 10-12°C more than the non-solarized control.

F. Effect on weed emergence

Due to elevated temperature in soil following solarization treatment it results in reduction in the population of weeds. The response to solarization in weeds varies with weed species. Soil solarization was most effective at controlling broad-leaved weeds than sedges and grasses.

G. Types of weeds controlled

The first sign of an effective soil solarization treatment could be seen by the amount of weeds grown in the treated plots. Soil solarization is effective in controlling most of the annual weeds however, the perennials, such as *Cynodon dactylon, Cyperusrotundus,* and *Convolvulusarvensis,* gradually recovered. Several studies over many years have revealed that many rainy and winter season annuals are susceptible to soil solarization.

H. Effect on weed seed bank

The reserves of dormant weeds in agricultural soils provide a source of seeds for persistent weed problems that often require repeated control measures. A reduction in the number of dormant weed seeds in the soil should also correspondingly reduce weed persistence and weed control requirements. Hence, soil solarization would be desirable as a means of reducing the dormant weed seed reserves in the soil. However, solarization was not effective in eliminating dormant weed seeds from the germination zone.

I. Effect on soilborne pathogens

During soil solarization, temperatures commonly reach up to 35-60°C depending on soil type, season, location, soil depth and other factors.

These high temperatures induce changes in soil volatile compounds that are toxic to organisms already weakened by high temperature.

J. Effect on nematodes

The efficacy of soil solarization is based on the sensitivity of nematodes to relatively high temperatures. Notwithstanding that under clear plastic mulch, temperatures higher than 50°C can be reached only in the top 5 cm of the soil, temperatures of 40-50°C have been reported up to 10-15 cm depth in hot seasons in several countries.

- Moreover, temperatures of 36-40°C can be reached at 20-30 cm depth in warm areas. Such temperatures, if prolonged, can be lethal to nematodes or at least may reduce their infectivity because of energy reserve depletion. Such weakened nematodes may also be more vulnerable to biotic and abiotic stresses. Further, nematode antagonists may prevail in the soil after solarization or they may colonize the solarized soils much faster than the non-solarized soils when incorporated artificially. In deeper soil profiles (30-40 cm) lethal or sublethal temperatures usually are not attained, where the temperature increases only 3-4°C. However, this may render nematodes more active, which in turn increases nematode infection by *Pasteuria penetrans* or nematode capture by some trapping fungi.
- Because of soil biotic and abiotic changes following solarization, the suppressing effect on nematodes may not become evident or can last for several months. Walker and Wachtel found that infection of *Meloidogyne javanica* juveniles by *P.penetrans* increases for ten months after soil solarization and Stapleton and DeVay observed a reduction of *Helicotylenchus digonicus* populations only three months after solarization treatment.
- The beneficial effect of nematode control is further enhanced because of the lack of or the reduced interaction of nematodes with soilborne diseases, such as those caused by *Verticillium* spp. and *Fusarium* spp.
- Such weakened nematodes may also be more vulnerable to biotic and abiotic stresses
- Nematode antagonists may prevail in the soil after solarization because they colonize the solarized soils much faster than the non-solarized soils

K. Effect on beneficial microbes

- Some thermophilic and thermotolerant biota (actinomycetes) may survive and even flourish under soil solarization, but poor soil competitors, such as many pathogens, are killed by soil solarization.
- Solarization initially may reduce populations of beneficial micro-organisms but their populations quickly recolonize solarized soil.
- Nitrogen fixing Rhizobium bacteria are also sensitive to high soil temperatures, and reduction in root nodulation of legumes in solarized soils is also temporary.

L. Effect on plant nutrients

- There is increased availability of plant nutrients and rhizosphere populations of favorable bacteria, such as *Bacillus* spp.
- Soil solarization increases N, Ca, P, K and Mg availability.
- An increase in soil nitrate nitrogen by more than 3000 kg/ha was obtained by adding poultry manure and growing mustard and incorporation in soil before soil solarization.

II. Effect of Soil Solarization in Improving Crop Productivity

As soil solarization has tremendous effect on soil-borne pathogens, nematodes and weeds, the treatment enables the crop to grow and yield better as compared to non-solarized field. The magnitude of increase depends upon the type of pest problem and the degree of control. Control of weeds alone due to solarization increased the yield of many crops. Solarization is very effective in controlling parasitic weed *Orobanche.*

HINTS FOR EFFECTIVE SOIL SOLARIZATION

- Solarization-4-6 weeks during summer season (hottest month)
- Land - thoroughly prepared, free from crop stubbles, clods, stones etc. and leveled
- A light irrigation (4-5 hours sprinkler or 50 mm irrigation) prior to tarping
- Transparent (not black or coloured) - 25-100 μm thickness
- Immediately after irrigation the polyethylene film should be trapped close to the soil
- All free edges of polyethylene should be inserted, buried in the furrows and sealed
- Any hole appearing in the polythene sheets should be sealed immediately
- Entry into mulched plots should be avoided
- After solarization, crop seeds should be sown without much soil disturbance
- Irrigation water should not be allowed to flow from non-solarized areas

ADVANTAGES OF SOIL SOLARIZATION

- Non-chemical method - no toxic effect on users or soil
- No harmful effect on environmental
- Integrated method of weed control
- Easy to understand and execute

Limitations

- Climate dependency
- Soil occupied by plastic for 3-6 weeks

REFERENCES

http://www.ext.colostate.edu/pubs/crops/00505.html

https://en.wikipedia.org/wiki/Soil_solarization

Stapleton, J. J. 2000. Soil Solarization in Various Agricultural Production Systems. *Crop Protection,* 19: 837-841.

FAO. 1990. Plant Production and Protection Paper. *In:* Proceedings of the First International Conference on Soil Solarization Amman, Jordan, pp. 19-25.

Land Reclamation, Soil Quality and Agriculture
Edited by: Dr. Pawan Kumar 'Bharti' and Alka Chauhan
ISBN: 978-93-5056-882-8
Edition: 2017
Published by: Discovery Publishing House Pvt. Ltd., New Delhi (India)

3

Upshotsof Age of Oil Spill and the Influence of Physico-chemical Properties on the Diversity of Soil Dwelling Insects

[1]Uwagbae, Michael. A, [2]El Surtasi, Eman.I, [1]Rotimi, Johnny, [1]Dirisu, Abdul–Rahman, [3]Gbarakoro, Tembeke. N, [4]Richard, Glory, [5]Oratokhai, Rudolf. A and [6]Agwu, Julia, E.

ABSTRACT

Oil exploration in the Niger Delta as an important economic source to the Nigerian nation has increased lately but this has been exacerbated without regards to the estimation of the negative pollution impacts on agricultural and communal lands. Soil is the main habitat for any terrestrial ecosystem and any disturbance to itsphysico-chemical properties has noticeable feedback on its inhabitants. Physico-chemical properties were chosen as indicators for detecting the impact of oil spillage at different temporal scale of occurrence on insect community and diversity. Threeimpacted sites (7 months, 19 months and 38 months after spillage incidence) in comparison to a control site were located for extraction of insect for a period of two years. Insect fauna were identified into twenty eight taxa (5,488 individuals) belonging to four different orders and ten different families. There was a spatially significant difference ($P<0.005$) in the overall pattern of insect assemblage's diversity. Results from a multivariate constrained ordination technique showed negative correlation between total hydrocarbons and heavy metals (especially with Copper (Cu) and Nickel (Ni), Iron (Fe), Zinc (Zn)) and species composition and diversity in the impacted sites. While positive correlations wererecorded amongst macro nutrients (Potassium,

1 Department of Animal and Environmental Biology, Faculty of Life Sciences, University of Benin, Benin City, P.M.B 1154, Edo State, Nigeria
2 Department of Zoology, Faculty of Science, Damietta University, Damietta City, 34511, Egypt.
3 Department of Animal and Environmental Biology, College of Sciences, University of Port Harcourt, P.M.B 5323, Choba, Port Harcourt, Nigeria
4 Department of Community Medicine, Niger Delta University, P.M.B. 071, Wilberforce Island, Bayelsa State, Nigeria
5 Department of Agricultural Education, TayoAkpata University of Education, Ekiadolor, Edo State, Nigeria.
6 Department of Zoology, University of Nigeria, Nsukka, Nigeria.

Magnesium and Sodium) in the control site and the site with the oldest time of spill occurrence. However, among the physical characteristics of soil, silt, clay and pH were the most negatively correlated. Nonetheless, soil temperature, moisture and sand correlated positively with the impacted polluted sites. A gradual recovery of species, abundance and species diversity was recorded in the impacted sites alongside the time of occurrence. Despite the economic importance of the crude oil to a nation, the dangers of spillage and the bearingeffects of periodic range of spill occurrence on the surrounding ecosystem adversely restrainsinsect population as they play key roles in terms of biomass, diversity and ecosystem services in the terrestrial ecosystems than any another type of animal.

Keywords: Insect diversity, Niger Delta, Oil pollution,Nutrient, Ecosystem Services,

INTRODUCTION

The environment is the carrier and instrument of life support, especially inthe case of the Nigeria's Niger Delta region. Oil spillage in the Niger Delta area of Nigeria has become a public interest as a result of its frequent occurrence which has been associated with petroleum exploration and development activities. Cases of crude petroleum and refined petroleum products spill onto communal and agricultural lands and water ways through processes of production and transportation operations have been recounted (Odu, 1977; Awobajo, 1981, Grevy, 1995, Moffat and Linden, 1995, Obireand Nwaubeta, 2001, NAT. CONFAB. Report, 2014 and Uwagbae *et al.,* 2014). Oil pollution is so widespread in the Niger Delta that it is estimated that an equivalent of one Exxon Valdez size of crude is spilled every year in the Niger Delta (NAT. CONFAB. Report, 2014).

Paoletti and Bressan (1996) stated that disturbances caused by pollutants in the soil results in both qualitative and quantitative changes in faunal population and this is said to affect normal soil functioning. Sensitivity of soil organisms to petroleum hydrocarbons is based on the quantity and quality of oil spilled and as well as prior applications (Bossert and Bertha, 1984). Some soil organisms can tolerate oil contaminated environments because they can utilize petroleum hydrocarbon as an energy source (Song *et al.,* 1990). Other species may not be gradually eliminated (Amadi *et al.,* 1996). However, other species such as mites that can migrate to deeper soil profile in order to escape from the severity of pollution (Okiwelu *et al.,* 2012).

Various studies relating to the effect of crude oil spills on soil arthropods including insects in the Niger Delta region had revealed that Collembola abundance (mean per gram) at soil depths of 10 cm, 20 cm and 30 cm were statistically significant; using age of crude oil spill on impacted sites. Also, it was established that time course (age of spillage of crude oil) contributed tothe abundance and distribution of Collembola species that inhabit a typical tropical rain forest soil impacted by series of oil spills in the Niger Delta. Some soil insect species (Collembola) exhibited diverse preferences to crude oil spillage and showed differential responses to some soil physicochemical characteristics such as Total Hydrocarbon Content (THC), soil pH and soil moisture content (Iloba and Jarrett (2007), Iloba and Odon (2007), Rotimi *et al.*, (2014) and Uwagbae *et al.*, 2014). Besides, a significant direct correlation between mite abundance/density and depth of a twelve month old impacted site has been reported (Okiwelu *et al.*, 2012).

In addition, Rotimi *et al.*, (2014) recorded seven soil arthropod orders including insects from sites that had been impacted with crude oil over 7, 19 and 38 months at varied soil depths. The results showed that overall pattern of diversity of the studied sites were significantly different in species diversity, richness, evenness, dominance and abundance. The age of occurrence of spill detected was an important factor in reflecting the diversity; as the general diversity of insect orders demonstrated the negative feedback of crude oil spillage on species composition. This negative feedback diminishes with increase in the age of crude oil spill occurrence. Additionally, Gbarakoro *et al.*, (2012) recorded one collembolan species and six species of mites in a twelve month old impacted site and three collembolan species and thirteen mite species in a thirty-six month old impacted site in the Niger Delta.

Impacted sites at varied time course and soil physico-chemical characteristic shave significant influence on the diversity of insects in part of the Niger Delta where the states of polluted lands due to anthropogenic effects such as crude oil spillages arefamiliar sites. The study aims to reconnoiterthe impact of age of spill and also soil physico-chemical characteristics onsoil dwelling insects' species abundance, distribution and diversity.

MATERIALS AND METHODS

Study Area

The study sites were located in Yenagoa Local Government Area of Bayelsa State of Nigeria.The crude oil contaminated sites were located in Ikarama community (Lat. 05° 09′ 16″ N, Long. 06° 27′ 11″ E) a distance of about 12 km from Yenagoa Town, which is the State capital ofBayelsa State, Nigeria. Ekeki community (Lat. 05° 55′ 47″ N, Long. 06° 17′ 54″ E), a residential district within Yenagoa Town, served as the CONTROL, called "SITE D" (Plate 1). The three polluted sites sampled in the study were located within Ikarama community; and all impacted sites had oil wells at an approximate distance of 20 meters from sampled site.

Table 3.1: Spatial Variation of Abundance (Relative Change to the Control Site %). Species Richness, Diversity and Evenness of Insect Assemblage Extracted from the Different Study Sites During the Study Period.

Study sites	Age after disturbance (spill)	Abundance (relative change %)	Species Richness	Species Evenness	Simpson diversity
SITE A	less than 1 year ago (7 months)	472 (83.32%)	24	0.5994	0.9013
SITE B	19 months (1year 7 months)	901 (68.16%)	28	0.5392	0.9064
SITE C	38 months (3 years 2 months)	1285 (54.57%)	28	0.5579	0.9085
SITE D	Control site	2830	28	0.5066	0.9001

Values within columns having the same letter are significantly different at P< 0.05.

Spatial variation of soil arthropods in Simpson diversity index ($F_{(3,95)}$= 6.60, P< 0.001), abundance ($F_{(3,95)}$=50.38, P< 0.000001), species evenness ($F_{(3,95)}$= 6.60, P< 0.001), species richness ($F_{(3,95)}$= 90.82, P< 0.00001) at different sites of the study area.

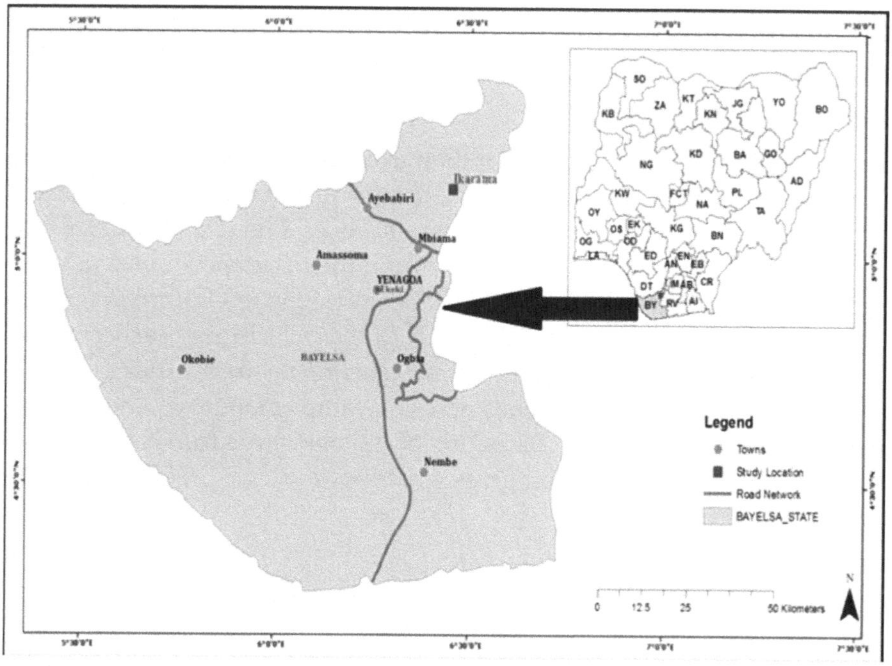

Fig. 3.1: Map of Bayelsa State showing where the study sites are located. Inset: Map of Nigeria showing different states

(Source: modified from Fatoba *et al.*, 2015)

Major environmental contamination at the sites appears to be the result of oil spills from equipment failure of oil companies' well heads (Plate 2). Soil texture ischaracteristically sandy-loam (MOEN, 2008). A total of three polluted sites were selected based on varied time of occurrencefrom the time of the study. The sites were classified as follows: less than 1 year ago (7 months) after spillcoded "SITE A" (Plate 3), 19 months (1 year 7 months) after spill coded "SITE B" (Plate 4), and 38 months (3 years 2 months) of yet after spill designated "SITE C" (Plate 5). Each of the selected polluted sites had experienced some estimated 50litres (0.32 barrels, Calculateme.com, 2008) of Brass blend crude. Results of time of occurrence (age of spill) and quantity of crude oil spilledwere affirmed from reports of the Field Joint Investigation Team (FJIT). All the four sites were uncultivated lands dominated by*Andropogongyanus* (gamba grass).

Topographic and Climatic Disposition of Study Sites

The study sites are typically moist lowland rain forest within floodplain topography on the southern flank of Niger Delta, crisscrossed with tidal creeks. The climatic region lies in the mainly wet equatorial climatic zone of Nigeria, with high cloud cover and sunshine hours are low and air is moist for most part of the year because of the very high relative of about 95% to 100%. Temperatures are moderated by the cloud cover and by the generally clammy air. Nonetheless, mean annual temperatures are as high as 22–31°C. Rain falls all months of the year with a short dried out spell in the months of January–March.

Land Use and Vegetation

Family and communally-owned lands make up most of the available lands in Ikarama community. Landsareused mainly for agricultural activities involving the cultivation of principal crops such as: Yam (*Dioscoreasp*), Cassava (*Manihotesculenta*), Maize (*Zea mays*), Tomatoes (*Lycopersiconescullentum*), Pepper (*Capsicum sp.*) and *Piper nigrum*), Beans (*Vigna sp.*) Pumpkin (*Cucurbita maxima*), other vegetables like Spinach (*Spinaciaoleracea*), cash crop such asPlantain(*Musasp*), Raphiapalm (*Raphiafarinifera*) and other foodcrops. The floristic composition stretches across swamp, mangrove and rainforest ecosystems with *Elaeisguineensis* as one of its major tree forms. Uncultivated lands are dominated by gamba grass (*Andropogongyanus*), *Sidaacuta*and herb like *Chromolenaodorata*.

Sampling and Extraction of Soil Insects

Use of soil corer

In order to quantify soil arthropod population at varied depths of 0-10 cm, 10-20 cm and 20-30 cm; soil samples were collected monthly (1st week) from each site (control and polluted sites) for two years (24 months), using a cylindrical core sampler (diameter 7.5 cm). Sampling wasconducted once a month for the entire period to allow for proper environmental stabilization after perturbation (adopted from Maraun *et al.*, 2003).

Sampling grid (10 m × 10 m) was marked out on both the control and polluted sites. Each grid was subdivided into one hundred 1 m^2 microplots, after random sampling, a microplot on the north and southern positions were sampled as replicates. In each microplot, three cores were taken using a 7.5 cm diameter soil corer. The first core was taken between 0-10 cm soil layer, the second core between 10-20 cm soil layer and the third core, 20-30 cm soil layer. This was a modified procedure of Battigelli and Marshall (1993). Each core was carefully sealed in a separate well labeled polythene bag and taken to laboratory for extraction. Extraction methods were designed to suit, behaviours and body structures of the organisms (Wallwork, 1970). The Berlese Tullgren funnel extractor was best for extracting soil micro arthropods with efficiency of about 90% (Hopkins, 1997). Berlese-Tullgren Funnel (dynamic) method with suitable modifications was used for the extraction of soil arthropods and the fauna were collected in vials on account of their negative phototropic behavior (Hopkins, 2002).

The samples were placed in the funnels for about five days and the soil arthropods collected in containers with 70% alcohol mixed in propylene glycol. Before the soil micro-arthropods were extracted and collected, sorting of larger sized soil arthropods was done with the aid of a binocular dissecting microscope (AmScope SM-1TS-144S-M Dissecting Circuit 144-LED Zoom Stereo Microscope). Individual species were sorted from the debris by means of a fine camel hairbrush under a microscope and by suction using sucking pipette. Soil arthropods were placed in glass specimen bottles containing 70% alcohol mixed in propylene glycol. Specimens were labelled appropriately. Slides of the micro-arthropods were prepared and insects identified by use of keys.

Identification of collembola followed Christiansen *et al.*, (2004), while other soil arthropods were identified with the help of a research faculty in Entomology Unit of the Department of Biological Sciences, Niger Delta University (NDU), Amassoma, Bayelsa, Nigeria . The subject of analysis was to ascertain the effect of age of spillandthe diversity of species in the sampled biomes.

Use of Pitfall Traps

To record the activity densities of mobile, ground-dwelling arthropods, pitfall traps were set (16 sampling days per season). The traps (plastic cup, diameter: 8.5 cm, height: 12 cm) were filled up to one third with a formalin solution (3%) and a few drops of detergent to kill and conserve the animals. Traps were set randomly not > 5 m apart from each other) and level with the surface of the soil. Furthermore, the pitfall traps remained open and were thus entirely exposed to the entry of litters. In total, there were four treatments with ten replicates of each (altogether making 40 traps). The catches were sorted and preserved in 70% ethanol as specimens.

Laboratory Analyses

Physicochemical characteristics (soil pH, moisture content) were determined as described by Osuji and Nwonye, (2007). Total Hydrocarbon Content (THC) was determined by extraction and spectrometric methods described by Osuji *et al.*, (2005).

Statistical Analysis

Overall diversity of soil insect was expressed as species richness, abundance, evenness and Simpson diversity index. Species richness and diversity patterns are a fundamental point for any scientific act in conservation biology (Bestelmeyer *et al.*, 2003; Leather *et al.*, 2008). Species richness represents the simplicity of describing communities at different scales and its broadly understood meaning. The complementary picture of overall diversity pattern of any community was documented by information about the abundance of species, the evenness of communities across the sampling region or the dominant species. Abundance is the kind of diversity measures that has inclusively been considered as equivalent to biodiversity per se (Peet, 1974) and referred to the sum of individuals in area. However, Simpson diversity index (D) is nearly the most tractable and statistically useful calculation (Lande, 1996):

$$\lambda = \Sigma p_i^2 \; D = 1 - \lambda$$

Where D is Simpson diversity index, λ is an index of dominance. p_i is the proportion of the community occupied by the ith species.

The Jaccard index, also known as the Jaccard similarity coefficient, is a statistic measurement used for comparing the similarity and diversity of sample sets (Jaccard, 1901). It is based entirely on the presence or absence of species at the locality. It also reflects species shifts and trends between stations; applicable at low population densities or sample size; it can be adapted to qualitative data; minimizes the effects of seasonal or annual variation on population trends (Hocutt *et al.*, 2004).

Cluster analysis is a technique for classifying numerical data using similarity indices between localities and sites within localities depending up on the similarity, distances between groups and plotted using the Hierarchical cluster analysis. Ordination techniques have been widely used to assess their ability to portray patterns of differences among sites whose environmental characteristics may vary to describe the differences in species composition among individual sampling units (Okland, 1999). Ordination is the collective term for multivariate techniques that arrange sites along axes on the basis of data on species composition" (TerBraak, 1986).

Non-metric multidimensional scaling NMDSwas equally used in this study. It is an ordination method based on ranked distances between objects and was used because of its flexibility with any distance metric as well as its performance with non-normally distributed species data (Legendre and Legendre, 1998). It was used for detecting the variationamong community composition of insects in the studied sites. However, Canonical Correspondence Analysis (CCA) is a multivariate method, which relates the community species composition to environmental variables. Its results were displayed as a CCA tri-plot of species, sample habitats and environmental variables and the axes of the ordination were constrained to optimize their linear relationships to the environmental variables. Longer the line (and more parallel) is with an axis, the more important variable(s) is for structuring the insectspecies composition. A permutation test with 1000 iterations was performed to test for significance of the species and the environmental variables.

All parameters of diversity were calculated by PC-ORD program 4.14 (McCune & Mefford, 1999). Grouping and ordination analysis were carried out by PAST V. 1.92 software running on Windows® XP. (Hammer *et al.*, 2001). However, analyses of variance (ANOVA) were used to test for differences.

RESULTS

Overall Soil Insect Diversity

The overall pattern of diversity was estimated through diversity indices (2.684 in Simpson diversity index and 0.907 in Shannon diversity indices), species evenness (0. 54) and dominance index (0.0931) in the study area. About 5,488 individuals (28 species) were identified (Appendix 1) throughout the study period. Twenty eight species were identified into four different orders and ten different families. Collembola ranked the highest percentage of families (41.66 %), individuals (74.2%) and species (39.3%) among the sampling orders. Moreover, insect species exhibited a spatially significant difference in abundance among different sampling orders ($F_{(3,15)} = 5.44$, $P< 0.01$). Where the control site (SITE D) had the highest insect abundance in represented orders of collections from theSites, while the lowest collection occured at SITE A.

Spatial pattern of variation in diversity of the insect assemblage

The spatial variation in diversity index clarified table (3.2) among the study sites, of which very high significant differenceswere observed amongst Simpsondiversity index ($F_{(3,95)} = 6.60$, $P< 0.001$), abundance ($F_{(3,\ 95)} = 50.38$, $P< 0.000001$), species evenness ($F_{(3,95)} = 6.60$, $P< 0.001$), species richness ($F_{(3,95)} = 90.82$, $P< 0.00001$). Among the study sites, (SITE C) (38 months after disturbance) had the maximum value of diversity index (0.91) on the reverse, SITE A (7 months after disturbance) had (0.901). Also, SITE A, was characterized with the minimum value of species richness (21 species) and abundance

(453 individuals) and the maximum value of species everuiess (0.5994), while on the reverse, the maximum values of species richness and abundance (26 species made up of 2,647 individuals) and minimum value of species evenness (0.5066) was recorded at the control site "SITE D".

Temporal pattern of variation in diversity of the insect assemblage

As clarified in figure (3.1a&b), temporal variation in species richness ($F_{(11,47)}$ = 2.0933, *P<0.00001*), and species abundance ($F_{(23,95)}$ = 2.0932, *P*<0.0002) showedmarkedly significant differences between the study sites. In contrast to the control site (SITE D). SITE A ranked a sharp decrease in the species richness (between 25- 76.92308 %), abundance (75.3-91.3%), while the "SITE C" recorded the less percentage of change range (0-43.75% in species richness and 47.25-69.4% in abundance of species). Also, the mean decrease change of diversity index (figure 3.1c) was 5.5% in SITE A and this reduced with the increase in the age after spill (2.5% in SITE B and 1.019% in SITE C) with significant difference ($F_{(11,47)}$ = 2.09*P*<0.007), among the study sites.

Similarity of study sites

Bray-Curtis index of similarity (table 3.3) clarified that the degree of similarity depends on the insect composition among the study sites, where the most similarity was clarified between control sites (SITE D and SITE C-38 months after spill. On the contrary, the lowest similarity was shownbetween the control site (Site D)and SITE A (7 months after spill).

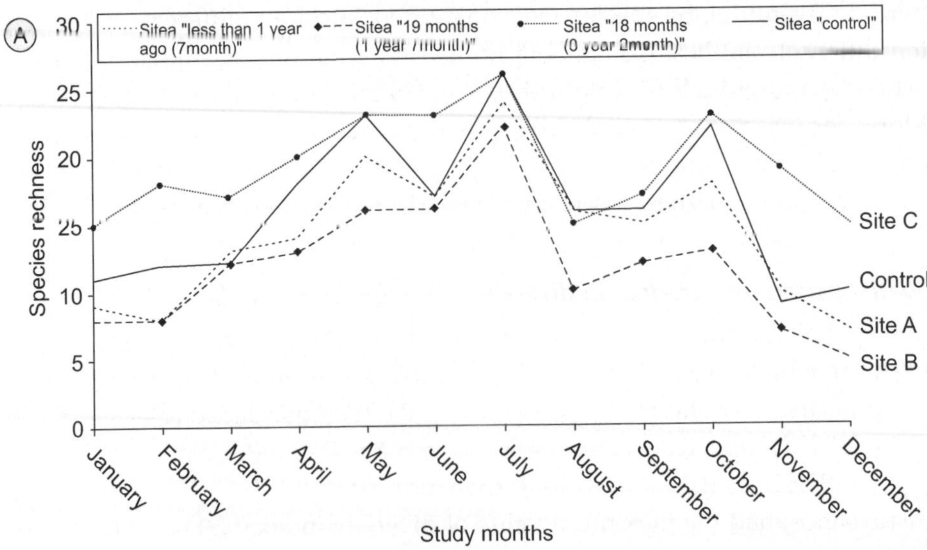

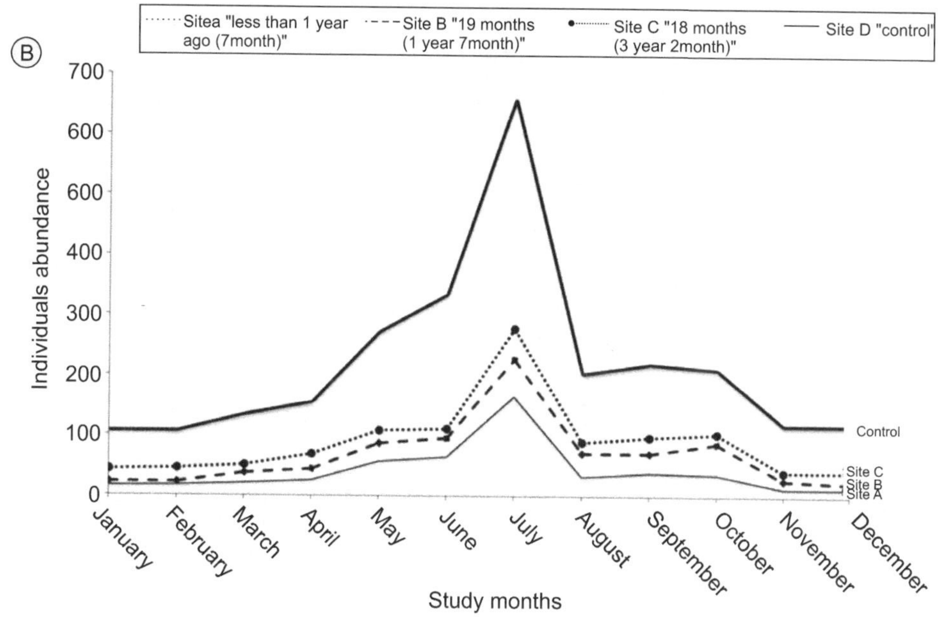

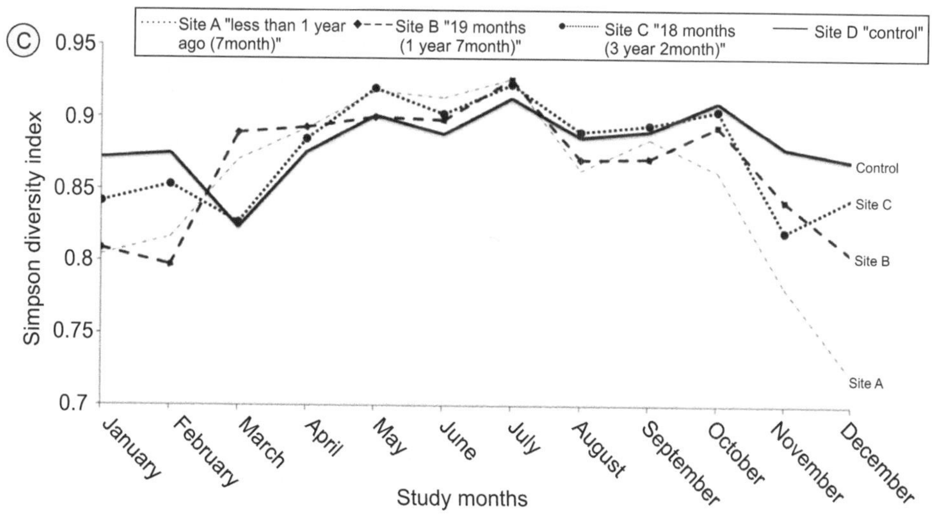

Fig. 3.1(a,b&c): Temporal variation in species richness ($F_{(23,95)}$=25.039, *P*< 0.00001), species abundance ($F_{(23,95)}$=9.11, *P*< 0.00001), and Simpson diversity index ($F_{(23,95)}$=4.64 *P*< 0.0001), among the study sites.

Grouping and ordination analyses

The Hierarchical Cluster analysis figure (3.2) visualized a marked differentiation among the different study sites. The average pair-wise similarity was 96%.

Table 3.2: Spatial Variation of Abundance (Species Richness) of Collected Families Among the Study

The collected groups/orders	SITE A	SITE B	SITE C	SITE D	Total of abundance (species richness)
Coleoptera	39 (8)	4(4)	25(8)	38(8)	106(8)
Collembola	2244 (11)	364(11)	598(11)	867(11)	4073(11)
Hymenoptera	348(7)	85(7)	203(7)	266(7)	902(7)
Isoptera	199 (2)	19(2)	75(2)	114(2)	407(2)

SITE A "less than 1 year ago (7 months)"; SITE B "19 months (1 year 7 months)"; SITE C "38 months (3 years 2 months)" and SITE D "Control site"

Table 3.3: The Similarity (Bray-Curtis Index) of Species Assemblages Between the Different Study Sites

		SITE A	SITE B	SITE C	SITE D
Sites of different ages oil spills	**SITE A "less than 1 year ago (7 months)"**	1	0.29226	0.46964	0.55546
	SITE B "19 months (1year 7 months)"	0.29226	1	0.64949	0.56126
	SITE C "38 months (3 years 2 months)"	0.46964	0.64949	1	0.80739
Control site	SITE D	0.55546	0.56126	0.80739	1

The grey dotted values indicate the highly similarity index between the different locality.SITE A "less than 1 year ago (7 months)"; SITE B "19 months (1 year 7 months)"; SITE C "38 months (3 years 2 months)" and SITE D "Control site"

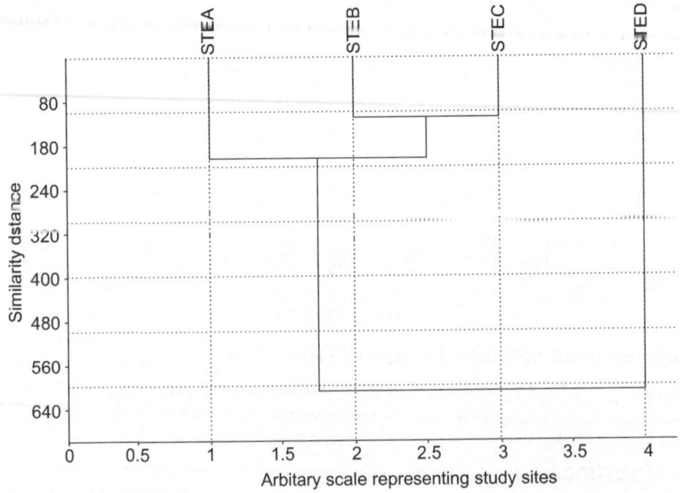

Fig. 3.2: Hierarchical Cluster Analysis of insect species using the Euclidean similarity with linkage method grouping sites depending upon the similarity distances. ***The length of each node in the dendrogram is the similarity between the pair of clusters whose fusion corresponds with the node.***

dependent upon insects' composition. The control site (SITE D) was far away from the three different sites where spills occurred. Moreover, non-metric multidimensional scaling clarified differentiation between the control site and sites of different ages of impacted oil spills through two axes (axis1; Eigen-value = 0.99 and axis1; Eigen-value = 0.01, and stress = 0) (figure 3.3). The axis one differentiated the control site (SITE D) on the negative part far away from the others on the positive part. Also, the minimal spanning tree clarified the closely similarity distance (SITE C) is to the control site.

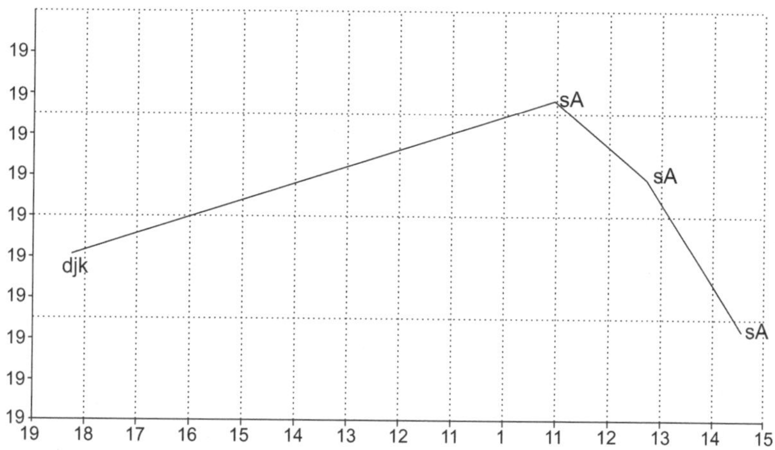

Fig. 3.3: Non-metric multidimensional scaling of species composition among the study sites. The unstraight line refers to minimal spanning tree.

Canonical correspondence analysis (CCA)

The Canonical Correspondence Analysis explained the distribution of species composition of different study sites and correlation to the different environmental variables throughout three axes. The first two axes displayed 49% of insects composition, and 24% throughout axes 2 (Eigen-value = 0.024) and axis 3 (Eigen-value = 0.004).

As shown in table (3.4a), the study sites were very correlated (96%) to the first two axes, where the control site (SITE D) spread out to the negative partition of axis (1), while the three impacted sites were on the positive partition of the same axis.

About 75% of the insect fauna correlating to different physical characteristics of soil are displayed in figure (3.4a) and table (3.4b). Silt content and soil pH were the most negatively correlated with axis 1 while the reverse was positively correlated to soil temperature and sand. Moreover, the moisture of soil and clay content were the most positively and negatively correlated factors respectively with axis 2. However, the permutation results of CCA analysis created a Trace value of $P = 0.397$ and P-value of 0.07; species were not linearly related to the environmental variables.

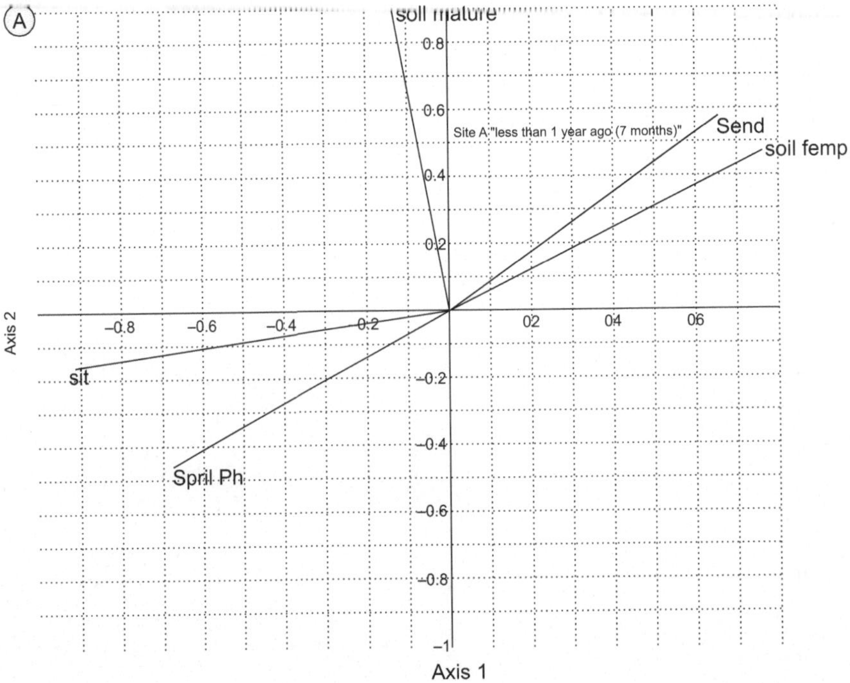

Fig. 3.4A: Canonical Correspondence Analysis (CCA) results for the environmental variables and study sites and physical variables of soil analysis.

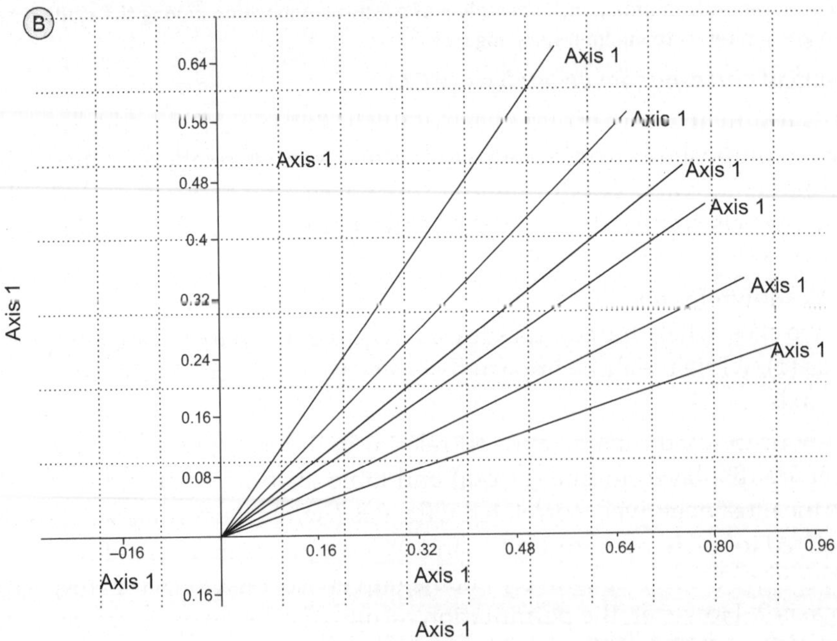

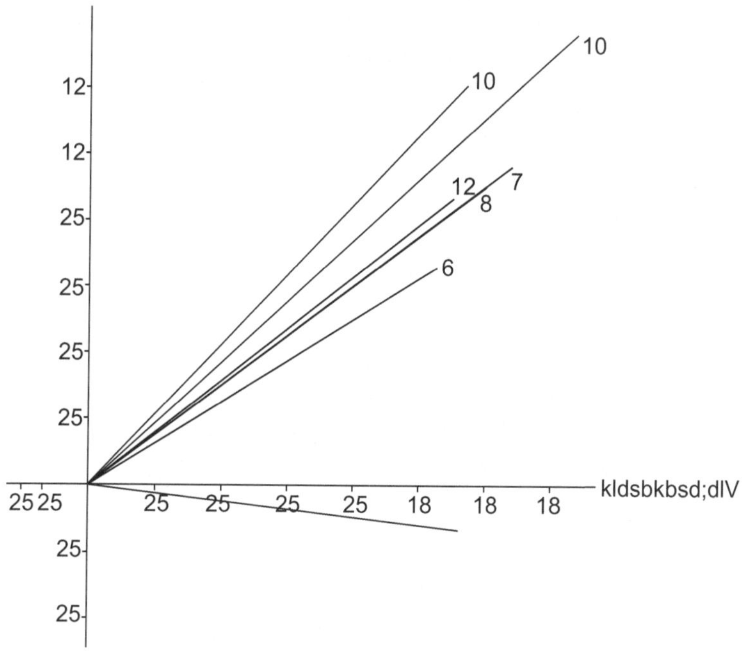

Fig. 3.4B & C: Canonical Correspondence Analysis (CCA) resultsfor the environmentalvariables and study sites (b) marconutrients and organic matter (c) heavy metals and THC. ***(Longer the line (and more parallel) is with an axis, the more important that variable(s) is for structuring the beetles species composition).***

The importance of macronutrients was clarified throughout figure (3.4b), the first four axes explained 99% of the insect fauna. All variables are positively correlated with axis 1 and 2. The permutation results created a Trace value of $P = 0.7$ and P-value of 0.05; species were linearly related to the environmental variables. Potassium, Magnesium and Sodium are the most positively correlated with axis 1, while phosphorus and organic matter content were the most positively correlated with axis 2.

On the contrary, the measured heavy metals and total hydrocarbons (T.H.C) correlated negatively with control site (SITE D) and positively with the three different oil spill sites through the first two axes (figure 3.4C). The correlation between the measured environmental factors visualized that is Iron (Fe), Zinc (Zn), and total hydrocarbons were the most prominent environmental factors. These factors are positively correlated with SITE B and SITE C and axis 1. While Copper (Cu) and Nickel (Ni) were the most prominent heavy metals that positively correlated with axis 2, were increased toward SITE A. The first four axes explained 73% of the insect fauna. The permutation results created a Trace value of $p = 0.339$ and p-value of 0.07; species were not linearly related to the environmental variables.

Table 3.4a: The Correlation of the Different Study Sites with Three Axes of CCA Analysis.

CCA term	Age of oil spill	Axis 1	Axis 2	Axis 3
SITE A	less than 1 year ago (7 months)	0.014	0.5137	0.004
SITE B	19 months (1year 7 months)	0.257	–0.046	0.125
SITE C	38 months (3 years 2 months)	0.267	–0.044	–0.085
SITE D	Control site	–0.202	–0.054	–0.002

Table 3.4b: The Correlated Environmental Factors in Related to Different Study Sites and Three Axes of CCA Analysis Grey Dotted Values Represent the Most Important Variable for that Axis.

	Environmental factor	CCA term	Axis 1	Axis 2	Axis 3
Fig. (4A)	Physical variables	*Soil temperature*	0.766	0.473561	0.172079
		Soil moisture	–0.132	0.893479	0.402819
		Soil pH	–0.678	–0.46063	–0.47371
		Sand	0.657	0.576079	0.284306
		Silt	–0.917	–0.16253	–0.28645
		Clay	0.003	–0.97265	–0.10374
Fig. (3.4B)	Marco nutrientients and organic matter content	*Calcium*	0.753096	0.497	0.1259
		Magnesium	0.853806	0.341	0.1463
		Sodium	0.790758	0.442	0.1498
		Potassium	0.901314	0.251	0.0912
		Nitrogen	0.731258	0.481	0.3095
		Phosphorus	0.55203	0.662	0.3212
		Organic matter content	0.664703	0.569	0.2788
Fig. (3.4C)	Heavy metals and total hydrocarbons (T.HC)	*Lead (Pb)*	0.763	0.476	0.181
		Chromium (Cr)	0.769	0.4538	0.241
		Copper (Cu)	0.652	0.5852	0.272
		Nickel (Ni)	0.737	0.5075	0.192
		Zinc (Zn)	0.792	0.4367	0.172
		Iron (Fe)	0.806	0.421	0.133
		Total hydrocarbons	0.788	0.4451	-0.025

DISCUSSION

Quantifying patterns of species diversity and understanding the processes that determine these patterns are important goals in ecology. As a result, a major focus has been whether species diversity is a consequence of the random assembly of species, or whether these assemblages are a product of biotic or abiotic factors (Connor and Simberloff, 1979; Sousa, 1979; Pacala and Roughgarden, 1984). Disturbance is one dangerous factor that has threatened the diversity of any ecosystem which performs as new microhabitat to species. Disturbance is responsible for the changes in vegetation, soil and native species as well as may give a chance to recolonization of some species having existence power (El-Surtasi, 2012). The intensity and frequency of the disturbances are important factors determining the changes in the structure and/or composition of natural communities (Pickett and White, 1985). The present study detected the dangers of crude oil spillage and the impact of its periodic range on the surrounding ecosystem and the diversity. Insects were chosen in the current study because they play key roles in terms of both biomass and diversity and have a greater impact on terrestrial ecosystems than any another type of animal (Solue, 1990; LaSalle and Gauld, 1991). Pitfall trapping was the suitable sampling tool in this evaluation. It is known as a good predictor of mean biomass, the quantitative importance of ground active species and highly reliable indicators of spatial or temporal changes (Dufrêne and Legendre, 1997; Bromham *et al.*, 1999; Thomas *et al.*, 2001).

Throughout the study, twentyeight species from four orders and ten families were identified. Among the identified orders, Collembolahad the most dominant and, abundancespecies. As reported byIloba and Jarrett (2007), Iloba and Odon (2007), Rotimi *et al.*, (2014) and Uwagbae *et al.*, (2014) who all confirmed the dominance of Collembola among soil dwelling insects.

The changes of species community and composition as previously detected in the study sites impacted on species diversity. As the most common method of using a multispecies approach to evaluate changes in an ecosystem is by determiningspecies diversity, measured either by species richness or indices such as the Simpson's Diversity Index (1949) and Shannon indices (Shannon and Weaver, 1949). The natural habitat (control sites) recorded the highest in species richness and abundance with the minimum value of evenness while the reverse was the case for the short term exposed site after the pollution (7 months). As concluded by many authors who explained such results with the characteristics of natural sites with different microhabitat heterogeneity, stability, resource availability and non-human disturbance (Brown, 2003; Lassau *et al.*, 2005; Apigian *et al.*, 2006; González Megías *et al.*, 2007; D'Amato *et al.*, 2009; Janssen *et al.*, 2009; Torchote *et al.*, 2010). On the other hand, disturbance and diversity theory has traditionally been applied to understanding patterns of species richness or diversity (Odion and Sarr, 2007). Indeed, increasing the age after exposure to any impact decreases the negative effect of impact. The current study detected the gradually recovery and increase of species, abundance and species diversity alongside the age of site impacted with extremely significant differences among the study sites (*with the oldest impacted site – Site C-38 months after spill recording the most significant difference while the Site A-7 months after spill site recorded the least*). Such sequence of partial recovery after an oil spill resulting in a significant positive correlation between total soil mite and collembolan densities and the length of the intervention periods between occurrence of spill and commencement of study has also been described (Gbarakoro *et al.*, 2012).

Ordination (or inertia) methods, like principal component and correspondence analysis, clustering and classification methods are currently used in many ecological studies (Whittaker, 1967; Anderson, 1971; Orlóci, 1978; Gauch, 1982; Legendre and Legendre, 1998). The application of ordination and similarity were applied for detection of the degree of similarity between the controlsite and three polluted sites depending upon the variation of insect diversity and species composition. Clearly separation was between the control and polluted sites, but the closest one to the Control site was the oldestimpacted site after pollution (38 months after spill). This confirms that the recovery in species composition and community structure were correlated with the time of spill occurrence.

Canonical Correspondence Analysis (CCA) is a direct ordination for explaining the importance of physico-chemical properties in species diversity and composition and also could suggest a negative feedback of pollution. As detected in the current results, the increase of total hydrocarbons and heavy metals especially, Copper (Cu) and Nickel (Ni), Iron (Fe), Zinc (Zn) as the main soil properties in the polluted sites was negatively correlated with the species composition and diversity. This is not strange, as it is earlier reported in accordance with the conclusions of Del Val *et al.*, (1999), Syrek *et al.*, (2006), Beyrem *et al.*, (2007) and Piolaand Johnston (2009) who explained that such scenario eliminates the most sensitive species and promote thetolerance of opportunistic species or invasive species. On the reverse, the positive increases of macronutrients (potassium, magnesium and sodium) were detected in the control site and the oldest site after spill (Site C-38 months after spill).

Also, Canonical Correspondence Analysis showed that there were increase of soil temperature, moisture and sandy texture in addition to phosphorus and organic matter content towardsthe most recent site age after pollution (Site A-7 months after spill site). Grzés (2009) clarified these results by reporting that pollution by metals can favour species with affinity for humidity by reducing the microbial activity, thereby allowing an accumulation of organic matter.

CONCLUSION

In conclusion, the evaluation of the impact of oil spillage occurrenceinsites at varied times is important for modeling the short and long term effects of these impacts on any ecosystem especially with soil insects. Besides, this study drew our attention to the impactof the changes of soil physico-chemical properties and insect diversity as well as composition as corresponding to deleteriousconsequenceof oil spill.

Conflict of Interest

The authors declarethat there was not any conflict of interestin this study.

REFERENCES

Amadi, A., Abbey, S.D., Nwa, A., (1996): Chronic Effects of Oil Spill on Soil Properties and Microflora of a Rainforest Ecosystem in Nigeria. *Water Air Soil Pollut*. 86, 1–11.

Anderson, A. (1971): Ordination Methods in Ecology. *The Journal of Ecology*. 59: 713-726

Apigian, K. O.; Dahlsten, D. L. and Stephens, S. L. (2006): Biodiversity of Coleoptera and the Importance of Habitat Structural Features in a Sierra Nevada Mixed-conifer Forest. *Environmental Entomology*, 35(4): 964-975

Awobajo, A. O. (1981): An Analysis of Oil Spill Incidents in Nigeria. *Proceedings of National Seminar on Petroleum Industries and Nigerian Environment*, Warri. pp. 57 – 63.

Battigelli,J.P and Marshall,V.G (1993): Relationships Between Soil Fauna and Soil Pollutants. In: *Proceedings of Forest Ecosystem Dynamics Workshop*. February 10-11. FRDA II, Report 210. Province of British Columbia, Canada, pp. 31-34.

Bestelmeyer, Brandon T., Joel, R. Brown, Kris, Havstad M, Robert Alexander, George, Chaveh and Jeffery E. Herrick (2008): Development and Use of State-and-Transition Models for Rangelands. *Journal of Range Management*. 56(2): 114 – 126.

Beyrem, H, Mahmoudi, E. E, N, Hedfi, A, Boufahja, F, Aïssa, P. (2007): Individual and Combined Effects of Cadmium and Diesel on a Nematode Community in a Laboratory Microcosm Experiment. *Ecotoxicology and Environmental Safety*.68:412–418.

Bossert, I., Bertha, A.S., (1984): Hydrocarbon in Soil Ecosystems. In: Altas, R.M. (Ed.), Petroleum Microbiology. *Macmillan Publ.*, New York, pp. 458–474.

Bromham, L.; Cardillo, M.; Bennett, A. F. and Elgar, M. A. (1999): Effects of Stock Grazing on the Ground Invertebrate Fauna of Woodland Remnants. *Australian Journal of Ecology*, 24(3): 199-207.

Brown, B. L. (2003): Spatial Heterogeneity Reduces Temporal Variability in Stream Insect Communities. *Ecology Letters*, 6(4): 316-325

Christiansen, K. A., Janssens, F., Pomorski, R.J., Greenslade, P. (2004): Checklist of the Collembola: key to the Genera. http://www.collembola.org (*Accessed January, 2015*)

Connor, E. F. and Simberloff, D. (1979): The Assembly of Species Communities: Chance or Competition? *Ecology*: No Vol. Number 1132-1140

D'Amato, A. W.; Orwig, D. A. and Foster, D. R. (2009): Understory Vegetation in Old-growth and Second-growth Tsugacanadensis Forests in Western Massachusetts. *Forest Ecology and Management*, 257(3): 1043-1052.

Del Val, C.; Barea, J. and Azcón-Aguilar, C. (1999): Assessing the Tolerance to Heavy Metals of Arbuscularmycorrhizal Fungi Isolated from Sewage Sludge-contaminated Soils. *Applied Soil Ecology*, 11(2): 261-269.

Dufrêne, M. and Legendre, P. (1997): Species Assemblages and Indicator Species: The Need for a Flexible Asymmetrical Approach. *Ecological Monographs*, 67(3): 345-366

El- Surtasi, E. I. (2012): Impact of Anthropogenic Activities on the Ground Insect's Biodiversity in New Damietta Region, Egypt. Faculty of Science, Damietta Branch, Mansoura University. Master Degree. 75pp

Fatoba, Paul O., Ogunkunle, Clement O. and Ihaza, Cynthian O. (2015): Assessment of Metal Pollution of Soil and Diagnostic SpeciesAssociated with Oil Spills in the Niger Delta, Nigeria.

Environmental Research, Engineering and Management, 71(3), 13-22.

Gauch, H. G. (1982): *Multivariate Analysis in Community Ecology, Cambridge University Press.* 109pp

Gbarakoro, T.N., Okiwelu, S.N, Umeozor, C O., Badejo, A.(2012): Soil Microarthropods in A Secondary Rainforest, Rivers State, Nigeria - III-Partial Recovery after an Oil Spill. *International Journal of Ecosystem*. 2(2):1-4.

González Megías, A.; María Gómez, J. and Sánchez Piñero, F. (2007): Diversity Habitat Heterogeneity Relationship at Different Spatial and Temporal Scales. *Ecography*, 30(1): 31-41.

Grevy, P. (1995). The Niger Delta Nigeria Pollution Assessment Study. *Report to the World Bank*. Carl Bro International Glostrup Denmark, Pg. 125.

Grzeœ, I. M. (2009): Ant Species Richness and Evenness Increase along a Metal Pollution Gradient in the Boles³aw Zinc Smelter Area. *Pedobiologia*, 53(1): 65-73.

Hammer O, Harper D.A. Tand Ryan PD: PAST (2001): Paleontological Statistics Software Package for Education and Data Analysis. *Palaeontologia Electronica*; 4(1): 1-9pp.

Hopkins, S. (2002): A Key to Springtail of Britain and Ireland. AIDGAP. 105pp.

http://www.calculateme.com/Volume/Barrels(Petroleum)/ToLiters.htm (Accessed January 2014)

Iloba, B.N. and Jarrett, I.E. (2007): Effect of Crude Oil Spills on the Abundance and Distribution of Soil Microarthropods at Different Depths. *Intern.Jour. Zoologic.Resear.* 3(1):24-32.

Iloba, B.N. and Odon, A.P. (2007): Studies on the Biodiversity of Soil Microarthropods and their Responses to Crude Oil Spills. *Intern.Jour. Zoologic.Resear.* 3(1):41- 47.

Janssen, P.; Fortin, D. and Hébert, C. (2009): Beetle Diversity in a Matrix of Old Growth Boreal Forest: Influence of Habitat Heterogeneity at Multiple Scales. *Ecography*, 32(3): 423-432

Lande, Russell (1996): Statistics and Partitioning of Species Diversity and Similarity Among Multiple Communities. *Oikos* 76: 5-13.

LaSalle, J. and Gauld, I. (1991): Parasitic Hymenoptera and the Biodiversity Crisis. *Redia*, 74(3, Appendix): 315-334.

Lassau, S. A.; Hochuli, D. F.; Cassis, G. and Reid, C. A. (2005): Effects of Habitat Complexity on Forest Beetle Diversity: Do Functional Groups Respond Consistently? *Diversity and Distributions*, 11(1): 73-82

Leather, S.R., Basset, Y. and Hawkins, B.A. (2008): *Insect Conservation & Diversity* – A New Journal for the Royal Entomological Society. *Insect Conservation & Diversity*, 1, 1-9.

Legendre, P. and Legendre, L. (1998): Developments in Environmental Modelling. *Numerical Ecology*, Volume 24, 41-46.

Maraun, Mark, Salamon, Jörg-Alfred, Schneider Katja, Schaefer, Matthias and Scheu, Stefan (2003): Oribatid Mite and Collembol an Diversity, Density and Community Structure in a Moder Beech Forest (*Fagussylvatica*): Effects of Mechanical Perturbations. *Soil Biology & Biochemistry* 35 (10): 1387-1394.

McCune, B. and Mefford, M. J (1999): PC-ORD. Multivariate Analysis of Ecological Data, Version 4.0 for Windows.

Ministry of Environment (MOEN) (2008): Oil Spill Logbook Investigated. Ministry of Environment, Bayelsa State, Nigeria. 10pp.

Moffat, D. and O. Linden, (1995): Perception and Reality: Assessing Priorities for Sustainable Development in the Niger River Delta. *Ambio*.24 (7-8): 527 – 532.

National Conference Report (NAT. CONFAB.), (2014): The National Conference 2014 Report of Committee on Environment. 148pp.

Odion, D. C. and Sarr, D. A. (2007): Managing Disturbance Regimes to Maintain Biological Diversity in Forested Ecosystems of the Pacific Northwest. *Forest Ecology and Management*, 246(1): 57-65.

Odu, C. T. I (1977): Pollution and the Environment. *Bull. Sci. Assoc. Nig*. 3(2) : 284 – 285 of *Orchesellacincta* (L.) (Collembola), *Arch. Environ. Cont. Tox*. 22 146–156.

Orlóci, L. (1978): *Ordination by Resemblance Matrices* (Eds.), Ordination of Plant Communities, *Springer*, pp.239-275

Okiwelu, S.N, Gbarakoro, T.N., Umeozor, C O., Badejo A.(2012): Soil Micro-arthropods in a Secondary Rainforest, Rivers State, Nigeria-IV-The Impact of Oil Pollution on Their Vertical Distribution. *Resources and Environment*. 2(2): 14-19.

Osuji, L.C., Egbuson, E.J. and Ojinnaka, C.M. (2005): Chemical Reclamation of Crude-oil-Inundated Soils from Niger Delta, Nigeria. *Chemistry and Ecology*, 21(1): 1–10.

OsujiL.C andNwoye I. (2007): An Appraisal of the Impact of Petroleum Hydrocarbons on Soil Fertility: the Owaza Experience. *African Journal of Agricultural Research* Vol. 2 (7), 318-324.

Pacala, S. and Roughgarden, J. (1984): Control of Arthropod Abundance by Anolis Lizards on St. Eustatius (Neth. Antilles). *Oecologia*, 64(2): 160-162

Paoletti, M.G., Bressan, M. (1996): Soil Invertebrates as Bioindicators of Human Disturbance. *Crit. Rev. Plant Sci*. 15, 21-26.

Peet, Robert (1974): The Measurement of Species Diversity. *Annual Review of Ecology and Systematics*.Vol. 5: 285-307.

Piola, R. F. and Johnston, E. L. (2009): Comparing Differential Tolerance of Native and Non-indigenous Marine Species to Metal Pollution using Novel Assay Techniques. *Environmental Pollution*, 157(10): 2853-2864

Rotimi, J., Agwu, E.J., El Bokl, M.M. and Uwagbae, M.A. (2014): Impact of Age of Crude Oil Spillage on Arthropod Diversity at Varied Soil Depths in Part of Niger Delta, Nigeria *Nigerian Journal of Life Sciences* 4 (1), 108-118.

Simpson, E. H. (1949): Measurement of Diversity. *Nature*. 168, 688.

Shannon, C.E. and Weaver, W. (1949): The Mathematical Theory of Communication. *University of Illinois Press*, Urbana. 134pp

Song, H., Wang, X., Bartha, R., (1990): Bioremediation Potential of Terrestrial Fuel Spills. *Appl. Environ. Microbiol*.56, 652–656.

Solue, M. E. (1990): The Real Work of Systematics. *Annals of the Missouri Botanical Gardens*, 77: 4-12

Sousa, W. P. (1979): Disturbance in Marine Intertidal Boulder Fields: The Non-equilibrium Maintenance of Species Diversity. *Ecology*, 60(6): 1225-1239.

Steen E. (1983), Soils Animals in Relation to Agricultural Practices and Soil Productivity, *Swed. J. Agr. Res.* 13, 157-165.

Syrek, D.; Weiner, W. M.; Wojtylak, M.; Olszowska, G. and Kwapis, Z. (2006): Species Abundance Distribution of Collembolan Communities in Forest Soils Polluted with Heavy Metals. *Applied Soil Ecology*, 31(3): 239-250.

TerBraak, C. J. F (1986): Canonical Correspondence Analysis: A New Eigenvector Technique for Multivariate Direct Gradient Analysis. *Ecology*. 67: 1167–1179.

Thomas, C. D.; Bodsworth, E.; Wilson, R. J.; Simmons, A.; Davies, Z. G.; Musche, M. and Conradt, L. (2001): Ecological and Evolutionary Processes at Expanding Range Margins. *Nature*, 411(6837): 577-581.

Torchote, P., Sitthicharoenchai, D. and Chaisuekul, C. (2010): Ant Species Diversity and Community Composition in Three Different Habitats: Mixed Deciduous Forest, Teak Plantation and Fruit Orchard. *Tropical Natural History*. 10: 37-51.

Uwagbae, M.A., Rotimi, J. and Agwu, E.J. (2014): The Pollution of a Terrestrial Ecosystem from Hydrocarbon Exploitation and Its Outcome on Collembola (Arthropoda: Insecta). *Asian Journal of Microbiology, Biotechnology & Environmental Sciences,16(3): 539 - 549.*

Wallwork, JA (1970): Ecol. Soil Animals. *McGraw Hill Publisher*, London. 106pp.

Pickett, S. and White, P. S. (1985): Natural Disturbance and Patch Dynamics. *Academic Press*. 76pp.

Whittaker, R. H. (1967): Gradient Analysis of Vegetation. *Biological reviews*, 42(2): 207-264.

Plate 1: Sampling site (SITE A) in Ekeki community in Yenagoa, Bayelsa State, Nigeria

Plate 2: A common incidence of oil spill at Ikarama community, flood of crude oil spilled over a stretch of 10km destroying farmand fallow lands, ponds, lakes and streams in the community

Plate 3: Sampling site (SITE A) (less than 1 year - 7 months after spill) in Ikarama community

Plate 4: Sampling site (SITE C) (19 months - 1 year and 7 months after spill) in Ikarama community

Plate 5: Sampling site (SITE D) (38 months - 3 years and 2 months after spill) in Ikarama community

Appendix 1: Spatial Distribution of the Taxonomic Species of Soil Arthropods Extracted from the Study Sites

Order	Family	Scientific name	Code	SITE D	SITE A	SITE B	SITE C
Coleoptera	Carabidae	*Amara sp.*	Sp1	4	1	4	5
Coleoptera	Carabidae	*Carabus* sp.	Sp2	4	0	3	5
Coleoptera	Carabidae	*Cicindela* sp.	Sp3	3	1	3	4
Coleoptera	Carabidae	*Cotalpa (larva)*	Sp4	2	0	3	5
Coleoptera	Carabidae	*Cotalpa* sp.	Sp5	5	1	2	3
Coleoptera	Carabidae	*Geopinu* sp.	Sp6	4	0	3	4
Coleoptera	Carabidae	*Pheropsophus* sp.	Sp7	5	0	2	3
Coleoptera	Scarabeidea	*Aphodius* sp.	Sp8	12	1	5	9
Collembola	Entomobryidae	*Entomobrya* sp.	Sp9	120	25	32	45
Collembola	Entomobryidae	*Lepidocyrtus* sp.	Sp10	92	60	38	56
Collembola		*Hypogastrura*sp.	Sp11	570	91	163	229
Collembola	Isotomidae	*Folsomia* sp.	Sp12	389	53	113	159
Collembola	Isotomidae	*Hydroisotoma*sp.	Sp13	153	16	40	51
Collembola	Isotomidae	*Isotoma* sp.	Sp14	147	24	48	69
Collembola	Isotomidae	*Isotomurus* sp.	Sp15	169	27	36	44
Collembola	Onchiuridae	*Mesophorura*sp.	Sp16	168	20	31	63
Collembola	Onchiuridae	*Onchiurus* sp.	Sp17	85	7	37	51
Collembola	Sminthuridae	*Sminthurus* sp.	Sp18	161	3	36	55
Collembola	Sminthuridae	*Sminthurinus*sp.	Sp19	190	38	24	45
Hymenoptera	Formicidae	*Camponotus* sp.	Sp20	13	8	14	26
Hymenoptera	Formicidae	*Formica* sp.	Sp21	131	25	66	47
Hymenoptera	Formicidae	*Lasiusniger*	Sp22	70	9	15	25
Hymenoptera	Formicidae	*Solenopsis* sp.	Sp23	79	23	89	136
Hymenoptera	Myrmicidae	*Meranoplus* sp. *(Juv.)*	Sp24	20	2	0	3
Hymenoptera	Myrmicidae	*Meranoplus* sp.	Sp25	15	7	7	12
Hymenoptera	Poneridae	*Ectatomma* sp.	Sp26	20	11	11	17
Isoptera		*Coptotermes* sp.	Sp27	134	12	59	92
Isoptera	Termitidae	*Macrotermes* sp.	Sp28	65	7	16	22
Abundance (mean ± SD)				2830 ± 127.1	472 ± 21.5	901 ± 27.96	12850 ±53.2
Species richness				28	24	28	28

SITE A "less than 1 year ago (7 months)" , SITE B "19 months (1year 7 months) ", and SITE C "38 months (3 years 2 months) "; different ages of spill impacted sites and SITE D "Control site".

Land Reclamation, Soil Quality and Agriculture
Edited by: Dr. Pawan Kumar 'Bharti' and Alka Chauhan
ISBN: 978-93-5056-882-8
Edition: 2017
Published by: Discovery Publishing House Pvt. Ltd., New Delhi (India)

4 Integrated Nutrient Management (INM) for Increasing Productivity under Dryland Conditions

[1]M. Pavithra, [2]Ashoka Reddy Yerva and [3]N. Meena

INTRODUCTION

India accounts for 2.2% of the global land and 16% of the world's population. The country's population has crossed the one-billion mark in 2001. While the population is likely to further increase at an alarming rate and, side by side, as the land for cultivation of crops will decrease tremendously in the following decades, it will result in an increased demand for food, fodder, shelter, energy, employment, etc. The long-term fertilizer experiments have shown that continuous application of suboptimal doses of chemical fertilizers alone to soil has resulted in the deterioration of soil health, thereby culminating in environmental pollution and stagnation in crop productivity. Hence, integrated use of organic manures with optimal levels of NPK fertilizer is the need of the hour, as it will not only improve the nutrient status and soil health, but also prove to be a boon in stabilizing the crop yields over a period of time. Therefore, integrated nutrient management (INM) system is the only way to maintain and improve the nutrient status of Indian soils. In other words, INM system is an ecologically, socially and economically viable approach, which on the whole is non-hazardous.

What is Integrated Nutrient Management?

The term INM is interpreted in the much broader more holistic sense of "land husbandry". It thus embraces soil, nutrient, water, crop, and vegetation management practices, tailored to a particular cropping and farming system, undertaken with the aim of improving and sustaining soil fertility and land productivity and reducing environmental degradation.

Integrated Nutrient Management aims to optimize the condition of the soil, with regard to its physical, chemical, biological and hydrological properties, for the purpose of enhancing farm productivity, whilst minimizing land degradation. There is now greater awareness that INM can, not only provide

1 Ph.D Scholar (Agronomy), TNAU, Coimbatore, Tamil Nadu, India
2 Ph.D Scholar (Agronomy), TNAU, Coimbatore, Tamil Nadu, India
3 Ph.D Scholar (Agronomy), TNAU, Coimbatore, Tamil Nadu, India

tangible benefits in terms of higher yields, but simultaneously and almost imperceptibly conserve the soil resource itself. The field level management practices considered under the heading of INM would include the use of farmyard manures, natural and mineral fertilizers, soil amendments, crop residues and farm wastes, agroforestry and tillage practices, green manures, cover crops, legumes, intercropping, crop rotations, fallows, irrigation, drainage, plus a variety of other agronomic, vegetative and structural measures designed to conserve both water and soil. The underlying principles on how best to manage soils, nutrients, water, crops and vegetation to improve and sustain soil fertility and land productivity and their processes are derived from the essential soil functions necessary for plant growth. The following are fundamental to the approach outlined in these guidelines:

1. Loss of soil productivity is much more important than the loss of soil itself, thus land degradation should be prevented before it arises, instead of attempting to cure it afterwards, i.e. the focus for IPNM should be on sustaining the productive potential of the soil resource.
2. Soil and plant nutrient management cannot be dealt with in isolation but should be promoted as an integral part of a productive farming system.
3. Under rainfed dryland farming conditions soil moisture availability is the primary limiting factor on crop yields, not soil nutrients as such, hence INM requires the adoption of improved rainwater management practices (conservation tillage, tied ridging etc.), so as to increase the effectiveness of the seasonal rainfall.
4. With declining soil organic matter levels following cultivation, the adoption of improved organic matter management practices are a prerequisite for restoring and maintaining soil productivity (improved soil nutrient levels, soil moisture retention, soil structure and resistance to erosion).

INM - The Concept

The basic concept underlying the integrated nutrient management system (INMS), nevertheless, remains the maintenance and possible improvement of soil fertility for sustained crop productivity on long term-basis and also to reduce inorganic (fertilizer) input cost. The three main components of INMS as defined by FAO, 1998 are:

1. Maintain or enhance soil productivity through a balanced use of fertilizers combined with organic and biological sources of plant nutrients.
2. Improve the stock of plant nutrients in the soils.
3. Improve the efficiency of plant nutrients, thus, limiting losses to the environment.

Thus, integrated nutrient supply/management (INS) aims at maintenance or adjustment of soil fertility and of plant nutrient supply to an optimum level for sustaining the desired crop productivity through optimization of benefit from all possible sources of plant nutrients in an integrated manner.

Requirement of a crop for a nutrient is decided by the rooting behavior and its mining ability, the native soil status, the potential yields as decided by the soil-agroclimatic situations, the targeted yields and nutrient management. Therefore, an INMS is the most efficient and practical way to mobilize all the available, accessible and affordable plant nutrient sources in order to optimize the productivity of the crops/cropping systems and economic return to the farmer.

COMPONENTS OF INTEGRATED NUTRIENT MANAGEMENT

Bulky Organic Manures

In India, the estimate production of rural compost is about 226 million tons and urban compost of 6.6 million tons annually. Aggregate stability, decrease in pH, resistance to compaction, infiltration and water holding capacity. Proper methods of preparation of FYM/Compost therefore have to be popularized.

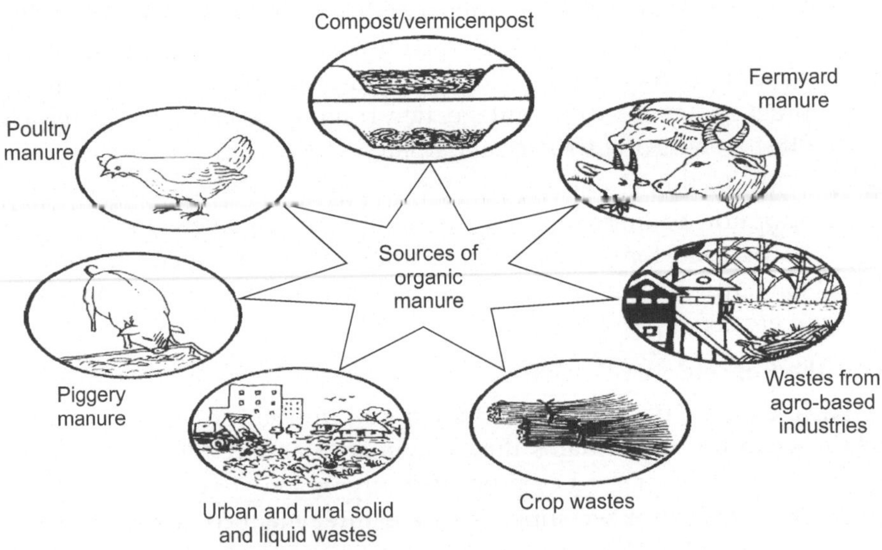

Different sources of organic manure for INM

Recycling of Organic Wastes

Substantial quantities of crop residues (350 million tons) are produced in India every year. Crop residues in combination with organics have been shown to improve availability of plant nutrients, soil organic matter, aggregate stability, infiltration rate, microbial population etc.

Bio-fertilizers

Bio-fertilizers such as rhizobium culture is an effective source of N supply to leguminous corps. Azotobacter and Azospirillium help in N fixation and supply to crops like rice, wheat, sorghum, maize, cotton, sugarcane, fruit corps and vegetables. Phosphate solubilising bacteria viz., *Bacillus aspergillus* help in making available soil P to the crops and increase the solubility of indigenous sources of P like rock phosphate. Blue green algae and Azolla have shown promise in low land rice. These are renewable and environment friendly supplementary sources of nutrients and are presently being used in quantities between 8-10 tons per year. *Vesicular arbuscular mycorrhiza* (VAM) has beneficial effect on plant growth, particularly in P deficient soils. Improved uptake of water, production of plant hormones and microbial activity are the prime benefits of mycorrhizal inoculations.

Govt. of India has been providing non-recurring grant-in-aid upto Rs. 20 Lakhs for setting up of biofertilizer production units of 150 MT capacity of annual production by industry, cooperatives, PSUs/NGOs etc. Under this scheme 68 BF units are funded by Ministry of Agriculture and 9 BF units are funded by Department of Fertilizer.Current production of Bio-fertilizer in the country is 10,000 metric tonne per annum against the production capacity of 18,000 metric tonne per annum.Average annual consumption of bio-fertilizers in the country is 64 g/ha.To ensure quality, standards have been notified by BIS and regular testing is also done by NBDC/RBDCs and State Government Laboratories.

Green Manuring

Green manuring is a cheap alternative to the use of fertilizer N. The process also makes a positive contribution to the maintenance of soil organic matter at a satisfactory level. The stem nodulating green manure plant, *Sesbania rostrata* (Danchia) can fix 100-250 kg/N/ha in 45 to 55 days and has great scope in rice culture. There is also greater scope for green-leaf manuring for rice and other crops from the lopping of various multipurpose trees popularized through afforestation and agro-forestry systems. Popularization of bio-gas plants, encouraging legumes in crop rotation and intercropping system and use of sewage, sludges and effluents for agriculture can also be the components of INMS.

Importance and Need of Integrated Nutrient Management

The increasing use of chemical fertilizers to increase the production of food and fibre is causing concern for the following reasons :

- Soils which receive plant nutrients only through chemical fertilizers are showing declining productivity despite being supplied with sufficient nutrients.
- The decline in productivity can be attributed to the appearance of deficiency in Secondary and micronutrients.

- The physical condition of the soil is deteriorated as a result of long-term use of chemical fertilizers, especially the nitrogenous ones. It also aggravates the problem of poor fertilizer nitrogen use efficiency (NUE).
- Excess nitrogen use leads to groundwater and environmental pollution apart from destroying the ozone layer through N_2O production.
- The recent energy crisis, high fertilizer cost and low purchasing power of the farming community have made it necessary to rethink alternatives.
- Unlike chemical fertilizer, organic manure and biofertilizer available locally at cheaper rates. They enhance crop yield per unit of applied nutrients by providing a better physical, chemical and microbial environment. This ultimately improves crop yield.
- The available quantity of animal excreta and crop residues cannot meet the country's requirements for crop production. Therefore, maximizing the usage of organic waste and combining it with chemical fertilizers and biofertilizers in the form of integrated manure appears to be the best alternative.

REFERENCES

Krishna Murthy, R. 2012. Productivity and Economics of Rainfed Rice as Influenced by Integrated Nutrient Management. *Madras Agric. J.* 99 (4-6): 266-270.

Kubsad, V.S., Hanumantharaya, L., Rudra Naik, V and Nekar, M.M.. Integrated Nutrient Management in Mungbean-safflower Sequence Cropping in Vertisols under Rainfed Conditions. 7th *International Safflower Conference*, Australia.

Lalith Kannan, R., M. Dhivya, M. Abinaya, M., Lekshmi Krishna, R and Krishnakumar, R. 2013. Effect of Integrated Nutrient Management on Soil Fertility and Productivity in Maize. *Bull. Env. Pharmacol. Life Sci.* 2 (8). 61-67.

Land Reclamation, Soil Quality and Agriculture
Edited by: Dr. Pawan Kumar 'Bharti' and Alka Chauhan
ISBN: 978-93-5056-882-8
Edition: 2017
Published by: Discovery Publishing House Pvt. Ltd., New Delhi (India)

5 Nutrient Needs of Different Crops Based on Targeted Yields

[1]M. Pavithra, [2]Ashoka Reddy Yerva and [3]D. Anitha

INTRODUCTION

By 2020, India will need 294 million tonnes of food grains as against a provisional production of 230 million tonnes in 2007-2008. Thus, an additional food grain production of 64 million tonnes has to be achieved from the same or even lesser land area, because some area will have to be diverted to civil works such as urban housing, roads, railways, industrial units etc. This additional production has, therefore, to come through efficient, judicious and balanced use of chemical fertilizer.

For this one should have a better understanding of the nutrient needs of the crops.

Nutrient Needs of Crops

A NPK ratio of 4:2:1 ($N:P_2O5:K_2O$) is generally considered ideal and accepted for macro-level monitoring of consumption of plant nutrients for the country as a whole. For producing a ton of cereal grains about 20 – 27 kg N, 8 – 19 kg P2O5 and 24 – 48 kg K_2O are required. Grain legumes remove much more N (two to four times of that in cereals) but most of it is fixed by the *Rhizobium* on their roots and very little N as fertilizer has to be applied, say, 20 – 25 kg N/ha as a starter. However, P and K removal is higher in pulses than in cereals.

Crop	Nutrient Requirement (kg) to produce 100 Crop kg of economic produce		
	N	P2O5	K20
Rice	2.01	1.12	3.00
Wheat	2.45	0.86	3.28
Maize	2.63	1.39	3.58
Sorghum	2.24	1.33	3.40
Fingermillet	2.98	1.13	3.90
Chickpea	4.63	0.84	4.96

[1] Ph.D Scholar (Agronomy), TNAU, Coimbatore, Tamil Nadu, India
[2] Ph.D Scholar (Agronomy), TNAU, Coimbatore, Tamil Nadu, India
[3] Ph.D Scholar (Agronomy), UAS, Raichur, Karnataka, India.

Soyabean	6.68	1.77	4.44
Groundnut	5.81	1.96	3.01
Potato	0.39	0.14	0.49
Cotton	4.45	2.83	7.47

The need of a cereal crop for added nutrients in a given field depends on:

- Yield of the crop
- Past fertilizer use
- Crop residue management
- Nutrients supplied by soil
- Nutrients in irrigation water
- Crop establishment and tillage
- Crop variety, such as its duration

The nutrient requirement of the crops yielding 3.5 t/ha will be certainly be much less (52 N, 29 P_2O_5 and 83 K_2O and 20 kg S) than crops targeted to yield 9.5t/ha (218N, 71 P, 309 K and 80 S). Depending on nutrient removal and soil nutrient supply, the difference has to be supplied through fertilizer at the efficiency with which the fertilizer nutrient is absorbed by the crop as determined by the genotype and quality of crop management. Achieving high yield targets are possible only when correct amount of nutrients is supplied at the right time matching with the crops nutrient demand during the season. Efficient nutrient management strategy should aim at maximizing crop uptake of nutrients, utilize crop residues/manures, and adopt good crop management strategies while correcting specific nutrient limitations through use of mineral fertilizers.

Soil as a Factor on NPK Uptake and Its Ratio in Crops

Soil due to native availability of NPK and other physical, chemical and biological properties also affects the supply and NPK uptake by crops. Soil tests for N most commonly used in India include organic C or alkaline permanganate oxidizable N, while for available P, Olsen's 0.5 M sodium bicarbonate extractable P is most widely used. 1 M ammonium acetate extractable or exchangeable K is the method for available K.

Soils are generally classified as low, medium and high in available nutrients. What is worth taking note, is that soil test values are relative and not absolute values and the amounts of NPK to be applied depends on how well a soil chemist can relate it to likely response of a crop to be obtained on a soil, and this is where real refinement comes into picture.

A procedure for such refinement was developed by *Dr. Ramamoorthy* at the Indian Agricultural Research Institute and is known as *'Targetted Yield Concept'* and has been widely used in *Soil Test Crop Response (STCR) studies.* The fertilizer dose determined on the basis of targeted yield concept gave higher yields than those obtained with RDF (recommended dose of fertilizer). At Hisar having sierozems (Aridisols) K application recommended on the basis of STCR for Raya was zero, while in Palampur having Hapludalfs (sub-montane soil) it was only 5 kg/ha as compared to 40 kg/ha in the state RDF for *toria*. However, in Coimbatore having Vertic Ustochrepts (medium black) both N and K applications on STCR basis were much higher than state RDF for groundnut. At none of these research centres the recommended dose on STCR basis had a NPK ratio of 4:2:1. Application of targeted yield concept can also take into account the application of nutrients applied through FYM or made available through biofertilizers resulting in reduced NPK application ratio.

NUTRIENT DEFICIENCIES IN INDIAN SOILS

Nitrogen - Low in 228 districts, Medium in 118 districts, High in 18 districts.

Phosphorus - Low in 170 districts, Medium in 189 districts, High in 17 districts.

Potassium - Low in 47 districts, Medium in 192 districts, High in 122 districts.

Sulphur - Low in 130 districts.

Magnesium - Kerala, AP, Parts of Tamil Nadu and Very acid soils.

Zinc - More than 50 % soils.

Iron - In most of calcareous soils, Mainly in groundnut, sugarcane, sorghum and upland rice.

Boron - Parts of West Bengal, Assam, Bihar and Karnataka.

PREDICTING YIELDS USING NUTRIENT FUNCTIONS

Nutrient function Crop yield is a function of 4 major factors:

Yield = f (crop, soil, climate, management).

Nutrient functions are fitted using data obtained in experiments conducted either in *deductive* or *inductive* approach.

Deductive approach

Deductive approach utilizes the natural variation in soil fertility for calibrating soil test values. Multilocation trials are carried out with same set of treatments. The responses are then fitted in the fertilizer prescription models.

Colwell (1967) developed this approach on the basis that some variables, which affect the response of crop to fertilizers, if omitted from the correlation between soil test and crop response, led to poor correlations. To prevent this difficulty, a calibration model was suggested based on the generalization of coefficients of an *orthogonal polynomial yield-response model*, which can include all the variables affecting the responses to fertilizers.

Inductive approach

This approach is by creating fertility gradient artificially in a particular experimental location by addition of fertilizers. The approach of inducing *fertility gradient (Ramamoorthy, 1970)* aims at eliminating influence of the 3 out of 4 factors in the yield function, namely: crop, climate and management in the experimental location. A large field having wide variation in fertility is chosen in a location. It is divided into 4 strips, which are treated with 4 doses of N, P and K fertilizers, viz., control (N0P0K0), ½ normal dose (N½ P½ K½), normal dose (N1P1K1) and double dose (N2P2K2). The normal doses are fixed based on *nutrient fixing capacity* of the soil. Exhaustive crop like maize is grown. The calibration crop experiment is then laid out. For the purpose of correlation, 21 treatments having one untreated check plot are tested.

Percentage of yield maximum concept (sufficiency concept)

This is commonly known as Mitscherlich and Bray approach. An empirical relationship is developed between percent yield, soil test, and fertilizer maximum yield (Bray, 1944).

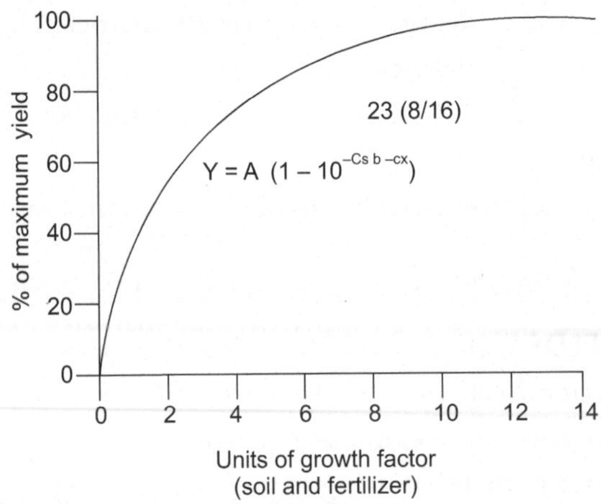

Presently, this approach is modified and used by the Department of Agriculture, Tamil Nadu for giving site-specific fertilizer recommendations.

The modified Mitscherlich-Bray equation is:

$$\text{Log}\,(A - Y) = \text{Log}\,A - Csb - Cx$$

Where, A = calculated maximum yield

Y = percentage yield

Cs = proportionality factor for soil nutrient

b = soil test value

x = dose of fertilizer added.

The maximum yield (A) is calculated by extrapolation

Targeted yield approach

Fertilizer recommendation must aim at providing balanced nutrition to crops. Balanced nutrition should ensure the nutrients to be present in available forms in adequate quantities and required proportion for the plant in order to produce maximum yield. The requirement of nutrient to produce the expected yield can be worked out based on *nutrient uptake.*

Liebig's law of minimum states that the growth of plants is limited by the plant nutrient element in the smallest quantity, when all others being present in adequate amounts. This forms the basis for fertilizer application for targeted yields, first advocated by *Troug (1960)* by significant *linear relationship* between the yield of grain and uptake of nutrients. Yield target can be projected within the linear region of the response function. This approach, popularly known as *Soil Test Crop Response* Function (*STCR*), implies that for obtaining a specific yield (grain or any other economic produce) a definite quantity of the nutrient must be taken up. This value can be determined by the magnitude of the expected yield (T in q/ha) and the nutrient requirement to produce unit quantity of that target (NR in kg/ha). Once it is known for a target yield, the fertilizer dose (FD kg/ha) can be estimated.

It is done by taking into account the efficiency of soil contribution (CS in percent) from the soil available nutrients (STV in kg/ha), and the efficiency of fertilizer of fertilizer contribution (CF in percent) from the fertilizer nutrients (FD in kg/ha) towards the total uptake.

$$FD = \frac{NR}{CF} \times 100T - \frac{CS}{CF} \times STV$$

Where

- FD - Fertilizer dose of N or P_2O_5 or K_2O (kg ha-1)
- NR – Nutrient requirement of N or P_2O_5 or K_2O (kg ha-1)
- CF – Per cent contribution from fertilizer N or P_2O_5 or K_2O
- T – targeted/expected yield [q/ha]
- CS – Per cent contribution from soil N, P, K.
- STV – Soil test value of N or P × 2.29 or K × 1.21 (kg/ha-1).

Law of Optimum

- The "Law of Optimum" is propounded as the unifying concept in Plant Nutrition for realizing"*Targeted yield of Crops*" through soil test based Nutrient management, as calibrated from a novel factorial field experiment technique, designed and used under the All India Coordinated Soil Test Crop Response (STCR) project investigations, on a range of soils and crops, in India over four decades.

- The "Law of Optimum" is defined as the concept of soil test based major plant nutrients (N, P and K) application to crops, by taking into account the percent contribution from the soil available nutrients as estimated by chemical soil tests and the percent contribution of nutrients from added fertilizers and manures and the nutrient requirement of the crop as estimated from plant uptake, for obtaining a specific yield target.
- Over 2000 demonstration trials in Farmers' fields conducted so far have validated this Law on the Targeted yield concept by realizing the yield target (s) within 10% deviation by followingsoil test based fertilizer use and adopting all other best Agronomic management practices.
- This Law harmonises the approaches namely, *'Fertilising the soil' versus 'Fertilising the crop'* ensuring for real balance (not apparent balance) between the applied fertilizer nutrients among themselves and with the soil available nutrients.
- The principles underlying the *"Law of Minimum", "Law of Diminishing returns" and the "Law of the Maximum".*
- Governing plant nutrition are not only embedded in the "Law of Optimum" but this Law also provides a basis for soil fertility maintenance consistent with high productivity and efficient nutrient management in "Precision Farming" for sustainable and enduring Agriculture.

Site Specific Nutrient Management

Concept: Nutrient Management and recommendation process in India is still based on response data arranged over large domains. The SSNM provides an approach for need based feeding of crops with nutrients while recognizing the inherent spatial variability. It involves monitoring of all pathways of plant nutrient flows/supply, and calls for judicious combination of fertilizers, bio fertilizers, organic manures, crop residues and nutrient efficient genotypes to sustain agricultural productivity. It avoids indiscriminate use of fertilizers and enables the farmer to dynamically adjust the fertilizer use to fill the deficit optimally between nutrient needs of the variety and nutrient supply from natural resources, organic sources, irrigation water etc. It aims at nutrient supply at optimal rates and times to achieve high yield and efficiency of nutrient use by the crop.

SSNM approach involves three steps:

- establishing attainable yield targets,
- effectively use existing nutrient sources and
- application of fertilizers to fill the deficit between demand and supply of nutrients.

Soil test based nutrient management

Evaluation of soil fertility and making fertilizer prescriptions for sustained crop production is of importance to the farming section. Considerable progress has been made to understand the contribution of soil and fertilizer to crop nutrition and the influence of nutrient levels and management on crop productivity and nutrient use efficiency. Soil testing to assess the nutrient supply capacity provided an opportunity for practical solutions to nutrient management. Soil test based recommendations will be useful only when it is based on important factors like soil, crop, variety, fertilizer and management interaction for a given soil condition. The soil test based crop response (STCR) project of ICAR provided the right impetus to understand the variability in the soil and crop with practical solutions to enhance nutrient use efficiencies narrowing down to each farm or field. The on-farm trials provided further need and scope for refinement, and development of more efficient soil test methodologies and decision support systems for adoption at all levels of technology transfer. Several models to predict changes in soil test values under a given environment were also developed. While the results for irrigated dry and rainfed crops were encouraging, in crops like wet land rice, soil test based fertilizer recommendation could not be that successful because of the unique system and chemistry that influenced soil nutrient availability.

SSNM for Rice

The SSNM approach for rice was developed across diverse irrigated rice-growing environments in Asia, where 90% of the world's rice is produced. Researchers developed the concept of SSNM in the mid 1990s. It was then evaluated and refined from 1997 to 2000 on about 200 irrigated rice farms in eight major rice-growing areas across six countries in Asia (Dobermann *et al.*, 2004). The need of a crop for fertilizer N, P or K was determined from the gap between the crop demand for sufficient nutrient to achieve a yield target and the nutrient supply from indigenous sources. A modification of the QUEFTS model (Janssen *et al.*, 1990) was used to predict the amount of fertilizer N, P and K required for a specific yield target. After 2001, the initial SSNM concept was systematically transformed into a plant-based approach with simple principles, tools and guidelines for enabling rice farmers to effectively supply their crops with nutrients as and when needed (IRRI, 2007).

Site-specific Nutrient Management for Nitrogen

Soils in India are deficient in N-supply and support not more than 3.0 t/ha of cereal grain production without nutrient application. Fertilizer N is invariably required to harvest higher yields but its vulnerability to losses makes it less efficient in terms of fertilizer N recovery (25-40%). The goal of N management is to maximize plant N use efficiency and minimize N losses. Key requirements include crop N demand with optimal internal use efficiency, potential indigenous N supply and its variation with climate, soil, cropping history and algorithms for N management strategy to match N supply and crop demand. At an approximate requirement of 15-22 kg N/ton of paddy and average recovery efficiency of 35%, rice would accumulate 150-220 kg N/ha to produce 6.0 t/ha of paddy with a base yield of 2.5 t/ha without N application. Given the requirement, the method, timing and quantity of N application becomes crucial.

- Depending on the season, duration of variety and site characteristics, split application of N (2-4) to match crop N demand at transplanting rice @ 30-50 % of recommended dose, rest top dressed at tillering and 3-5 days before panicle initiation in equal proportion is recommended.
- Early N application before 14 DAT or 21 DAS of rice depends on yield response, season and genotype - At yield responses of 1-3 t/ha apply 20-30 kg N/ha, or 25-30% of total N for >3.0 t/ha response as early N dose.
- Rest of the dose should be top dressed in 2-4 splits based on leaf color chart (LCC). Early N application (incorporation) should be increased for low tillering large panicle type varieties, for older seedlings of short duration varieties, for wider spaced crop and in areas of low temperature at transplanting time.
- Reduce or avoid early N application when high quality organic materials or composts are applied or in soils of high N supply capacity (soil OC > 2.0%).
- Real time N management using leaf color chart (LCC), as a guiding tool for proper timing substantially improved N efficiency and save fertilizer N to the extent of 15-30%.
- In areas of uncontrolled water situations (rain fed) soil placement of N or incorporation of urea coated with neem cake or its formulations have been very effective.
- Legumes in the cropping system, supplementation with available organic manures, recycling of crop residues and use of bio-fertilizers have proven to be very efficient substitutes for N and other nutrients with additional advantage of building soil quality.
- Rice hybrids with higher yield potential respond to higher nutrient application but are also reported to be efficient utilizers of nutrients. Additional dose of N at flowering is also recommended for hybrids to delay senescence and support large sink filling.
- In areas where top dressing of N is not feasible due to stagnant and uncontrolled water situations, N can be applied for quick recovery as spray @ 2-4% with knapsack sprayer or up to 15-20% when a high pressure low volume sprayers are used.

- Substitute 25-50% N through green manures/FYM/compost/bio-fertilizers to improve N economy and sustain soil and crop productivity.

Real Time N Management using LCC

- Leaf color chart (LCC) is used only for top dressing of N.
- Read the color of top few leaves at 7-10 days interval from early tillering to booting stage.
- Apply fertilizer N @ 50, 75, 100 or 125 kg urea/ha as top dressing, respectively for low, medium, high, or very high response environments each time at tillering and 3-5 days before panicle initiation stage.

Table 5.1: Guidelines for Estimating Total Fertilizer N Required for Rice Based on Hield Response to Fertilizer N and Efficiency of Fertilizer N Use

Efficiency of fertilizer N use (kg grain increase/kg applied N)→	15	18	20	25
Yield response (t/ha)↓	Fertilizer N rate (kg/ha)			
1	65	55	50	40
2	130	110	100	80
3	195	165	150	120
4	220	200	160	
5			250	200

SSNM for Phosphorous (P)

- The second most important plant nutrient, P is required for better root and shoot growth, starch mobilization and as source of energy.
- P is mobile within the plant and promotes tillering, root development, early flowering, and ripening. It is particularly important in early growth stages. Hence all recommended P should be applied as basal dose.
- Phosphorous is less available in coarse-textured soils containing small amounts of organic matter and small P reserves. Calcareous and saline soils, and acid laterites and acid-sulfate soils (strongly P-fixing).
- P deficiency reduces growth of roots and shoots; affected plants have few tillers with small, erect and dark green leaves with purple tint.
- Rice requires 5-9 kg P_2O_5/ton of grain and recovers about 15-25% of applied P with substantial residual effects.
- Depending on site characteristics, for a 6.0 t target yield/ha about 50 kg P_2O_5/ha fertilizer is required at native soil productivity of 4.0 t/ha, 6 kg P_2O_5/ton requirement and 25% recovery efficiency.
- Apply higher P dose in cold/*rabi* seasons and for legumes/oil seed crops in rotation.

- Being less mobile in soils and prone to fixation in calcareous and acid soils, the management of P needs careful consideration of total requirement of the cropping system, temperature regimes, and overall productivity.
- In acid soils of < 6.0 pH use low cost phosphate rock or its mixture with SSP to economize P input cost.
- Supplementing with organics, dipping of rice seedlings in super phosphate soil slurry and use of phosphorous solubilising micro-organisms etc substantially insulate P against soil fixation, and improve P use efficiency.
- Organic manures (up to 20-30% of P dose) along with P fertilizer prevents P fixation in calcareous, clay and acid soils.
- Cultivate P efficient rice genotypes like Rasi, Vikas, IR 64 which are high yielding, early to mid early duration group, and suitable for rabi season.
- Integration of deep rooted crops like chick pea with upland rice in the cropping sequence and/or application of P to pre kharif green manure/ grain legume crops in lowlands mobilize P and prevent from soil fixation.

Table 5.2: Guidelines for the Application of Fertilizer P_2O_5 According to Yield Target and P-limited Yield in Omission Plots (Witt *et al.*, 2007)

Yield target (t/ha)→	4	5	6	7	8
P-limited yield (t/ha)↓	Fertilizer P_2O_5 rate (kg/ha)				
3	20	40	60	—	—
4	15	25	40	60	—
5	0	20	30	40	60
6	0	0	25	35	45
7	0	0	0	30	40
8	0	0	0	0	35

SSNM for Potassium (K)

- Potassium increases spike let fertility and root oxidizing power, influences translocation of sugars to the grain besides improving plants tolerance to pests and diseases.
- Indian soils though show medium to high K fertility, the outflow of K by crops and cropping systems is very high (at 20-25 kg K_2O/ton grain).
- At the current levels overall balance of K in the system is negative in majority of the crop systems needing K application in quantities sufficient to prevent depletion of the nutrient to acute levels.

- For a target yield of 6 t/ha with 4.5 t/ha average yield at native soil fertility about 65-70 kg K_2O/ha is required (table 5.10-5.12).
- Recommended sources of K are MOP (50%) and paddy straw (50%).
- Half of the recommended K should be applied as basal and remaining half at panicle initiation stage especially for hybrid rice.
- Recycling of crop residues rich in K, split application in high productivity systems (eg. Hybrids) (table 5.13), additional dose of K in acid soil environments prone to iron, Al, sulfide toxicity etc all benefit the crop system and support high crop production.

Table 5.3: Guidelines for the Application of Fertilizer K_2O According to Yield Target and K-limited Yield in K Omission Plots (Witt *et al.,* 2007)

Rice straw inputs	Yield target (t/ha) →	4	5	6	7	8
	K-limited yield (t/ha) ↓	Fertilizer P_2O_5 rate (kg/ha)				
Low (<1 t/ha)	3	45	75	105	—	—
	4	30	60	40	120	—
	5	0	45	75	105	135
	6	0	0	60	90	120
	7	0	0	0	75	105
	8	0	0	0	0	90
Medium (2-3 t/ha)	3	45	75	105	—	—
	4	30	60	90	120	—
	5	0	20	50	80	110
	6	0	0	35	65	95
	7	0	0	0	50	80
	8	0	0	0	0	65
High (4-51 t/ha)	3	45	75	105	—	—
	4	30	60	90	—	—
	5	0	30	60	90	—
	6	0	0	10	35	70
	7	0	0	0	25	55
	8	0	0	0	0	40

Table 5.4: Plant Nutrient Recommendations Based on Soil Tests and Yield Goals for Soybeen and Other Oilseed Production

<table>
<tr><th rowspan="4">Crop</th><th colspan="9">Recommended Nutrients Based on Soil Tests</th><th rowspan="4">Suggested method of application</th></tr>
<tr><th colspan="5">Soil phosphorus level</th><th colspan="4">Soil potassium level</th></tr>
<tr><th rowspan="2">Nitrogen (N) pounds</th><th>Low</th><th>Med-ium</th><th>Opti-mum</th><th>Exce-ssive</th><th>Low</th><th>Med-ium</th><th>Opti-mum</th><th>Exce-ssive</th></tr>
<tr><th colspan="4">P_2O_5 pounds per acre</th><th colspan="4">K_2O pounds per acre</th></tr>
<tr><td>Soybean (full season)
(40 bu/A yield goal)</td><td>0*</td><td>80-120</td><td>45-80</td><td>20-45</td><td>0</td><td>80-125</td><td>40-80</td><td>20-40</td><td>0</td><td>Broadcast or banded at planting</td></tr>
<tr><td rowspan="3">Canole
A. Lodging not expected</td><td>120-150</td><td>—</td><td>60-80</td><td>40-60</td><td>20-40</td><td>60-80</td><td>40-60</td><td>20-40</td><td>0</td><td>Total</td></tr>
<tr><td>20-40</td><td>—</td><td>60-80</td><td>40-60</td><td>20-40</td><td>60-80</td><td>40-60</td><td>20-40</td><td>0</td><td>Broadcast</td></tr>
<tr><td>100-110</td><td>—</td><td>0</td><td>0</td><td>0</td><td>0</td><td>0</td><td>0</td><td>0</td><td>topdress</td></tr>
<tr><td rowspan="3">B. Lodging expected</td><td>70-100</td><td>60-80</td><td>40-60</td><td>20-40</td><td>0</td><td>60-80</td><td>40-60</td><td>20-40</td><td>0</td><td>Total</td></tr>
<tr><td>20-40</td><td>60-80</td><td>40-60</td><td>20-40</td><td>0</td><td>60-80</td><td>40-60</td><td>20-40</td><td>0</td><td>Broadcast</td></tr>
<tr><td>50-60</td><td>0</td><td>0</td><td>0</td><td>0</td><td>0</td><td>0</td><td>0</td><td>0</td><td>topdress</td></tr>
<tr><td>Sunflower 0.5 ton seed/A yield goal)</td><td>50</td><td>30</td><td>20</td><td>0</td><td>0</td><td>30</td><td>20</td><td>0</td><td>0</td><td>Broadcast at planting</td></tr>
</table>

Comparision of SSNM Approach and STCR Approach

SSNM approach	STCR approach
N management through LCC based on leaf colour where optimum time is taken	Soil test based on optimum time is taken care by split doses.
P & K management based on missing plot yield of previous year of some season	P & K management based on soil test values
In wet land rice, normal soil testing results do not correlate with nutrient supply/uptake, hence, actual nutrient uptake in nutrient omission plots.	Plot omission technical is not followed. Nutrient uptake by plant in control treatment is taken into consideration.
Fertilizer nutrient required = Total nutrient requirement-soil Nutrient supply	Based on soil test values, contribution from fertilizer plant nutrient requirement and desired yield of the
Recommendation are only rice	Technology is available or almost all crops including cereals, pulse, oilseeds, some vegetable crops tested in farmers' field and demonstrated for 2-3 years also.
Direct estimation of Nutrient supplying capacity of soil for a particular crop and location	For a crop and location validation of target yield equation are required.

Every farmer must conduct omission plot experiment during previous year to workout the fertilizer recommendation of current year which is very difficult.	Farmer need not conduct omission plot trial during previous year.
SSNM encourages the use of locally available nutrient sources particularly nutrient sources particularly organic and biological sources	This INM approach involves locally available organic and biological sources.
Less N losses N in more split doese is applied.	Almost similar in N losses.
Soil moisture should be sufficient when crop based on LCC. Thus more number of irrigations requirement especially in case of wheat.	Less number of irrigation
Regular monitoring by skilled person is required.	Not required for this purpose.
More split doese increases the cost of N fertilizer application	Cost does not increased

CASE STUDIES

Case Study-1

Effect of Site Specific Nutrient Management [SSNM] Through Targeted Yield Approach on Quality Parameters of Chilli [*Capsicum Annuum* L.]

A field experiment was conducted during kharif season 2007-08 on farmer's fields at Rottigawada village in Kundagol taluka of Dharwad district [Karnataka] to study the effect of site specific nutrient management on quality parameters of chilli *[Capsicum annuum L.]* through targeted approach.

Table 5.5: Ascorbic Acid (mg/100 g fruit), Oleoresin (%) and Colour Value (ASTA Units) as Influenced by Different Targeted Yield Levels of Chilli

Sr. No.	Targeted yield levels of chilli (q/ha)	Experimental location in farmers' fields at rottigarada village											
		Ascorbic acid (mg/100 g fruit)				Oleorresin content (%)				Colour value (ASTA units)			
		Location 1	Location 2	Location 3	Pooled	Location 1	Location 2	Location 3	Pooled	Location 1	Location 2	Location 3	Pooled
1.	10	153.6	156.2	149.8	153.2	15.50	15.00	14.75	15.08	224.5	226.3	219.0	223.3
2.	15	167.1	168.7	158.0	164.6	16.25	17.00	16.00	16.42	243.0	248.8	240.0	243.9
3.	20	179.4	180.6	170.2	176.8	18.25	19.00	17.75	18.33	282.5	290.0	278.8	283.8
4.	25	183.6	188.9	177.2	183.3	16.50	17.25	15.75	16.50	318.8	323.3	315.0	319.0
5.	30	191.1	191.3	189.6	190.7	16.00	17.00	15.50	16.17	314.5	317.8	313.3	315.2
	S.E±	3.5	3.4	2.7	1.8	0.83	0.95	0.79	0.45	3.9	4.9	5.5	3.1
	C.D (P = 0.05)	10.7	10.6	8.1	5.6	2.57	2.92	2.45	1.38	12.0	15.1	16.8	9.5

Abhilash K. Deshmukh *et al.*, An Asian Journal of Soil Science, [December 2009 to May 2010] Vol. 4 No. 2 :217-219

*Pooled data of three experimental locations

The Calculated Fertilize Dose for S.S.N.M. Treatment for Different Targeted Yield Levels of Chilli in Different Locations

	Treatment	Location 1	Location 2	Location 3
		$N:P_2O_5:K_2O$ (kg/ha)	$N:P_2O_5:K_2O$ (kg/ha)	$N:P_2O_5:K_2O$ (kg/ha)
1.	Targeted yield level 10 g/ha	90:39:98	88:38:97	97:390:97
2.	Targeted yield level 15 g/ha	164:84:165	161:85:164	163:85:164
3.	Targeted yield level 20 g/ha	236:132:231	231:131:230	235:130:232
4.	Targeted yield level 25 g/ha	309:177:298	304:178:297	310:179:296
5.	Targeted yield level 30 g/ha	382:223:364	376:224:363	381:222:363

[Asian J. Soil Sci. 4(2) Dec. 2009 to May 2010] *Hind Agricultural Research and Training Institute

CONCLUSION

The pooled data of three experimental locations indicated that Ascorbic acid [190.7 mg/100 g fruits] and colour value [319.0 ASTA units] were higher at targeted yield of 30 q ha^{-1} and 25 q ha^{-1}, respectively but higher oleoresin content [18.33%] was recorded in targetedyield level treatment of 20 q per ha.

Case Study–2

Targeted Yield Approach Under Integrated Nutrient Management for Assessing Fertilizer Requirement of Rice

Poonam Gautam*, Ajaya Srivastava, Sobaran Singh and Anil Kumar Saxena

G.B.Pant University of Agriculture and Technology, Pantnagar-263145, Distt. U.S. Nagar, Uttarakhand.

CONCLUSION

Response of rice to the selected combinations of four levels of N, P, K and three levels of FYM with simultaneous variations in initially available soil forms of these three nutrients were studied under soil test crop response. Grain and straw yield and soil analysis data were utilized to formulate the prescription equations for fertilizer doses under integrated nutrient management system with varying yield targets at different fertility levels. Besides, follow up trials were conducted to test the validity of these equations. Results of these trials clearly indicate the superiority of yield target approach over other approaches.

Table 5.6: Economics of Follow up Trials for Rice (Variety Pant Dhan-4)

Treat-ments	Ferti-liser dose N-P-K (Kg ha^{-1})	Actual Mean yield (t ha^{-1})	Addi-tional yield (t ha^{-1})	Value of addi-tional yield (Rs.)	Cost of fertilizer (Rs.)	B.C ratio	Net benefit (Rs.)	Repo-nse ratio	Yield devia-tion
FP	140-30-20	3.08	0	0	0	0.00	0.0	0	0
GRD	150-60-40	3.65	0.56	8538	2968.20	1.88	5569.8	2.3	0
TY1	70.1-35-4-4.7	3.89	0.81	12168	1424.37	7.54	10743.6	7.4	−2.78
TY2	83.0-46-11.6	4.34	1.25	18846	1812.57	9.40	17033.4	8.9	−3.47

FP- Farmers' practice, GRD- General recommended dose TY1- yield target 4.0 t ha^{-1} TY2 - yield target 4.5 t ha^{-1}

Case Study–3

Influence of Targeted Yield Approach on Yield, Yield Attributes, Nutrient Uptake and Economics of Maize

The experiment was conducted during *kharif* 2011 in sandy clay loam soil at Zonal Agricultural Research Station, UAS, GKVK campus, Bengaluru, Karnataka to study yield attributes, nutrient uptake and yield of maize (*Zea mays* L.) hybrid NAH 1137 (Hema) and economics of maize cultivation as influenced by nutrient management through various fertilization approaches.

The investigation consisted SSNM through fertilizers for targeted yield of 8 and 10 t ha-1, SSNM through INM for targeted yield of 8 and 10 t ha-1, STCR through fertilizers for targeted yield of 8 and 10 t ha-1, STCR through INM for targeted yield of 8 and 10 t ha-1. These eight treatments were compared with 100 per cent RDF and100 per cent RDF + FYM @ 10 t ha-1, and were replicated thrice.

Table 5.7: Grain Yield and Yield Parameters of Maize at Harvest as Influenced by Targeted Yield Approach

Treatment	Grain yield (t ha−1)	%YA (cm)	Cob length	NGRC	NGR	NGP	100 GW (g)
T1; 100% recommended dose of fertilizer							
(150:75:40 kg N:P_2O_5 K_2O ha^{-1})	4.04	–	16.5	13.6	31.4	426.7	21.4

T2: 100% Recommended dose of NPK + FYM							
(150:75:40 kg N.P_2O_5 K_2O ha^{-1} 10t FYM)	5.93	–	16.7	14.7	33.4	489.6	22.9
T3: SSNM through fertilizers for targeted yield of 8 t ha^{-1}							
(210:119 2:286.4 kg N.P_2O_5 K_2O ha^{-1})	7.69	96.17	18.4	16.2	35.0	569.3	26.6
T4: SSUM through fertilizers for targeted yield or 10 t ha^{-1}							
(263: 140.4.358 kg N:P_2O_5: K_2O ha^{-1})	9.77	97.67	20.3	20.5	41.3	891.2	32.9
T5: SSNM through INM for targeted yield of 8 t ha^{-1}							
(210.119.2.286.4 kg N.P_2O_5. K_2O ha^{-1})	7.53	94.13	18.3	16.1	34.9	564.4	25.3
T6: SSNM through INM for targeted yield of 10 t ha^{-1}							
(263:140.4:358 kg N.P_2O_5. K_2O ha^{-1})	8.43	84.33	18.8	19.0	38.5	797.8	29.5
T7: STCR through fertilizer for targeted yield of 8 t ha^{-1}							
(73.4.54.3:71.9 kg N.P_2O_5. K_2O ha^{-1})		7.16	89.54	15.1	34.5	517.3	25.1
T8: STCR through fertilizer for targeted yield of 10 t ha^{-1}							
(160.2:85.8.94.9 kg N.P_2O_5. K_2O ha^{-1})	8.56	85.57	19.8	19.2	37.0	802.9	29.8
T9: STCR through INM for targeted yield of 8 t ha^{-1}							
(73.4:54.3:71.9 kg N.P_2O_5. K_2O ha^{-1})	6.87	85.96	17.3	33.9	498.9	24.0	
T10: STCR through INM for targeted yield of 10 t ha^{-1}							
(160.2.85 8:94.9 kg N.P_2O_5. K_2O ha^{-1})	8.06	80.63	18.5	16.6	38.0	796.8	28.1
S.Em±	0.77	–	0.6	0.6	1.2	32.2	2.0
CD (P=0.05)	2.32	–	1.9	1.8	3.5	96.6	6.1

NGRC: number of grain rows per cob. % YA: per cent yield achieved over 100% RDF, NGR: Number of grain per row. 100 GW: 100 grain weight (g) and NGP: Number of grains per plant

Ashok Biradar *et al.*, Madras Agric. J., 100 (1-3): 146-149, March 2013

CONCLUSION

Among the treatments, SSNM through fertilizers for targeted yield of 10 t ha-1 recorded higher dry matter production (501.4 g), cob length (20.3 cm), number of grain rows cob-1 (20.5), number of grains row-1 (41.3), number of grains plant-1 (891.2) test weight (32.9 g) and significantly higher grain yield (9.77 t ha-1) as compared to other treatments. Whereas, significantly lower cob length (16.5 cm) number of grain rows cob-1 (13.6), number of grains row-1 (31.4), number of grains plant-1 (426.7) test weight (21.4 g), Grain yield (4.04 t ha-1) were recorded in the treatment with the application of 100 % RDF. Significantly higher nutrient uptake (504.8, 103.1 and 212.3 N, P and K kg ha-1) was recorded in SSNM through fertilizers for targeted yield of 10 t ha-1 over 100 % RDF (219.4, 32.2 and 73; N, P and K kg ha-1) and economics.

Case Study–4

Yield Target Approach Under Integrated Nutrient Management for Assessing Fertilizer Requirements of Onion in Mollisols of Uttarakhand

The response of onion to the selected combinations of 4 levels of N, P, K and 3 levels of FYM with simultaneous variations in initially available soil forms of these nutrients were studied under soil test crop response (STCR) The bulb and leaves yield with plant and soil analysis data were utilized to formulate equations each for inorganic and organic mode connecting the fertilizer doses with varying yield targets at different fertility levels.The validity of the equations has been tested in the valedictory trial, targeted and actual yields have been shown to be within ± 4.14% and target yield gave higher yield, net benefit and B/C ratio with or without FYM over farmer's practice. The results of valedictory trial clearly indicate the superiority of yield target over other approaches.

Treatment	Fertil-izer dose N-P-K-FYM (kg/ ha)	Actual mean yield (t/ha)	Addi-tional yield (t/ha)	Value of addi-tional yield (Rs.)	Cost of ferti-lizer (Rs.)	B:C ratio (Rs)	Net bene-fit (Rs)	Res-ponse ratio	Yield devia-tion (%)
Farmer's practice (T_1)	60-0-0-0	26.30	-	-	-	-	-	-	-
GRD (T_2)	100-50-50-0	28.35	2.05	10.250	2,854.0	2.59	7,396.0	10.3	-
FYM 20t/ ha (T_3)	0-0-0-20	26.80	0.50	2,500	1,000.0	1.50	1,500.0	12.5	-
Target 30t/ ha (T_4)	58-14-17-0	29.00	2.70	13,500	978.2	12.80	12,521.8	30.6	-3.333
Target 35 t/ ha (T_5)	91-22-28-0	33.55	7.2	36.250	1.553.7	22.33	34.696.3	51.5	-4.143
Target 30 t/ ha +	58-14-17-20	4.25	21,250	1,978.2	9.74	19,271.8	33.2	+1.833	
20 t FYM/ha (T_6)									

Target 35 t/ ha +	91-22-28-20	36.20	9.90	49,500	2,553.7	18.38	46.946.3	54.8	+3.429
20 t FYM/ha (T_7)									
CD at 5%		3.74							
Rate N = 10.5 P_2O_5 = 18.5 and K_2O = 7.08 Rs. /kg. Onion bulbs Rs. 2.00/t (2006-07)									

Anil Kumar Saxena et al., Indian J. Hort. 65(3), September 2008: 302-306

REFERENCES

Limin Chuana, Ping Heab,", Mirasol F. Pampolino. *Establishing a Scientific Basis for Fertilizer Recommendations for Wheat in China: Yield Response and Agronomic Efficiency,* Field Crops Research 140 (2013) 1–8.

NAAS (2006) Low and Declining Crop Responses to Fertilizers. Policy Paper 35: 1-8

DRR (2007;2008) Progres Report Soil Science. Vol. III

B. Ramamoorthy' and M. Velayutham2* *The "Law of Optimum" and Soil Test Based Fertiliser Use for Targeted Yield of Crops and Soil Fertility Management for Sustainable Agriculture,* Madras Agric. J., 98 (10-12): 295-307, December 2011.

IRRI (International Rice Research Institute). 2009a. Nutrient Manager for Rice.

http://www.irri.org/nmrice. Accessed 29 November 2009.

IRRI (International Rice Research Institute) (2009b) Site-specific Nutrient Management.

http://beta.irri.org/ssnm. Accessed 29 November 2009.

IRRI. 2007. Site-specific Nutrient Management. www.irri.org/irrc/ssnm. Accessed 28 February 2007.

Dobermann, A., C. Witt and D. Dawe (eds). 2004. Increasing the Productivity of Intensive Rice Systems Through Site-specific Nutrient Management. Enfield, NH (USA) and Los Baños (Philippines): Science Publishers, Inc., and International Rice Research Institute (IRRI).

K.N. Singh, N.S. Raju, *Prescribing Optimum Doses of Nutrients for Targeted Yield Through Soil Fertility Maps in Andhra Pradesh (AP),* J fnd Soc Agril Statist. 59(2). 2005 131-140

Land Reclamation, Soil Quality and Agriculture
Edited by: Dr. Pawan Kumar 'Bharti' and Alka Chauhan
ISBN: 978-93-5056-882-8
Edition: 2017
Published by: Discovery Publishing House Pvt. Ltd., New Delhi (India)

6

Agroforestry for Wasteland Development

[1]Alok Kumar Patra and [2]Amita Rani Patra

ABSTRACT

The demand for food and fodder is increasing due to ever increasing human and livestock population. But there is little scope to increase food production by increasing the area under cultivation. Because the land resources are decreasing due to various reasons like conversion of agricultural lands to wastelands as a result of erosion, salinisation and water logging and infra-structural developments. In this context, agroforestry has now been recognized as an effective tool for wasteland development. Agroforestry is being viewed as a restoration agent, rehabilitation process, bioremediation, and mechanism to high input agriculture on fragile lands. In this chapter an attempt has been made to enumerate the biological measures for management and development of various categories of wastelands like eroded gullied and ravinous land, sand dune, coastal wastelands, mining and industrial wastelands, degraded pasture, waterlogged and marshy land, etc.

Keywords: Agroforestry, degraded lands, wastelands

INTRODUCTION

India shares 16.7% of the world's human and 16.2% of livestock population, while its land is only 2.4% of the total geographical area of the world. Naturally, the pressure on the land is often beyond its carrying capacity. Therefore, the productive lands, especially the farmlands in India are in the constant process of various degrees of degradation and are fast turning into wastelands. At present, approximately 68.35 million hectare area of the land is lying as wastelands in India (NRSA, 2005). Out of these lands, about 50% lands are such non-forest lands, which can be made fertile again if treated properly. In the last 60 years

1 Associate Professor (Agronomy), All India Coordinated Research Project on Integrated Farming Systems, Orissa University of Agriculture and Technology, Bhubaneswar-751003, Odisha, India

2 Scientist, Krishi Vigyan Kendra, Orissa University of Agriculture and Technology, Baliapal, Balasorer-756023, Odisha, India

it is India's lush green village forests and woodlots have been deforested to the maximum. It is precisely to restore this ecological imbalance by developing the degraded non-forest wastelands, Government of India had created the Department of Wasteland Development during July, 1992 under the Ministry of Rural Development, which has been subsequently reorganized and renamed Department of Land Resources, with a broader mandate.

WASTELANDS

Land degradation or deterioration of land quality for agricultural production and environmental protection has been a matter of concern for land users. Land degradation assessment undertaken by the various Central and State agencies resulted in the generation of databases on the degraded and wastelands. But these agencies had used varying definitions of land degradation, data sources, classification systems, methodologies and scales that resulted in diverse estimates of degraded and wasteland areas (Maji, *et. al.*, 2010). The earliest assessment of the area affected by the land degradation was made by the National Commission on Agriculture at 148 M ha, followed by 175 M ha by the Ministry of Agriculture (Soil and Water Conservation Division). The NBSS&LUP

Table 6.1: Land Degradation Assessment by Different Organizations

Agency	Estimated extent (M ha)	Criteria for delineation
National Commission on Agriculture (NCA, 1976)	148.09	Based on the secondary data
Ministry of Agriculture (1978) (Soil and Water Conservation Division)	175.00	Based on the NCA's estimates. No systematic survey was undertaken
Society for Promotion of Wastelands Development (SPWD) (Bhumbla and Khare, 1984)	129.58	Based on the secondary estimates
NRSA (1985)	53.28	Mapping on 1 : 1 million scale based on the remote-sensing techniques
Ministry of Agriculture (MOA, 1985)	173.64	Land degradation statistics for states
Ministry of Agriculture (MOA, 1994)	107.43	Elimination of duplication of area. Area reclaimed counted
NBSS&LUP (1994)	187.70	Mapping on 1 : 4 million scale based on the Global Assessment of Soil Degradation (GLASOD) guidelines
NBSS&LUP (2004) (revised)	146.82	1 : 1 million scale soil map
Department of Environment (Vohra, 1980)	95.00	
National Wasteland Development Board (1985)	123.00	

Source: Gautam and Narayan, 1988

(National Bureau of Soil Survey and Land Use Planning) estimates projected an area of 187 M ha as degraded lands in 1994 following GLASOD (Global Assessment of Soil Degradation) methodology (Oldeman, 1988), and revised it to 147 M ha in 2004. The National Wasteland Development Board estimated an area of 123 M ha under wastelands.

National Wasteland Development Board was established in 1985, mainly to tackle the problem of degradation of lands, restoration of ecology and to meet the growing demands of fuel wood and fodder at the national level. The Board was reconstituted in August 1992 and was made responsible for mainly development of wastelands in non forest areas in totality by involving local people at every stage of development. It aims at creating a scenario where the Government acts as a facilitator and the people at the grass root level become the real executioner of the programme. The degradation of environment in the fragile Indian sub-topical eco-system is basically attributed to the following factors.

1. Increasing biotic pressure.
2. Absence of adequate investments and appropriate management practices.
3. High rate of population growth and high incidence poverty in rural areas.
4. Over-exploitation of national resources.
5. The break-down of traditional institutions for managing common property resources and failure of new institutions to fill the vacuum.
6. Faulty land use practices.

The consequences of this environmental degradation are soil erosion and land degradation, depletion of natural resources, lower productivity, ground water depletion, shortage of drinking water, reduction in species diversity and increase in the extent of wastelands. Development of wastelands mainly in non-forest areas aimed at checking land degradation, putting such wastelands of the country to sustainable use and increasing biomass availability especially that of fuel wood, fodder, fruits, fiber and small timber. Government of India is taking up this colossal task through its Integrated Wasteland Development Project by revitalizing and reviving village level institutions and enlisting people's participation. The basic objective of this scheme is an integrated wastelands development. These plans are prepared after taking into consideration the land capability, site condition and local needs of the people. The major activities taken up under the scheme include:

1. In situ soil and moisture conservation measures like terracing, bunding, trenching, vegetative barriers and drainage line treatment.
2. Planting and sowing of multi-purpose trees, shrubs, grasses and legumes.

3. Encouraging natural regeneration.
4. Promotion of agroforestry and horticulture.
5. Wood substitution and fuel wood conservation measures.
6. Drainage line treatment by vegetative and engineering structures.

Wastelands are broadly classified into culturable and unculturable wastelands. The lands that cannot be developed for vegetative cover are called unculturable wastelands, which include barren rocky areas, snow covered glacier areas and steep sloppy areas. The lands those are capable of vegetative cover but not being used due to different constraints of varying degrees are called culturable wastelands. These lands can be put to some productive use after proper treatment and reclamation measures. National Wasteland Development Board classified the culturable wastelands into the following categories.

1. Eroded gullied and ravinous land
2. Undulating upland
3. Waterlogged land
4. Salt affected saline and alkali soils
5. Shifting cultivation areas
6. Degraded forest areas
7. Degraded non forest plantation area

Table 6.2: Categories of Wastelands in India

Category	Area (in sq. kms.)
Barren Rocky/sheet rock	64584.77
Degraded land under plantation crop	5828.09
Degraded/pastures/grazing land	25978.91
Gullied/or ravinous land	20553.35
Land affected by salinity/alkalinity	20477.38
Mining/industrial wastelands	1252.13
Sands-inland/coastal	50021.65
Shifting cultivation land	35142.20
Snow covered/glacial	55788.49
Steep sloping area	7656.29
Underutilized/degraded notified forest land	140652.31
Upland with or without scrub	194014.29
Water logged and marshy	16568.45
Total	**638518.31**

Source: http://www.mospi.gov.in

8. Sand dunes, sand bar and coastal sand
9. Mine spoils and industrial wastelands
10. Strip lands
11. Pasture and grazing lands

A management system needs to be devised that is capable of producing food from marginal agricultural land and wastelands and is also capable of maintaining and improving quality of producing environment. The shrinking of land per capita, huge demand supply gap of various kind of forest products, food products as well as fodders are making agroforestry viable and alternative land use option.

AGROFORESTRY CONCEPT

Agroforestry is a new name for a set of old practices. The general concept of agroforestry is to integrate trees and agriculture so as to create a more diversified landscape, while providing the producers with new environmental and economic benefits. In other words agroforestry is a method of farming that allows trees and shrubs to grow along with crops and/or livestock, therefore blending agriculture and forestry in the same production system (Bene, 1977). In fact, man's association with forest is much older than with agriculture. First man was a food gatherer and hunter. Then he realized that seeds of the food he collected germinated, grew into plants and bore the fruits, and started to cultivate foods. Man's desire to live in co-existence in a community created settled agriculture (Tejwani, 2008).

The pressure on the agricultural lands has increased manifolds due to the increasing population, expansion of urban area and the industrialization process. The environment has also been disturbed. Soil is losing its productivity and the biodiversity is threatened. Farming community is trying all means to increase the land productivity. Chemical fertilizers and pesticides are applied in higher proportion, causing environmental pollution hazards. Under all these circumstances agroforestry has shown that besides sustainable agriculture it can also help promote a better environment. Trees have always played an important role in mankind's survival. This relatively young science known as agroforestry was brought from the realm of indigenous knowledge into the forefront of agricultural research three and half decades ago and was promoted widely as a sustainability-enhancing practice that combines the best attributes of forestry and agriculture.

Several definitions of agroforestry have been suggested since its conceptualization as a land use approach in 1977. But in short, agroforestry is generally perceived as the deliberate cultivation of several productive components, of which at least one is a woody perennial, on the same piece of land, combined either spatially or sequentially.

In the early 1980s International Council for Research in Agroforestry (ICRAF) defined agroforestry as "a collective name for land-use systems and technologies where woody perennials (trees, shrubs, palms, bamboos, etc.) are deliberately used on the same land management units as agricultural crops and/ or animals, in some form of spatial arrangement or temporal sequence". This definition gained wider acceptance and it was used till the mid 1990s. Then in 1996 ICRAF redefined agroforestry as "a dynamic, ecologically based natural resource management system that, through the integration of trees on farms and in the agricultural landscape, diversifies and sustains production for increased social, economic and environmental benefits for land-users at all levels". Thus, in agroforestry systems there are both ecological and economical interactions between the different components (Lundgren and Raintree, 1982).

Moreover, there are three attributes which, theoretically, all agroforestry systems possess (Nair, 2008).

1. *Productivity:* Agroforestry systems aim to maintain or increase production of preferred commodities as well as productivity of the land.
2. *Sustainability:* Agroforestry can achieve and indefinitely maintain conservation and fertility goals by conserving the production potential of the resource base, mainly through the beneficial effects of woody perennials on soils.
3. *Adoptability:* Improved or new agroforestry technologies that are introduced into new areas should fit the social as well as environmental characteristics of the land use system for which it is designed and also confirm to local farming system.

Benefits from Agroforestry

Agroforestry systems play a great role in conservation of natural resources, especially soil. Agroforestry has both productive and service functions. Among the productive functions, food, fuel wood, timber and fodder are the most important besides gums, resins, medicines, fibres and a host of other economic base and greater food security. The service functions include shade, reduction in wind speed, control of erosion and maintenance and improvement of soil fertility. Agroforestry systems increase nutrients inputs through nitrogen fixing trees and nutrient uptake from deep soil horizons. They reduce nutrient leaching losses through tree root and micorrhizal systems. Agroforestry systems recycle nutrients through decomposition of litter, pruning and root residues. Agroforestry is a medium and a combination of agricultural and forestry technologies to create integrated, diverse and productive land use systems (Garrity and Agus, 2000). Benefits from agroforestry can be grouped under three broad categories - environmental, economic or social benefits.

Environmental benefits

1. Reduction of pressure on natural forests
2. More efficient recycling of nutrients by deep rooted trees on the site
3. Better protection of ecological systems
4. Reduction of surface runoff, nutrient leaching and soil erosion through impeding effect of tree roots and stems on these processes
5. Improvement of microclimate, such as lowering of surface soil temperature and reduction of evaporation of soil moisture through a combination of mulching and shading
6. Increment in soil nutrients through addition and decomposition of litter
7. Improvement of soil structure through the constant addition of humus from decomposed litter

Economic benefits

1. Increment in outputs of food, fuelwood, fodder, fertilizer and timber
2. Reduction in incidence of total crop failure, which is common to single cropping or monoculture systems
3. Increase in levels of farm income due to improved and sustained productivity

Social benefits

1. Improvement in rural living standards from sustained employment and higher income
2. Improvement in nutrition and health due to increased quality and diversity of food outputs
3. Stabilization and improvement of communities through elimination of the need to shift farm activities from one site to other

Need of Agroforestry

Forest cover in India is 67.71 million ha, constituting 20.60% of its total geographical area against the ideal coverage of 33.3%. Out of this, very dense forest (>70% canopy density) constitute 5.44 million ha (1.66%), moderately dense forest (40-70% canopy density) 33.26 million ha (10.12%) and open forest (40-70% canopy density) 28.99 million ha (8.82%). The forest cover in the hilly districts is only 35.85% compared with the desired 66% area. The per capita availability of forests in India is one of the lowest, 0.08 hectares as against an average of 1.07 hectares for developed countries and 0.64 hectares for the world as a whole. Thus to bridge the gap between desired and available forest coverage in the country agroforestry is the best intervention.

The carrying capacity of the arid and semi-arid regions is overstressed. The grazing lands in almost all parts of India have to support animals beyond their carrying capacity. Repeated grazing by animals hardly leaves any vegetation unless specially protected. The consequence is destruction of environment leading to desertification. Inclusion of fodder tree species with suitable grasses in the agroforestry system in wastelands will check overgrazing. Agroforestry interventions hold the key to check soil erosion and leaching loss of nutrients and to improve the soil productivity through biological nitrogen fixation, organic matter addition and efficient nutrient cycling.

Soil is the most precious natural non-renewable resource. Soil erosion is the major cause of land degradation and loss of productivity. Erosion control has always started with tree and grass planting. Tree roots bind the soil and their leaves break the force of wind and rain on soil. Trees fight soil erosion, conserve rainwater and reduce water runoff. Trees also absorb dangerous chemicals and other pollutants that have entered the soil. Trees can either store harmful pollutants or actually change the pollutant into less harmful forms. Trees filter sewage and farm chemicals and reduce the effects of animal wastes. Thus, agroforestry practices are most suited for sustainability. Heavy fertilization coupled with high irrigation frequencies leads to soil loss, nutrient loss and degradation of land whereas in forest cover land upgradation is a continuous process, it restores soil and moisture conservation and there is a gain from all angles.

There is a global crisis of energy and man is striving hard to find out some alternative source of energy. Fuel wood is one of the established sources to meet energy requirement. About 90% people in the developing countries depend upon wood as source of fuel. But in these regions deforestation is five times more than afforestation. If this continues a time may come when there will be sufficient food but not the fuel to cook. So the only solution is to promote agroforestry in degraded and wastelands. About 87% of the annually harvested wood in India is used as firewood. At present in rural India 60-80 million tonnes of dry cow dung is utilized as fuel, equivalent to 300-400 million tonnes of freshly collected manure. Acute shortage of fuelwood can be met through agroforestry practices in wastelands (Patra, 2013).

Area not presently available for arable cropping can be put to agroforestry practices. It is estimated that out of 120.72 million ha wasteland and degraded land in India 104.14 million ha is arable lands and 16.53 million ha is open forest land. Out of this area water erosion affects the largest proportion followed by salinization and terrain deformation. The extent of degraded forests in the country is more than 40 million ha. Besides these, about 50 m ha area is degraded due to mining activity. These areas can be reclaimed by adoption of suitable agroforestry practices. Since land holding becoming smaller and smaller due to demographic pressure, forest area in the vicinity of the thickly populated villages is diminishing as human demands for fuel, fodder, small timber and other forest minor products are met from the forest. By adopting agroforestry in the wastelands near the villages the pressure on natural forest could be greatly reduced.

MANAGEMENT OF WASTELANDS

The characteristics of the wasteland and their development vary with the categories. Agroforestry is being viewed as a restoration agent, rehabilitation process, bioremediation, and mechanism to high input agriculture on fragile lands. This system involves the conscious and deliberate use of land for the concurrent production of agricultural crops including tree crops and forest crops.

Gullied and Ravinous Land

A narrow deep gash formed due to concentrated runoff is called gully and it is considered as the severest form of water erosion. Very deep and wide gullies with steep sides are known as ravines. The ravines are classified as shallow, medium or deep based on gully depth, bed width and area. Ravinous lands are mainly confined to the states of Uttar Pradesh, Madhya Pradesh, Rajasthan and Gujarat. Clearance of forest for agriculture, faulty soil works for agriculture, uncontrolled grazing, low annual rainfall and extreme dryness of soil due to easy and fast drainage and high soil porosity are the major causes of ravine formation.

The ravinous lands can be managed through integrated approach of soil conservation and afforstation. Maintaining dense multistoried vegetation is considered highly effective. This reduces slash erosion, reduces runoff, increases infiltration and improves soil structure through addition of organic matter. Shallow and medium gullies can be put under silvipastoral system with suitable tree and grass species. The deep and narrow gullies are best controlled by putting them to permanent vegetation. Gully heads and sides are stabilized by planting grasses. Reducing the slopes of the gullies and diverting the surface flows are essential for successful afforestation programme in the gullied and ravinous lands. The gullies have to be plugged with suitable mechanical measures to check soil erosion and conserve soil moisture.

The suitable tree and shrub species for these wastelands are *Eucalyptus* spp., *Dalbergia sissoo, Gmelina arborea, Emblica officinalis, Acacia auriculiformis, Acacia nilotica, Acacia catechu, Albizia lebbeck, Albizia procera, Leucaena leucocephala, Azadirachta indica, Dendrocalmus strictus, Prosopis juliflora, Prosopis chilensis, Pongamia glabra, Tectona grandis* and *Ailanthus excelsa*. Among the grasses and legumes *Cenchrus ciliaris, Cenchrus setigerus, Chrysopogon fulvus, Dicanthium annulatum, Sacharum spontaneum, Pennisetum pedicellatum, Cynodon dactylon, Heteropogon contortus, Stylosanthes* spp. are found suitable for such lands.

Shifting Cultivation Areas

Shifting cultivation is a cyclic land use practice of felling trees and burning of forest areas for growing agricultural crops leading to land degradation.

Shifting cultivation areas are characterized with high rainfall, steep slopes and shallow soils. This system is prevalent in several parts of north-eastern hill regions of Arunachal Pradesh, Meghalaya, Mizoram, Manipur, Nagaland and Tripura. It is also practised in some parts of Andhra Pradesh, Assam, Odisha, Jharkhand and Madhya Pradesh. Burning of vegetation in shifting cultivation alters plant nutrients from organic to inorganic forms. Some nutrients are lost by volatization and a sizable quantity of nutrients is also lost through blown off ash due to strong wind velocity during dry period. Wrong tillage practices lead to runoff and soil erosion. Thus, shifting cultivation causes deforestation and denudation of hilly slopes. Integrated approach of conservation measures and improved farming including suitable agroforestry systems should be adopted for management of these degraded lands. Agrisilviculture (herbaceous crop + tree), silvipasture (tree + forage crop), hortisilviculture (horticultural crop + tree) and hortisilvipasture (horticultural crop + tree + forage crop) are the best suited agroforestry systems in shifting cultivation.

The main objective of introducing agroforestry systems in shifting cultivation fallows is to recover depleted soil nutrients. The best species for the fallow system should include good nitrogen fixation in soil. Plants included should be compatible with future crops, free of any negative physical or chemical effects on the soil and not in competition with the crops to be planted later on the same site. This include direct seeding of clean tilled, harvested plots, selective cutting of bush, followed by enrichment planting with tall seedlings. *Acacia catechu, Dalbergia sissoo, Anacardium occidentale, Bombax ceiba, Santalum album, Acacia nilotica, Schima wallichii, Michelia doltsopa, Pterocarpus dalbergioides, Albizia lebbek,* etc. are suitable for planting in the degraded soil (Balasubramaniyan and Palaniappan, 2001).

The silvipastoral system comprising *Alnus nepalensis,* short duration fruit crops like pineapple and forage crops like *Panicum maximum* (guinea grass) and *Setaria sphacelata* (nandi grass) coupled with *Stylosanthes guyanensis* (stylo) could be sustainable agroforestry system for hilly areas with 30-60% slope. Lower areas of hilly slope are terraced and stabilized with mechanical measures and planted with fodder grasses and legumes like *Stylosanthes hamata, Stylosanthes guyanensis, Setaria sphacelata, Clitoria ternatia, Panicum maximum* and *Panicum polystachion* on risers. Suitable field crops like rice, maize, millets, sesame, groundnut, blackgram, greengram, horsegram, and root crops like arrowroot, ginger and turmeric are grown on the terraces according to the requirement of the farmers.

Sand Dune

In India, about 22.7% of total geographical area comes under sandy areas, mainly confined to Rajasthan, Gujarat, Punjab and Haryana. The sand dunes and sandy undulating plains are responsible for the creation of sandy wastelands. The new wastelands are being created due to faulty tillage and agricultural operations, cutting and lopping of trees and overgrazing of natural rangelands in arid and semiarid areas. These wastelands are characterized by loose structureless sands, poor fertility and water holding capacity and presence of alternate layers of calcium carbonate. The region is subjected to severe wind erosion, high temperature, scanty and erratic rainfall, frequent drought and high rate of evaporation.

These wastelands can be rehabilitated by suitable agroforestry practices. The plant species chosen should have deeply buried rhizomes or prostrate growth with stem anchored by abundant adventitious fibrous roots for rehabilitation of sand dunes. *Prosopis cineraria, Prosopis chilensis, Acacia tortilis, Acacia radiance, Acacia nilotica, Zyzyphus mauritiana, Erianthus munja, Dalbergia sissoo, Albizia lebbeck, Azadirachta indica, Leucaena leucocephala, Tamarix* spp. and *Parkinsonia aculeate* are the important tree species for these areas. Grass species like *Cenchrus ciliaris, Cenchrus setigerus, Lasiurus sindicus, Panicum turgidum, Panicum antidotala,* etc. are suitable for silvipastoral system.

Coastal Wastelands

Coastal sandy area in the form of a narrow strips along the eastern and western coasts occupy about 8.4 million hectare in the country. The soil of this area is characterized with alkaline in reaction, high sodium salt content, poor in nutrients and low in water holding capacity. The water table is generally high. The occurrence of cyclones is a common phenomenon in the coastal area. Thus afforestation of coastal areas in one kilometer width is recommended to moderate the effects of cyclones. *Casuarina equisetifolia* is the best recommended tree species for plantation along coastal sandy areas. Planting *Casuarina equisetifolia* in the outer area and growing perennial fruit crops like coconut (*Cocos nucifera*) and cashew nut (*Anacardium occidentale*) in the inner area is generally practised along the coast. Plantations are done in raised mounds where water table is high. Other species found suitable are *Pongamia glabra, Nipa fruiticans, Avicennia officinalis, Casuarina jhunjhuniana, Acacia auriculiformis, Acacia tortilis, Acacia mangium, Eucalyptus tereticornis,* etc. are suitable for plantations in coastal wastelands. In silvipastoral and hortisilvipastoral systems grass species *Panicum maximum, Cynodon dactylon, Sorobolus* spp., *Cenchrus* spp., *Chloris* spp., *Spinifex squamosus, Sporobolus* spp., etc. are most suited.

Mining and Industrial Wastelands

A large area in the states of Madhya Pradesh, Chhattisgarh, Bihar, Jharkhand, Odisha, Karnataka and other states are subjected to degradation due to open-cast mining of coals, bauxite, limestone, slate, etc. Surface mining requires operation of heavy machines to excavate the earth which leads to complete destruction of vegetation and the entire soil profile is disturbed. After mining these areas are left with boulders, lateritic heaps, stones, and pits of various dimensions which give a very desolate look. Highly undulating topography with irregular slopes causes heavy water and soil erosion. Reclaiming these wastelands is a challenging task due to disturbed ecosystem with poor physical, chemical and biological soil properties. The species found suitable with high survival rate are *Eleagnus umberilata, Coriaria nepalensis, Indigofera pulchella, Acacia auriculiformis, Dalbergia sissoo, Eucalyptus camaldulensis, Grevillea robusta, Grevillea pteridifolia, Albizia lebbeck, Prosopis chilensis* and *Cassia siamea*. The area should be levelled to some extent with the help of dozer before undertaking plantation. Pits of one cubic feet are opened at the spacing of 2 m × 2 m. The pits are filled with the forest soils for mycorrhizal inoculation in case of plantation of tree legumes. Application of compost or farm yard manure 5 kg and plant nutrients N, P_2O_5 and K_2O at the rate of 50 gram each per pit helps in early establishment and quick growth of the seedlings. Silvipastoral system with suitable grass species is found highly successful in mined out wastelands.

High Altitude and Steep Sloppy Areas

Indiscriminate grazing by cattle especially sheep and goat is the major cause of soil erosion in the hilly areas. In high altitude regions, the soil suffers from excessive runoff during monsoon and moisture stress during dry periods. Hedge row planting is required under hilly terrain. Nitrogen fixing tree and shrubs suitable for agroforestry systems may be planted in closer spacing. To stabilize the structure and to make productive use of the land, in steeply sloping lands the risers or terraces are densely planted with multipurpose trees for fruit, fodder and fuelwood. The trees species are *Grevillea robusta, Acacia catechu, Pinus roxburghii, Acacia modesta, Prosopis juliflora, Populus alba, Populus nigra, Populus candicans, Populus ciliata, Alnus nepalensis, Leucaena leucocephala*, etc. are suitable. Fruit trees planted are ber, papaya, dwarf mango, guava, citrus, etc. The space between trees and within the rows may be utilized for growing with perennial grasses.

Waterlogged and Marshy Land

In the waterlogged areas, stagnation of water occurs for most part of the year because of imperfect drainage. The central Board of Irrigation defined waterlogging as an area where the water table rises to an extent that the soil pores in the root zone of a crop becomes saturated resulting in restriction of the normal circulation of air, decline in the level of oxygen and increase in the level of carbon dioxide. Large areas in the Punjab, Haryana and western Uttar Pradesh have become waterlogged due to canal irrigation. Some areas in high rainfall zones where drainage is poor gradually become waterlogged. Waterlogged areas are also developed in the coastal areas mainly in the estuaries of rivers, in creeks and lagoons and lower reaches of tidal streams. Marshy lands are permanently or periodically inundated by water and characterized by vegetation which includes grasses and aquatic weeds. Proper drainage is important to reclaim these areas. Tree species suitable for waterlogged areas are *Eucalyptus robusta, Sygygium cumini, Salix babylonica, Populus nigra, Terminalia arjuna, Alnus cremastogyne, Alnus trabeculosa, Morus alba, Taxodium scandens* and *Acacia nilotica*. In marshy places, tree species best adopted are *Baringtonia* spp., *Bischofia javania, Taxdoium distichum, Eucalyptus robusta, Eucalyptus rudis, Casuarina equisetifolia* and *Lagerstroemia flosreginea*.

Arid and Semi-arid Lands

The arid and semi-arid lands are spread over the Rajasthan, Gujarat, Punjab, Haryana, Maharashtra, Karnataka, Telengana and Andhra Pradesh. These lands are characterized by hostile environmental conditions viz. productivity potential of the land is low, soils are immature, structureless, coarse in texture and poor nutrient status with low water holding capacity. Correct selection of trees is of prime significant in this region for the development of agroforestry. The trees should have drought tolerance mechanism like deep root system, leaf shedding in summer to conserve moisture, water binding mechanism and other xerophytic characteristics. Tree crops should also have tolerance to salinity and saline water and alkalinity which are common features of these areas. The best trees suitable for these wastelands are *Tamarix articulata, Prosopis juliflora, Prosopis tamarugo, Salvadora oleoides, Eucalyptus spp., Dalbergia sissoo, Acacia nilotica, Albizia lebbeck* and *Azadirachta indica*. Horticultural fruit trees for arid areas are *Zizphus mauritiana, Punica granatum, Psidium guajava, Phoenix dactylifera, Aegle marmelos, Annona squamosa*. Agricultural crops for agrisilvicultural system in arid areas are pearl millet, cowpea, sorghum, cluster bean, black gram, green gram, etc. The suitable grass species for silvipasoral or hortisilvipastoral systems are Diplachure fusca, *Sporobolus* spp., *Brachiaria mutica* and *Chloris gyana*.

Undulating Land with or without Scrub

These lands occupy high areas of topography but exclude mountainous terrain. The soils in these regions are highly prone to degradation and erosion. It is mainly associated with plateau and laterite formations in the states of Maharashtra, Andhra Pradesh and Rajasthan. These areas are characterized with high rainfall and undulating terrain. The causes for the formation of such lands include deforestation and its rehabilitation is possible only through agroforestry. The tree species suitable these wastelands are *Eucalyptus* spp., *Dalbergia sissoo, Gmelina arborea, Acacia auriculiformis, Emblica officinalis, Albizia procera, Anogeissus pendula* and *Dendrocalamus strictus*. *Agave sisalana* that has high efficiency to protect soil from erosion is also recommended with perennial forage grasses as intercrops.

Degraded Pasture

This type of wasteland are found mainly on rocky topography, saline alluvial plains and eroded uplands and are characterized by stunted plant growth, irregular slopes, sandy and loamy soils. Overgrazing, deforestation, runoff and wind erosion are responsible for natural pasture and rangeland degradation. The recommended remedial measures for this type of wastelands are establishing soil and water conservation measures like windbreaks, shelterbelts, mulching, contour bunding, etc. to upgrade soil productivity followed by tree cover with species like *Acacia Senegal, Acacia tortilis, Acacia nilotica, Butea* spp., *Indigofera cordifolia, Heteropogon* spp., etc.

Degraded Notified Forest Land

These lands are characterized by eroded and undulating topography with very steep slopes and are highly prone to water and wind erosion. The growth of trees and shrubs is very poor. To restore the productivity of land nitrogen fixing tree species like *Acacia nilotica, Terminalia* spp., *Albizia lebbeck, Albizia saman* are found highly effective.

Barren Rock Hill Ridges

The rock exposure is often barren and devoid of soil cover and vegetation. There is low canopy coverage at the top of hill due to slow growth as there is very little or no soil in the hills. The soils of these areas are very shallow, coarse, poor, eroded and degraded. The species suitable for barren rock hill ridges are *Dendrocalamus strictus, Eucalyptus tereticornis, Melia azadarach, Albizia lebbeck, Acacia catechu, Ailanthus excels, Hardwickia binata, Cassia nsiamea, Prosopis chilensis, Dalbergia sissoo,* etc. Tree species such as Robinia pseudoacacia, Populus ciliate and Pinus roxburghii are suitable for the areas of high elevation. The suitable grass species are *Cenchrus ciliaris, Cenchrus setigerus, Dicanthium annulatum, Panicum antidotala, Pennisetum pedicellatum,* etc.

Snow Covered Areas

These are created mainly by glacial and fluvial glacial activities in mountainous area. These lands are covered by extensive snow. The recommended species for rehabilitation are *Pinus gerardiana, Daplux acuminate, Desmodium* spp., *Butea minor*, etc.

CONCLUSION

Agroforestry has both productive and protective functions. It has now been recognized as an effective tool for producing food and fodder from marginal agricultural land and wastelands and is also capable of maintaining and improving quality of producing environment. Adoption of suitable agroforestry in various categories of wastelands like degraded forest and non-forest plantation area, eroded gullied and ravinous land, mine spoils and industrial wastelands, pasture and grazing lands, salt affected saline and alkali soils, sand dunes, sand bar and coastal sand, shifting cultivation areas, undulating upland marshy and waterlogged land, etc. will bridge the gap between desired and available forest coverage in the country, besides meeting food and fodder requirements. By adopting agroforestry in the wastelands near the villages the pressure on natural forest could greatly be reduced. Agrisilviculture, silvipasture, hortisilviculture and hortisilvipasture are the best suited agroforestry systems for wasteland management.

REFERENCES

Balasubramaniyan, P. and Palaniappan, SP. 2001. Principles and Practices of Agronomy. Agrobios India, Jodhpur.

Bene, J.G., Beall, H.W. and Cote, A. 1977. Trees, Food and People: Land Management in the Tropics, International Development Research Centre, Ottawa, Canada.

Garrity, D.P., and Agus, F. 1999. Natural Resource Management on a Watershed Scale: What can Agroforestry Contribute? pp. 165-193 (In): Lal, R. (ed.) Integrated Watershed Management in the Global Ecosystem, CRC Press, Washington, D.C.

Gautam, N.C. and Narayan, L.R.A. 1988. Wastelands in India, Pink Publishing House, Mathura, India. pp. 96.

GOI. 2012. Compendium of Environment Statistics India. Ministry of Statistics and Programme Implementation, Government of India, New Delhi.

http://en.wikipedia.org

http://forestry.about.com

http://www.agroforestry.co.uk

http://www.centerforagroforestry.org/practices

http://www.fao.org/forestry

http://www.mospi.gov.in

http://www.overstory.org

http://www.treesofstrength.org

http://www.worldagroforestry.org

Lundgren, B.O. and Raintree, J.B. 1982. Sustained Agroforestry. (In): Nestel, B. (ed.). Agricultural Research for Development: Potentials and Challenges in Asia. International Service for National Agricultural Research, The Hague, Netherlands.

Maji, A.K., Obi Reddy, G.P., Sarkar, Dipak. 2010. Degraded and Wastelands of India: Status and Spatial Distribution. Indian Council of Agricultural Research, New Delhi and National Academy of Agricultural Sciences, New Delhi. pp. 158.

Nair, P. K. R. 2008. An Introduction to Agroforestry. Springer (India) Pvt. Ltd., New Delhi.

NCA. 1976. Report of the National Commission on Agriculture: Part V, IX and Abridged. Ministry of Agriculture and Irrigation, New Delhi.

NRSA. 2005. Wasteland Atlas of India. Ministry of Rural Development and National Remote Sensing Agency Publication, NRSA, Hyderabad.

Oldeman, L.R. (ed.) 1988. Global Assessment of Soil Degradation (GLASOD). Guidelines for General Assessment of Status of Human-induced Soil Degradation. ISRIC, Wageningen. Working Paper and Reprint no. 88 (4), pp. 12.

Patra, A.K. 2013. Agroforestry: Theory & Practices. New India Publishing Agency, New Delhi. 242 pp.

Tejwani, K. G. 2008. Agroforestry to Meet the Challenges of the Indian Agriculture. *Abstracts*. National Symposium on Agroforestry Knowledge for Sustainability, Climate Moderation and Challenges Ahead (15-17 December, 2008), NRC for Agroforestry, Jhansi, U.P.

Land Reclamation, Soil Quality and Agriculture
Edited by: Dr. Pawan Kumar 'Bharti' and Alka Chauhan
ISBN: 978-93-5056-882-8
Edition: 2017
Published by: Discovery Publishing House Pvt. Ltd., New Delhi (India)

7 Mitigation of Abiotic Stress Through Nutrients and Hormones

[1]M. Pavithra, [2]Ashoka Reddy Yerva and [3]M. Jyostna Kiranmai

STRESS

Any change in Environmental conditions that might adversely effect the Growth and Development of a plant or any factor potentially unfavorable to living things.

CLASSIFICATION

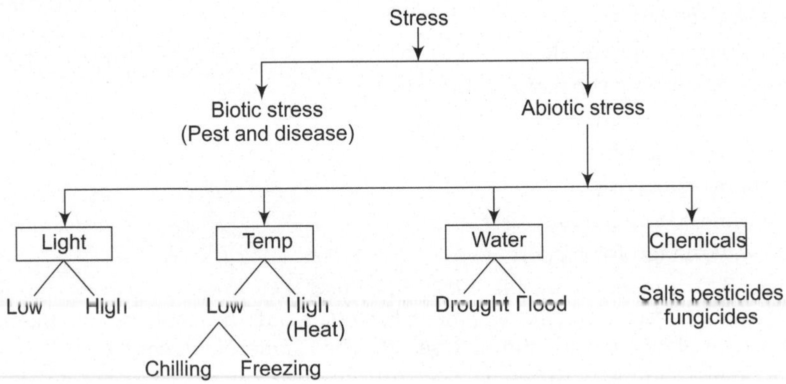

Phytohormones: Key mediators of plant responses to abiotic stresses.

They include:

- Auxin (IAA)
- Cytokinins (CKs)
- Abscisic acid (ABA)
- Ethylene (ET)
- Gibberellins (GAs)
- Salicylic acid (SA)
- Brassinosteroids (BRs) and jasmonates (JAs).

1 Ph.D Scholar (Agronomy), TNAU, Coimbatore, Tamil Nadu, India.
2 Ph.D Scholar (Agronomy), TNAU, Coimbatore, Tamil Nadu, India.
3 MSc (Ag), (Agronomy), TNAU, Coimbatore, Tamil Nadu, India.

- The strigolactone (SL) are relatively new phytohormones.

Abscisic Acid (ABA), the Abiotic Stress Hormone

- It is termed a "stress hormone."
- ABA is considered an essential messenger in the adaptive response of plants to abiotic stress.
- Under water-deficit conditions, ABA plays a vital role in providing plants the ability to signal to their shoots that they are experiencing stressful conditions around the roots, eventually resulting in water-saving antitranspirant activity, notably stomatal closure and reduced leaf expansion.
- ABA is also involved in robust root growth and other architectural modifications under drought stress and nitrogen deficiency.
- In maize, Saab *et al.*, in 1990 observed that stress-induced abcissic acid (ABA) accumulation appeared to promote root growth in addition to its effect on stomatal closure.
- ABA regulates the expression of numerous stress-responsive genes and in the synthesis of LEA proteins, dehydrins, and other protective proteins.
- ABA upregulates the processes involved in cell turgor maintenance and synthesis of osmoprotectants and antioxidant enzymes conferring desiccation tolerance.
- A proportional increase in ABA concentration is reported upon exposure of plants to salinity.

Auxins

- IAA plays an integral part in plant adaptation to salinity stress.
- It increases root and shoot growth of plants growing under *salinity or heavy metal stresses.*

Cytokinins

- Alteration of endogenous levels of CKs in response to stress indicates their involvement in abiotic stress, including drought and salinity.

Ethylene (ET)

- Essential regulator of Abiotic stress responses including *low temperature* and *salinity* alter endogenous ET levels in plants.
- ET also plays a major role in the defense response of plants to *heat stress.*
- Environmental stress induces ET accumulation which increases plant survival chances under these adverse conditions.

Water Stress: Drought

Since water is a main factor in biological and metabolic processes in plants, moisture deficiency during critical growth stages will adversely affect the growth and development of crops which may therefore reduce the quantity and quality of yield. If there is drought, the soil cannot provide enough moisture to maintain the water movement in the plant.

Crop under moisture stress will therefore close its stomates and eventually stop photosynthesis. Because photosynthesis provides the plant's food supply, limiting or completely stopping it can lead to a general decrease in the development of the plant. This is usually observed in a drought-prone area where the crops are smaller than the same type where water supply is sufficient. If not relieved, drought leads to interrupted reproductive development, premature leaf senescence, wilting, desiccation and death. Drought therefore, is a major limiting factor in farming.

Water Stress and Vegegrow Biostimulant

Plant hormones are defined in plant physiology as *natural organic substances* produced in one part of the plant and translocated in other parts where at very low concentration stimulates physiological response. On the other hand, substances that elicit the same response but are *chemically synthesized* are called *plant growth regulators (PGR's)*.

Water stress, as mentioned earlier, results in altered level of plant hormones and plant growth. Although these alterations and adjustments enable plants to survive during stress, with regards to cultivated plants, these adaptive mechanisms still result in low productivity and losses. It is therefore imperative to help crops increase their water stress resistance. One way is exogenous application of plant hormones through biostimulants.

Biostimulants are defined as materials, other than fertilizers, that promote plant growth when applied in small quantities; they are also referred to as metabolic enhancers. Biostimulants contain one or all of the following: carbohydrates, amino acids, macro & micronutrients, vitamins, plant hormones, plant compounds such as betaines etc.

Vegegrow is a natural plant food and biostimulant derived from seaweeds in a unique formulation designed to maximize the derived amount of essential nutrients, growth hormones and other beneficial compounds. Vegegrow Seaweed Extract is considered a biostimulant because it contains these beneficial compounds plus well-balanced and readily available macro & micronutrients.

Vegegrow is prepared using natural extraction, combining the essential properties of three (3) seaweed species namely.

- Eucheuma cottoni
- Eucheuma Spinosum and
- Sargassum polycystum.

Application of vegegrow throughout the critical growth stages can help crops withstand abiotic stress such as drought. The plant hormones and beneficial compounds like betaine in vegegrow can help improve drought tolerance in crops. It is best to start vegegrow application as early as possible to help crops establish in the field by promoting vigorous roots and healthy shoots. Continuous application, in small concentration but more frequent, maximize the efficacy of the product.

Vegegrow also produces a synergistic effect with other inputs that are applied in the crops. This means better protection by enhancing and promoting the natural defense mechanism of the crops when stress is imminent. While exogenous application of vegegrow provides plant hormones that trigger this defense mechanism, the crops are also provided with the essential nutrients that the crops cannot take by root absorption, since vegegrow is at the same time a plant food source. It is important to remember however, that the mitigating effect of biostimulant is building up and triggering of natural defense mechanism and acquired resistance, the action is preventive, and intervention must always start at earliest possible time to have the best results.

General Recommendation

- As foliar spray – 8-12 ml per liter of water 2*x*-4*x* a month
- As Soil conditioner – 25-30 ml per liter of water once a month
- As Seed Soak & Rooting Solution – 10-20 ml per liter of water
- As Transplant solution – 15-20 ml per liter of water

Effect of Silicon in Mitigation of Abiotic Stresses

- *Silicon nutrition* alleviates many abiotic stresses including physical stresses such as drought, UV radiation, high temperature, flood, lodging, freezing and chemical stresses such as salt, metal toxicity and nutrient imbalance.
- Tisdale *et al.*, (1985) reported that silicon in plants acts as a window as it filters harmful *ultraviolet radiation* reaching to the leaf surface.
- Wheat plants which were subjected to drought stress and treated with silicon maintained higher stomatal conductance, relative water content, water potential and leaves were also larger, thicker thereby reduced the water loss through transpiration.
- Silicon fertilizer has been reported to increase *frost tolerance capacity* in lemon and sugarcane.
- Silicon fertilization helps in the development of secondary and tertiary cells of the endodermis and allows better root resistance in dry soils and faster growth of roots.
- *Calcium silicate* obtained as a byproduct of steel and phosphorus production is one of the most widely used silicon fertilizer.

- *Potassium silicate* is highly soluble and can be used in hydroponic culture for research related laboratory experiments.
- Other sources of silicon have been used commercially are *silica gel* and *calcium silicate hydrate.*

Salinity Stress

Salinity is one of the most serious abiotic stress factors limiting crop productivity. Worldwide, 100 million ha or 5% of the arable land is adversely affected by high salt concentrations reducing crop growth and yield.

Case Study

Mitigation of Salt Stress in Lettuce *(Lactuca sativa L. var. Crispa)* by Seed and Foliar 24-epibrassinolide Treatments

Melek Ekinci *et al.*, 2012

Objective of this Study

- To determine the effect of 24-epibrassinolide (24-EBL) applications on growth, chlorophyll, and mineral content of lettuce (Lactuca sativa L. var. Crispa) grown under salt stress.
- The study was conducted in pot experiments under greenhouse conditions.
- Lettuce seedlings were treated with seed and foliar 24-EBL applications at different concentrations (0, 1, 2, and 3 mM).
- Salinity treatments were established by adding 0, 50 and 100 mM of sodium chloride (NaCl) to a base complete nutrient solution.

Results

- Salt stress negatively affected the growth and mineral content of lettuce plants.
- Seed and foliar applications of 24-EBL resulted in greater shoot fresh weight, shoot dry weight, root fresh weight, and root dry weight as well as higher stem diameter than the control under salt stress.
- Salinity treatments induced significant increases in electrolyte leakage of plant, but foliar 24-EBL application reduced leaf electrolyte leakage and has determined lower values of leaf electrolyte leakage than non-treated ones.
- In regard to nutrient content, it can be inferred that 24-EBL applications increased nutrient content in leaves and roots of lettuce plants under salt stress.
- Generally, the greatest values were obtained from *3 mM 24-EBL* application.

REFERENCES

Kaya C, Tuna L, Higgs D. 2006. Effect of Silicon on Plant Growth and Mineral Nutrition of Maize Grown under Water-stress Conditions. *J. Plant Nutr.* 29:1469-1480.

Sanjay Rawal., Rana, N.S. and Devendra Kumar.2007. Mitigation of Heat Stress in Potato Through Calcium Nutrition. *Potato J.* 34 (1-2) : 111-112.

Chanchal Malhotra, C.H., Riti Thapar Kapoor., Deepak Ganjewala, 2016. Alleviation of Abiotic and Biotic Stresses in Plants by Silicon Supplementation. *Sci. Agri.*13 (2) : 59-73.

Melek Ekinci, Ertan Yildirim, and Atilla Dursun.2016. Mitigation of Salt Stress in Lettuce (Lactuca sativa L. var. Crispa) by Seed and Foliar 24-epibrassinolide Treatments. *Hortscience* 47(5):631–636.

Land Reclamation, Soil Quality and Agriculture
Edited by: Dr. Pawan Kumar 'Bharti' and Alka Chauhan
ISBN: 978-93-5056-882-8
Edition: 2017
Published by: Discovery Publishing House Pvt. Ltd., New Delhi (India)

8

Pollution and Pollutants
An Indian Scenario

[1]Abhishek Swami

INTRODUCTION

Pollution has become a household word that calls up images of despoiled water, air, or land. Pollution eludes simple definition, because it may involve hundreds of factors that arouse from numerous sources. Some changes, such as contamination of drinking water, air that we inhale and food material that we take regularly, may directly affect human health and well being. Others may affect humans in a more indirect way, such as carbon dioxide emissions affecting the climate, which in turn may affect food production, or change in the nutrient levels causing some population to die out and others to explode. Thus pollution may be defined as *"The unfavorable alteration of our surroundings, wholly or largely as a by product of man's action." Pollution may also be defined as "Addition of any foreign material (inorganic, biological or radiological) or any physical change in the natural environment which may adversely affect the living resources directly or indirectly, immediately or after sometime or after a very long time."* One definition of pollution is "An undesirable change in the physical, chemical or biological characteristics of air, water and soil that may harmfully affect the life or create a potential health hazard for any living organism". Pollution is thus direct or indirect change in any component of biosphere that is harmful to the living component (s), and in particular undesirable for man, affecting adversely the industrial progress, cultural and natural assets or general environment.

Every organism in a natural ecosystem produces potentially polluting waste products. What makes natural ecosystem sustainable is that the waste from one kind of organism becomes food and or raw material for another. In balanced ecosystems, waste do not accumulate to produce unfavorable alterations, they are broken down and recycled. Through much of their history humans have relied on the same natural process to dispose of their wastes. But the situation has become extremely unbalanced. Exploding human population coupled

[1] Department of Applied Science, Dronacharay Group of Institutions, Greater Noida (UP), India

with increasing use of materials and energy have led to enormous volumes of wastes and other materials being discharged in to the environment. Even when materials are biodegradable, that is, of a kind that can be assimilated and recycled by organisms, sheer volumes overwhelm the capacity of natural system to cope. Aggravating the problem is the production of increasing amounts and kinds of non-biodegradable materials, which are not readily broken down and assimilated by the natural processes.

India today is one of the first ten industrialized countries of the world. Today we have a good industrial infrastructure in core industries like metals, chemicals, fertilizer, petroleum, food etc. What has come out of these? Pesticides, detergents, plastics, solvents, fuels, paints, dyes, food additives etc. are some examples. Due to progress in atomic energy, there has also been an increase in radioactivity in the biosphere. Besides these, there are a number of industrial effluents and emissions particularly poisonous gases in the atmosphere. Mining activities has also added to this problem particularly as solid waste.

Clearly, pollution involves so many different factors from so many sources that there is no single or simple remedy. Pollution is an evil which has born out of development. Lack of development of a culture of pollution control, has resulted a heavy backlog of gaseous, liquid and solid pollution in our country. It is to be cleaned. Thus pollution control in our country is a recent environmental concern. Not only in India, but also in the undeveloped Western World, pollution is a scare-word, which is a man-made problem, mainly of affluent countries. The developed countries have been in a mad race to exploit every bit of natural resource to convert them into goods, for their comfort, and to export them to needy developing world. In doing so, the industrialized countries dump lot of materials in their environment which becomes polluted. In one way pollution has been in fact "exported" to developing countries.

The following reports give the ststus of our air, water and soil which is so much so polluted that immediate steps need to control the situation: About 7000 tonns of solid waste is generated in Mumbai, the metro also generates about 3000 million liters of sewage every day, half of which is not treated. In water samples tested in 2003, 19% were found unfit for drinking. The Sulpher-dioxide levels in the metro exceeds 24 hours standards by 2 to 8%, nitrogen oxide by 17 to 56%, SPM by 31 to 83% and lead by 1 to 3%. The noise pollution of the metro exceeds all standards.

Similarly, Centre for Science and Environment (CSE) have reported harmful pesticides like lindane, DDT, Chloropyrifos and melathion in popular brands of bottled water in Delhi and Mumbai. In one of the brand, pesticide residues were 104 times higher than the prescribed norms of Europian Union. These pesticides get accumulated in the huan body and cause cancer, nervous disorders and weaken the immune system.

POLLUTANTS

Substance which are responsible for a change in the natural environment or conditions, which are harmful to the nature or particularly to the human beings are called pollutants. A pollutant may thus include any chemical or geo-chemical (dust, sediment, grit etc.) substance, biotic component or its product, or physical factor (heat) that is released intentionally or unintentionally by man into the environment in such a concentration that may have adverse harmful or unpleasant effects. A pollutant has also been defined as "any solid, liquid or gaseous substance present in such concentration which may be or may tend to be injurious to the environment". Pollutants are the residues of things we make, use and throw away. There are many sources of such pollutants. The lakes and rivers are polluted by wastes from chemical and other factories, and the air by gases of automobile exhausts, industries, thermal power plants etc. As the clean air moves across the earth surface, it collects the products of both natural events such as dust storms, volcanic eruptions etc. and human activities such as vehicular emissions etc. These potential pollutants, called *primary pollutants,* mix with the churning air in the troposphere. Some may react with one another or with the basic components of air to form new pollutants called *secondary pollutants*. Long lived pollutants can travel great distances before they return to the earth surface as solid particles, droplets, or chemicals dissolved in precipitation.

The following pollutants have been identified as most wide spread and serious:

(*i*) *Particulate:* Particulate are tiny solid or liquid particles suspended in the air. These particles can be seen as smoke or haze. Other pollutants present as gas or vapor are not visible except in the case of nitrogen oxide, which is a brownish gas. Particulate may carry any or all of the other pollutants dissolved in or adhering to their surfaces.

(*ii*) *Hydrocarbons and other volatile organic compounds:* These include materials such as gasoline, paint solvents and organic cleaning solutions that evaporate and enter the air in a vapor state.

(*iii*) *Carbon monoxide:* This is a highly poisonous gas.

(*iv*) *Nitrogen oxides:* These include several nitrogen-oxygen compounds, all in gaseous forms.

(*v*) *Sulfur oxides:* Sulfur di-oxide is a poisonous gas to both plants and animals.

(*vi*) Lead and other heavy metals.

(*vii*) Ozone and other photochemical oxidants: Ground level ozone is a serious pollutant.

(*viii*) Acid droplets.

(*ix*) *Metals:* Mercury, lead, iron, zinc, nickel, tin, cadmium, chromium etc.

(*x*) *Agrochemicals:* Pesticides, herbicides, fungicides, nematicides bactericides, weedicides and fertilizers etc.

(*xi*) Various effluents and solid wastes which are not treated prior to their discharge.

(*xii*) Radioactive waste.

(*xii*) Noise.

On the basis of their being bio-degradable or non-degradable nature the pollutants may be grouped in one of the following two categories:

1. *Non-degradable pollutants:* These are the materials and poisonous substances like aluminum cans, mercuric salts, long-chain phenolics, DDT etc. that either do not degrade or degrade only very slowly in nature. They are not cycled in ecosystem naturally. They not only accumulate but also are often biologically magnified with their subsequent movement in food chains and biogeochemical cycles.
2. *Biodegradable pollutants:* They are the domestic wastes than can be rapidly decomposed under natural conditions. They may create problems when they accumulate (i.e. their input into the environment exceeds their decomposition).

In United Nations Environment Program document following order of priority of different pollutants has been indicated:

S. No.	Order of priority	Medium
1.	SO_2+ suspended particle, strontium, cesium.	Air and food
2.	OzoneDDT and other organochlorine compounds	AirBiota, Man
3.	NO_{3s}.NO_{2s} Nitrogen oxides	Drinking waterAir
4.	Mercury compoundsLead and cobalt	Food, WaterFood, Air
5.	Petroleum hydrocarbonsCarbon monoxide	SeaAir
6.	Fluorides	Water (fresh water)
7.	AsbestosArsenic	AirDrinking Water
8.	Mycotoxins and microbial contaminants	Food

TYPES OF POLLUTION

Pollution may be classified on the basis of the type of environment that is being polluted. Thus we may have air pollution, water pollution and soil or land pollution. Another classification of pollution may be on the basis of type of pollutants such as sulfur dioxide pollution, fluoride pollution, carbon monoxide pollution, smoke pollution, lead pollution, mercury pollution, solid waste pollution, radioactive pollution, noise pollution etc. Organisms do have the capacity to deal with certain amount or level of pollutants without suffering ill effects. The level of a pollutant below which no ill effects are observed is called the *threshold level*. Above the threshold level effects begin to be observed. However, the effects caused by a pollutant depends on its concentration and time of exposure. Higher levels may be tolerated if the time of exposure is less. Thus the threshold level may be high for shorter exposure, but gets lower as the time of exposure increases. There are three factors which determine the level of exposure:

(*i*) Inputs of pollutants into the air.

(*ii*) Amount of space into which pollutants are dispersed and diluted.

(*iii*) Mechanisms by which these are removed from the air.

AIR POLLUTION

Our atmosphere has received smoke and other pollutants for millions of years from many natural processes such as volcanoes, natural fires and dust storms. But the biosphere does have means for removing, assimilating and recycling these natural pollutants. They disperse and dilute in the atmosphere. Then they settle or come down to earth via precipitation, and poisonous gases are converted to harmless products by soil micro-organisms. Thus keeping the natural inputs of pollution well below threshold level. However, the human inputs of pollutants are overloading the natural system and it has been calculated that human sources exceed those from natural sources by 10 to 1000 fold, depending on the particular pollutant.

Earth's Atmosphere: The earth is the only planet in the solar system and in the universe, known so far, to have the unique atmosphere where life can sustain. Its distance from the sun and its atmosphere makes its environment warm and inhabitable. It is the only planet where water exists in all three forms. The composition of the earth's atmosphere is determined by biological processes together with physical and chemical changes. Temperature profile is used to distinguish different regions of the atmosphere in terms of layer characteristics and by specific vertical temperature gradients. It has thus been divided into the following layers:

Troposphere: From the earths surface, the mean temperature decreases with height up to about 10 to 16 km. This region is known as the troposphere. The boundary where temperature decrease ceases is known as the tropopause. The general distribution of temperature at the tropopause is such that a minimum value is found at the equator and a maximum value in the polar regions. The troposphere acts as a source of heat resulting from the absorption of the visible sun light. It is characterized by its negative temperature gradient of about 6 degree K/km.

Stratosphere: The tropopause marks the end of troposphere and the beginning of the stratosphere, the atmosphere's second layer, which extends from about 17 to 48 km above the earth's surface. Although the stratosphere contains less matter than the troposphere, its composition is similar with two notable exceptions: its volume of water vapor is about 1000 times less and its volume of ozone is about 1000 times greater. The presence of ozone in the stratosphere keeps about 99% of the suns harmful UV radiations from reaching the earth's surface.

Mesosphere: The region between stratopause and about 85-90 km is known as the mesosphere and its upper boundary is called mesopause. The mesopause is the coolest region of the atmosphere.

Thermosphere: Above the mesopause, the region is known as the thermosphere. In this region, the temperature increases to reach highest value. The high temperature in the thermosphere are caused by very thin atmosphere.

There is no boundary between the atmosphere and void of outer space. About 75% of the earth's atmosphere lies within 16 km. of the surface and 99% of the atmosphere lies below an altitude of 30 Km. The atmosphere is an insulating blanket around the earth. It is sources of essential gases, maintains narrow difference of day and night temperatures and provides a medium for long-distance radio communication. It also acts as shield around the earth against lethal UV radiation's and meteors. Without atmosphere, there will be no lightening, no wind, no clouds, nor rains, no snow and no fire. Normal composition of clean air at or near sea is as given below:

Gases	Percent (by volume)
Nitrogen	78.084
Oxygen	20.9476
Argon	0.934
Carbon dioxide	0.0314
Methane	0.0002
Hydrogen	0.00005
Other gases	minute

However, it is very difficult to find such clean air and the concentration levels of different gases show variations due to addition of different types of pollutants in to the air which may be in the form of gases or particulates making it unfit for living organisms. In the western and more developed countries, it was realized in the 1950s and 60s that unrestricted discharge of pollutants in to the atmosphere could no longer be tolerated. In Indian cities, particularly in the metros, the layers of dust on almost all fixtures of the house, cleaned only a few hours back; the pungent, turbid air in areas of dense vehicular traffic; burning, watering eyes after a scooter ride are some examples which remind us that we may no longer be silent spectators to a situation where the environment is actually hitting back at us. Residents of our metropolitan cities are today exposed to some of the highest levels of air pollution in the country and perhaps in the world.

SOURCES OF AIR POLLUTANTS AND THEIR EFFECTS

In large measures, air pollutants are direct and indirect byproducts of burning coal, gasoline and other liquid fuels and refuse. These fuels and wastes are organic and with complete combustion, the byproducts are CO_2 and water vapor. However, their complete oxidation rarely takes place. In addition, fuels or refuse contain impurities or additives and these are also emitted into the air when burned. Some of these direct products further react within the atmosphere and produce additional indirect products. We may say that air pollution results from gaseous emissions from mainly industry, thermal power stations, automobiles, domestic combustion etc.

A. Industrial emissions: There are a number of industries which are source of air pollution. Petroleum refineries are the major source of gaseous pollutants. The chief gases are SO_2 and NO_x. The fertilizer industries release oxides of nitrogen and dust particles of microscopic size. Dust particles may be evolved from the process of drying, burning, calcining, grinding, screening, mixing and packaging. Cement dust is a common air pollutant around cement factories and construction sites which emit plenty of dust, which is potential heath hazard. Chemically it is a mixture of oxides of aluminum, silica, potassium, calcium and sodium. Stone crushers and hot mix plants also create a menace. The SPM levels in such areas of stone crushing are more than five times the industrial safety limits. There are many food and fertilizers industries, which emit gaseous pollutants. Many chemical manufacturing industries emit acid vapors in air. In the past two decades we have seen a tremendous increase in the number of industries in our metros particularly in Delhi, Bombay, Calcutta and Bangalore. Many of these are located in predominantly residential areas. The industries producing sulphuric acid, discharge large quantities of sulfur di-oxide in the air and pollute the atmosphere up to a few kilometers. The industries producing fluoride compounds have serious effects on plants, animals and human beings. The toxic effects of fluorides on live stocks arise from ingesting contaminated forage on which fluoride dust has settled. The various iron and steel industries emit sulfur dioxide, oxides of metals and carbon mono and di-oxides. Acids are also produced in the atmosphere due to reaction of sulpher di-oxide and nitrogen oxides with water vapors.

B. Automobiles: Starting from the 1950s, when there was a mushrooming use of cars for commuting, the metropolitan areas increasingly became enshrouded in a brownish haze on a daily basis. This haze is called smog, or more properly, photochemical smog, because sun light is involved in its formation. Certain weather conditions intensify the smog levels, the most important being temperature inversions. Normally, air temperature decreases with increasing elevation. In this situation, the warm air near the ground rises, carrying pollutants upward and dispersing them at higher altitudes. In a temperature inversion, a layer of cold air near the ground is covered by warm air. This situation develops as an influx of cooler air moves in under the warm air. With a temperature inversion, the upward movement of air carrying pollutants is blocked and pollutants accumulate in the cool air near the ground. The toxic vehicular exhausts are sources of considerable air pollution, next only to thermal power plants. The ever-increasing vehicular traffic density has posed a continue threat to the ambient air quality. There are over 300 million cars, trucks and buses in the world over and their number increasing rapidly. India, which is likely to have over 30 million vehicles, has more than 65% two-wheelers operating on petrol. In all the major cities of the country about 800 to 1000 tones of pollutants are being emitted into the air daily, of which 50% come from automobiles exhausts. In the major metropolitan cities, vehicular exhaust accounts for 70% of all CO, 50% of all hydrocarbons, 30-40%of all oxides and 30% of all SPM. In cities like Delhi, during peak traffic hours, automobiles of all classes emit as much as 700 Kg of CO, 250 Kg of hydrocarbons and 60 Kg of nitrogen oxides. The two-wheelers and three-wheelers contribute 60% of the total CO, and 83% of total hydrocarbons, whereas heavy traffic vehicles 55 to 80% of the oxides of nitrogen. It is estimated that a car (without cleaning device) on burning 1000 liter of fuel emits 350 Kg CO, 0.6 Kg SO_2, 0.1 Kg lead and 1.5 Kg SPM.

The sources of emission in automobiles are: (*i*) exhaust system, (*ii*) fuel tank and carburetor and (*iii*) crankcase. The exhaust produces many air pollutants including unburnt hyrocarbons, CO, NO_x lead oxides. There are also traces of aldehydes, esters, ethers, peroxides and ketones which are chemically active and combine to form smog in presence of light. Evaporation from fuel tank goes on constantly due to volatile nature of petrol, causing emission of hydrocarbons. The evaporation through carburetor occurs when engine is stopped and heat builds up, and as much as 12 to 40 ml of fuel is lost during each long stop causing emission of hydrocarbons. Some gas vapor escapes between walls and the piston, which enters the crankcase and then discharges into the atmosphere. This accounts for 25% of the total hydrocarbon emission of an engine.

C. Nuclear and thermal power stations: The catastrophic accident at Chernobyl in USSR in April 1986 is the biggest example of pollution that is being caused by thermal power stations. Radioactive emissions may penetrate through biological tissues in a manner analogous to tiny bullets. They leave no visible marks nor are they felt, but they are capable of breaking molecules within cells. In high doses, radiation may cause enough damage to prevent cell division. In low doses it may damage to DNA molecules. There are a number of thermal power stations and super thermal stations in the country. The National Thermal Power Corporation (NTPC) has setup mammoth coal-powered power stations to augment the energy generation of our country. The coal consumption of thermal plants is several million tones. The chief pollutants are fly ash, SO_2 and other gases hydrocarbons.

What Happens to Pollutants in the Atmosphere

Once the pollutants enter the troposphere, they are affected by four processes:

1. Transport, in which pollutants are carried down wind. The extent of this process depends on wind speed and direction, topographical features and how high in the atmosphere pollutants are injected.
2. Dilution, in which the turbulent motion of air mix and reduce the concentration of pollutants.
3. Transformation, in which pollutants undergo physical changes, including agglomeration, chemical changes and photochemical changes triggered by reaction with incoming solar energy.
4. Removal from the atmosphere by rainout, washout and fallout.

Choking of South Asia by a Blanket of Smog

India and rest of the South Asia is covered by a deadly, three km. deep blanket of pollution, which is readily changing monsoon patterns, causing draughts and literally killing hundreds of thousands of people by respiratory diseases. A group of scientists working with the United Nations Environment Program on the Asian Brown Haze has released this study. It said that the vast pollution parcel could endanger the economic success of South Asian Countries, particularly India. The haze has been identified as a deadly cocktail of ash, acids, aerosols and other particles. The study also says that the worst may be yet to come and the effects of the haze would intensify over the next 30 years. Already, higher levels of respiratory diseases are leading to several hundreds of thousands of premature deaths, as revealed by data from seven Indian cities, including Ahmedabad, Kolkatta, Delhi and Mumbai. The Indian data suggested some kind of air pollution was responsible for 24,000 annual premature deaths in the early 1990s, said the report. A few year later, the number rose to an estimated 37,000 per year.

UNEP executive director, Klaus Toepfer says, "In India they are expecting more than two million people to die because of the incomplete burning of biomass." The open fires used by the majority of ordinary Indians to cook their food also contribute to this. This pollution parcel, which stretches three kilometers high, can travel half way round the globe in a week, thus having global implications.

AIR POLLUTANTS AND THEIR EFFECTS

Some of the air pollutants and their effects have been discussed here below:

(a) Compounds of carbon: The two important pollutants are carbon dioxide and carbon monoxide.

1. Carbon dioxide: Human activities are responsible for the increasing amount of this gas in our atmosphere The concentration of CO_2 in the earth's atmosphere currently is 360μl/L, which is approximately 30% higher than the pre industrialization level and is conservatively projected to double by the end of first decade of 21 centuary. Around 1900, the concentration of CO_2 in air was 290 ppm, in 1960 it was about 315ppm and it is increasing at a rate of approximately 1.0 mg/kg/year. The reasons given for this situation are: (*a*) depletion of forest cover, (*b*) burning of fossil fuel, (*c*) increased number of living organisms and, (*d*) upset of balance in exchange of CO_2 between oceans and atmosphere.

Major amount of carbon dioxide is released in the atmosphere from burning of fossil fuel (coal, oil etc) for domestic cooking, heating etc. and the fuels consumed in furnaces of power plants, industries, hot-mix plants etc. From fossil fuel alone more than 18×10^{12} tones of CO_2 is being released into atmosphere each year. In our country, on an average, thermal power plants are likely to release around 50 million tones of CO_2 each year in the atmosphere.

To some extent an increase in CO_2 level in atmosphere increases the photosynthesis rate and consequently plant growth, acting as fertilizer especially in hot tropical climates. This potential of fertilizer effect may be exploited by using modified crop varieties and agricultural practices. However, an increase in CO_2 concentration in atmosphere may result into disastrous effects also.

Greenhouse effect: The term green house effect was coined by Jean Fourier more than 100 years ago. Since CO_2 is confined exclusively to the troposphere, its higher concentration may act a serious pollutant. Under normal conditions (with normal CO_2 concentration) the temperature at the surface of the earth is maintained by the energy balance of the sun rays that strike the planet and heat that is radiated back into space. The earth's surface and atmosphere receive energy from the sun. This energy comes in the form of radiation mainly in the visible region, 1 = 400 – 700 nm. Much of UV light (1 < 400 nm) from the sun is filtered out in the stratosphere and warms the air there rather than at surface of earth. Besides visible light, we receive some infra red (IR) light in the region 800-4000 nm. Of the total incoming light that impinges upon the earth, about 50% reaches the surfaces and is absorbed by it. About 20% of the incoming light is absorbed by gases in the atmosphere, such as, UV light by ozone in stratosphere and IR by CO_2 and water vapor in air. The remaining 30% is reflected back in to space by clouds, ice, snow and other reflecting bodies without being absorbed.

Like any other warm body, the earth emits energy, the amount of the energy that the planet absorbs and the amount that it releases must be equal if the temperature is to remain constant at earth. The emitted energy is neither visible nor UV, it is IR light having wavelength in the range of 4000-5000nm which is called thermal infra red region.

Some gases in the air such as CO_2, temporarily absorb thermal infra red light and, therefore, not all IR emitted from the earth's surface and atmosphere escape directly in to space. Shortly after its absorption by CO_2 molecules, this thermal

IR light is remitted in all directions. Thus some thermal IR is redirected back towards the earth's surface and is reabsorbed, and consequently further heats to both, the surface and the air. This phenomenon of redirection of thermal IR towards the earth is called the green house effect. Thus, the green house effect is trapping of heat caused by gases such as carbon di-oxide and water vapor which are transparent to incoming solar radiations but re-emit the infra red radiations from earth's surface. This is responsible for keeping the temperature of earth's surface at +15° C rather than –15° C (if there would had been no atmosphere).

The phenomenon that worries us is that, increasing the concentration of trace gases in atmosphere, that absorb thermal IR, would result in the redirection of even more of the out going thermal IR energy and would increase the average temperature of earth surface beyond +15° C. Most of the heat is absorbed by CO_2 layer and waters vapors in the atmosphere, which adds to the heat that is already present. CO_2 increases the earth temperature by 50% while CFCs are responsible for another 20 % increase and there are enough CFCs up there to last in 120 years.

The heat trap provided by atmospheric CO_2 probably helped to create the conditions necessary for the evolution of life and the greening of earth. Compared to moderately warm planet, Mars, with too little CO_2 in its atmosphere, is frozen cold and Venus with too much is a dry furnace. The excess CO_2 to some extent is absorbed by the oceans. But with the industrialization of West and increased consumption of energy, CO_2 was released into atmosphere at a faster rate than the capacity of oceans to absorb it. Thus its concentration increased. According to some estimates CO_2 in air may have risen by 30% since the middle of 19th century. It may even be doubled by 2030 A.D.

There are some difference of opinions, however, about the extent of rise in earth's temperature due to increasing CO_2 levels. According to some computerized models, doubling the CO_2 level will increase the global mean temperature (15°C) by 2°C. But, some others say that this will be less than one quarter of a degree. However, even a change of two degrees may disrupt the earth's heat budget, causing catastrophic consequences.

Impacts of Enhanced Green House Effect

The enhanced green house effect will not only cause global warming but will affect various other climatic and natural processes.

1. *Increase in global temperature:* The global temperature has been observed to increase ever since systematic recording of this temperature has been initiated. The world temperature has increased by 0.7°C from 1860 to 1990AD. Where as temperature of tropical ocean has risen by 0.5°C for the last 30 to 50 years. It is estimated that the earth's mean temperature will rise between 1.5 t0 5.5 °C by 2050 if input of green house gases continue to rise at present rate.

2. *Climate change:* The global change in temperature will not be uniform everywhere and will fluctuate in different regions. The places in higher latitudes will be warmed up more during late autumn and winter than the places in tropics. Poles may experience 2 to 3 times more warming than the global average while warming in the tropics may be only 50 to 100% of the average. The increased warming at poles will reduce the thermal gradient between the equator and high latitude regions decreasing the energy available to the heat engine that drives the global weather machine. This will disturb the global pattern of winds and ocean currents as well as timings and distribution of rainfall. Disturbed rainfall will result in some areas becoming wetter and the others drier.
3. *Rise in sea level:* With the increase in global temperature sea water will expand. Heating will melt the polar ice sheet and glaciers resulting in further rise in sea level. Current modes indicate that an increase in the average atmospheric temperature of 3°C would raise the average global sea level by 0.2 to 1.5 m over the next 50-100 years. One meter rise in sea level will inundate low lying areas of cities like Sanghai, Cairo, Bangkok, Sydney etc. Life of millions of people will be affected by the sea level rise.
4. *Effects on human health:* The global warming will affect the distribution of vector of disease like mosquitoes. The diseases like malaria, filariasis and elephantiasis will increase. More temperature and humidity will increase respiratory and skin diseases.
5. *Effects on agriculture:* Tropical and subtropical regions will be affected more since the average temperature in these region is already on higher side. Even a rise of 2°C may be quite harmful to crops. Soil moisture will decrease, evapo-transpiration will increase which may drastically affect many crops.

2. *Carbon monoxide:* It is produced by the incomplete combustion of coal, charcoal, petrol and its products. The largest source of combustion producing CO are internal combustion engines. From combustion sources, the CO emission per year in the world is about 2.6×10^8 tones. Furnaces, stoves, open fires, factories, power plants give off CO. The source of atmospheric CO is the oxidation of methane. Anaerobic decomposition of organic matter produces methane, which is oxidised to produce CO. Photochemical decomposition of ozone and the reaction of atomic oxygen with water vapor produces hydroxyl radicals, which initiate oxidation of methane. Thus CO production in atmosphere is associated with photochemical reactions.

Carbon mono oxide combines with hemoglobin of blood, reducing its O_2 carrying capacity. The gas is fatal over 1000 ppm, causing unconsciousness in an hour and death in four hours. If this gas is inhaled for few hours at even a low concentration of 200 ppm, it causes symptoms of poisoning. Inhaled CO combines with blood hemoglobin to form *carboxyhemoglobin* about 210 times faster than O_2 does. Formation of carboxyhemoglobin decreases the overall O_2 carrying capacity of blood to cells resulting into oxygen deficiency-*hypoxia*. At about 200 ppm concentration for 6-8 hours, headache begins, and mental activity gets reduced; above 300 ppm, throbbing headache starts followed by vomiting and collapse; at 500 ppm, man reaches into coma and at 1000 ppm, is death occurs. The accepted maximum allowable concentration (MAC) for occupational exposure is 50 ppm for 8 hours. The increase in carboxyhemoglobin level form 1-2% to 3-4% may cause cerebral anoxia resulting into impairing of vision and psychomotor activity. Sub-lethal concentrations of this gas may be injurious due to prolonged exposure. In smokers, prolonged exposures may cause an adaptive response, even producing more hemoglobin, as high as 8%. At 10% carboxyhemoglobin in blood due to smoking there may be lowered tolerance to CO. Cigarette smokers have increased hematocrit (per cent volume of red blood cells), within minutes of smoking. In developed countries cigarettes are linked to at least 80% of all deaths from lung cancer. Most plants are not affected by CO levels known to affect man. At higher levels (100 to 10,000 ppm), the gas affects leaf drop, leaf curling, reduction in leaf size, premature aging etc. It inhibits cellular respiration in plants.

3. *Compounds of sulphur:* Sulpher remains in the atmosphere in three forms namely, sulphur dioxide, hydrogen sulphide and sulphate particles. Sulphur dioxide is produced mainly by the combustion of the fossil fuels like coal, mobile oil and petrol. The other S-compounds are carbonyl sulphide (COS), carbon disulphide (CS_2), dimethyl sulphide [$(CH_2)_2S$] and sulphates.

(a) Sulphur dioxide: It is a colorless gas with a suffocating and pungent odor. The major source of SO_2 emission are industrial processes and burning of sulpher containing coals in thermal power plants, smelting industries (smelting sulphur containing metal ores) and other processes as manufacturing of sulphuric acid and fertilizers. These account for about 75% of the total SO_2 emission. Most of the rest 25% emission is from petroleum refineries and automobiles. In U. S. A., in 1970 there was emitted 37 million tons of SO_2. It is believed that about 109 million tons of SO_2 are added each year into the global environment. In polluted areas its concentration may reach 3000 mg/m^3, but in non polluted areas the concentration usually remains 0.3 to 1.0 mg/m^3. In our country, SO_2 emission is on the increase over the years and it has almost doubled between 1979 and 2000 A.D. The life time of SO_2 in the atmosphere depends upon the rate at which it is oxidized On global scale, about half of the ambient SO_2 originates from the oxidation of hydrogen sulphide given off by decaying organic matter.

The chronic exposures to SO_2 causes intense irritation to eyes and respiratory tract. It is absorbed in the moist passage of upper respiratory tract, leading to swelling and stimulated mucus secretion. Exposure to 1 ppm level of SO_2 causes a constriction of the air passage, and causes significant bronocho-constriction in asthmatics even at a lower (0.05-0.50 ppm) concentrations. Moist air and fogs increase the SO_2 dangers due to formation of H_2SO_4 and sulphate ions; H_2SO_4 is a strong irritant (4-20 times) than SO_2.

Plants are affected at lower concentrations of SO_2 than human beings. Leaf bleaching, necroses and loss of yield are the main damages caused by SO_2. Growth of the ornamental plants *Calendula officinalis* and *Dahlia rosea* was adversely affected when exposed to 1to 2 ppm of SO_2 for two hours.

SO_2 is also involved in the erosion of building materials as limestone marble, the slate used in roofing, mortar and deterioration of statues. Petroleum refineries, smellers, Kraft mills deteriorate the adjoining historic monuments.

(b) Hydrogen sulphide: The chief sources of H_2S are decaying vegetation and animal matter, especially in aquatic habitats. Sulphur springs volcanic eruptions, coal pits and sewers also give off this gas. About 30 million tons of H_2S every year is released by oceans and 60 to 80 million tons per year by land. Industries emit about 3 million tons every year. The chief industrial sources of H_2S are, users of sulphur containing fuel. In polluted areas its concentration reaches 100 mg/m^3, while in unpolluted areas its concentration remains around 0.3 mg/m^3. It is generally believed that hydrogen sulphide is oxidised in to sulpher dioxide but there is not much evidence for this.

At a low concentration, H_2S causes headache, nausea, collapse, coma and finally death. Unpleasant odor may destroy the appetite at 5 ppm level in some people. A concentration of 250 ppm may cause conjunctivitis and irritation of mucus membranes. Exposure at 500 ppm for 15-30 minutes may cause colic diarrhea and bronchial pneumonia. This gas readily passes through alveolar membrane of the lung and penetrates the blood stream. Death occurs due to respiratory failures.

4. Nitrogen oxides (NO_x): Nitrogen oxides are major primary pollutants. There are measurable amounts of Nitric oxide, nitrous oxide and nitrogen dioxide present in the unpolluted atmosphere. Of these nitric oxide (NO) is the pivot compound. It is produced by combustion of O_2 and N_2 during lighting discharges and by bacterial oxidation of NH_3 in soil. Nitric oxide contacts with air and combines with O_2 or even more readily with O_3 to form the more poisonous nitrogen dioxide (NO_2). NO_2 may react with water vapor in air to form HNO_3. This acid combines with NH_3 to form ammonium nitrate. Fossil fuel combustion also contributes to oxides of nitrogen. About 95% of the nitrogen oxide is emitted as NO and remaining 5% as NO_2. In urban areas about 46% of oxides of nitrogen in air comes from vehicles and 35% from electric generation and the rest from other sources.

(i) Nitrous oxide (N_2O): This gas has so far not been implicated in air pollution problems. The concentration of N_2O remains more or less constant up to the troposphere and then decreases with increase in altitude.

(ii) Nitric oxide (NO): The chief source of this gas are the industries manufacturing HNO_3 and other chemicals, and the automobile exhausts. At high temperature, combustion of gasoline produces this gas. A large amount of this is readily converted in to more toxic NO_2 in the atmosphere by a series of chemical reactions. NO is responsible for several photochemical reactions in the atmosphere, particularly in the formation of several secondary pollutants like PAN, O_3, carbonyl compounds etc. in the presence of other organic substances.

(iii) Nitrogen dioxide (NO_2): It is a deep reddish brown gas, which is the only widely prevalent colored pollutant gas. This gas is the chief constituent of *photochemical smog* in metropolitan areas.

At lower concentrations plant absorb NO and NO_2 from air without any damage. The uptake rate of NO_2 is much greater than that of NO. Concentrations of NO_2 in access of 2 mg/kg of air causes leaf damage to sensitive plants. In some plants, photosynthetic activity is impaired at a concentration of 0.6 mg/kg. In high concentrations, the oxides of nitrogen cause irritation to the mucus membrane and damage to the respiratory system.

5. Photochemical products: The important photo chemical products which are produced in the atmosphere as a result of interlinking of oxides of nitrogen, hydrocarbons and ozone in the presence of light include Olefins, aldehydes, ozone, PAN and photochemical smog. Olefins are produced directly form the exhaust and in the atmosphere from ethylene. At very low concentrations of few ppb, they affect plants seriously. They wither the sepals of orchid flowers, retard the opening of carnation flowers and may cause dropping of their petals. At high levels they retard the growth of tomatoes. Aldehydes as HCHO and olefin, acroleins irritate the skin, eyes and upper respiratory tract.

Photochemical smog: It was first discovered in Los Angeles, USA and is, therefore, also called Los Angeles Smog. When the air pollutants such as hydrocarbons and nitrogen oxides react with one another in the presence of sun light, NO_2, ozone and a compound called PAN (peroxyacetyl nitrate)-photochemical smog is formed which appears as a yellowish brown haze. The term smog is used for mixture of smoke and moisture in the air. The key reactant is NO_2. The important hydrocarbons for the production of this smog are olefins. The major changes that occur in atmosphere are that hydrocarbons and NO are discharged in to the atmosphere from automobile exhaust in large amounts in the peak activity hours of day. With increasing intensity of solar radiations, the concentration of NO goes on decreasing, the concentration of NO_2 increases and so does the amount of aldehydes. Then a decrease in NO_2 concentration later in the day accompanies the occurrence of significant ozone concentration, which from mid day to afternoon goes on increasing along with aldehydes and hydrocarbons. Similar photochemical reactions between oxides of nitrogen and hydrocarbons result in the formation of Peroxy Acetyl Nitrate (PAN).

Photochemical smog adversely affects plants, human health and materials. The oxidants enter as part of inhaled air, and alter, impair or interfere with respiratory process and other processes. Serious outbreaks of smog occurred in Tokyo, New York, Rome and Sydney in 1970, causing spread of disease as asthma and bronchitis in epidemic form. *Tokyo-Yokohama asthma* occurred in 1946 in some American soldiers and families living in smoggy atmosphere of Yokohama, Japan. Another serious disease caused by smog is *emphysema*, a disease due to structural breakdown of alveoli of lungs. The total surface area available for gaseous exchange is reduced and this cause severe breathlessness.

The smoke and the particulate matters (fog, mist, dust, soot etc) in the smog reduce the visibility, damage crops and livestock, and cause corrosion of metals, stones, building materials, painted surfaces, textile, paper, leather etc.

6. *Particulate matter:* This is a discrete mass of any material, except pure water, that exists as liquid or solid in the atmosphere and is of microscopic or submicroscopic dimensions. Air borne matter results not only from direct emission of particles but also from emissions of some gases that condense as particles directly or undergo transformation to form particle. Thus particulate matter may be primary or secondary. Primary particulate matter includes dust, as a result of wind, or smoke particles emitted from some factory, Atmospheric particulate matter range is size from 0.001 mm to several hundred mm. Particulate matter in atmosphere arises from natural as well as man-made sources. Natural sources are soil and rock debris (dust), volcanic emission, sea spray, forest fires and reactions between natural gas emission.

There are four types of sources of particulate matter: (*i*) fuel combustion and industrial operations (mining, smelting, polishing, furnaces and textiles, pesticides, fertilizers and chemical production), (*ii*) industrial fugitive processes (materials handling, loading and transfer operation), (*iii*) non-industrial fugitive processes (roadway dust, agricultural operations, construction, fire etc.) and (*iv*) transportation sources (vehicle exhaust and related particles from fire, clutch and break wear).

In our country, there is much of flyash introduced to atmosphere from fossil fuel based plants chiefly thermal power plants. They also emit coal dust. Besides them stone-crushers introduce smoke and dust in the atmosphere.

The particulate matter is injurious to health. Soot, lead particles form exhaust, assents, flyash, volcanic emission, pesticides, H_2SO_4, mist metallic dust, cotton and cement dust etc when inhaled by man cause respiratory diseases such as tuberculosis and cancer.

In addition to the above there are also many kinds of biological particulate matter that remain suspended in atmosphere. These are bacterial cells, spores, fungal spores, and pollen grains. These cause bronchial, allergy and many other diseases in man, animals and plants.

7. *Acid rains:* The oxides of sulphur and nitrogen are important gaseous pollutants of air. These two react with water in the atmosphere producing sulphuric acid and nitric acid. These oxides are swept up into the atmosphere and can travel thousands of kilometers. The longer they stay in the atmosphere, the more likely they are to be oxidized into acids. These come down to the earth along with rain. The pH of acid rain may vary from 3 to 6. Natural rains are slightly acidic because rain water reacts with CO_2 in atmosphere and produces a weak acid, the carbonic acid. The acid rains contain sulphuric acid, nitric acid along with carbonic acid.

Effects of Acid Rains

(*i*) Acid rain makes the leaves of plants yellow and brown and accelerates senescence. Thus affecting the productivity of forests, grasslands and crops.

(*ii*) It affects the properties of soil, changes the distribution of organisms in it and causes damage to soil fertility.

(*iv*) It kills aquatic life forms and affects the productivity of aquatic ecosystems.

(*v*) It leads to respiratory and skin diseases.

(*vi*) It damages marble and lime stone monuments.

Ozone (O_3): In the atmosphere, ozone is largely found in the stratosphere. Ozone absorbs most of the UV radiation of the sun and thus acts as a shield, protecting the living organisms on earth from health hazards. The depletion of this O_3 layer by human activities may have serious implications and this has become a subject of much concern over the last few years. Ozone is also formed in the atmosphere through chemical reactions involving certain pollutants (SO_2, NO_2, aldehydes) on absorption of UV-radiations. The atmospheric ozone is now being regarded as potential danger to human health and crop growth.

The temperature decreases with increasing altitude in the troposphere (8 to 16 km. from earth surface), while it increase with increasing altitude in the stratosphere (above 16 km. up to 50 km). This rise in temperature in stratosphere is caused by the ozone layer. The ozone layer has two important and interrelated effects. Firstly, it absorbs UV light and thus protects all life on earth from harmful effects of radiation. Second, by absorbing the UV radiation the ozone layer heats the stratosphere, causing temperature inversion which limits the vertical mixing of pollutants, thereby causing the dispersal of pollutants over the large areas near the earth surface. It is why a dense clouds usually hang over the atmosphere in highly industrialized areas causing several unpleasant effects. The wastes spread horizontally relatively fast (than slow mixing vertically), reaching all longitudes of the world in about a week and all latitudes within months. There is, therefore, very little that a country can do protect the ozone layer above it. The ozone problem is thus global in scope. In spite of slow vertical mixing, some of the pollutants (CFCs) enter the stratosphere and remain there for years until they are converted to other products or are transported back to the stratosphere. The stratosphere could be regarded as a sink, but unfortunately, these pollutants (CFEs) react with the ozone and deplete it.

The ozone near the earth's surface in the troposphere creates pollution problems. Ozone and other oxidants such as peroxy acetyl nitrate (PAN) and hydrogen peroxide are formed by light dependent reactions between NO_2 and hydrocarbons. Ozone may also be formed under UV-radiation effect. These pollutants cause photochemical smog. Increase in O_3 concentration near the earth's surface reduces crop yields significantly. It also has adverse effect on human health. Thus, while higher levels of O_3 in the atmosphere protects us, it is harmful when its comes in direct contact with us and plants at earth's surface.

In plants, O_3 enters through stomata. It produces visible damage to leaves, and thus a decrease in yield and quality of plant products. At 0.02 ppm it damages tobacco, tomato, bean, pine and other plants.

Ozone alone and in combination with other pollutants like SO_2 and NO_x is causing crop losses of over 50% in several European countries. In Denmark, O_3 affects potato, clover, spinach, alfalfa etc. In limited pockets O_3 concentration can be potentially harmful. For instance, in West Germany 100-250 mg/m^3 O_3 is not uncommon. In the Netherlands, O_3 concentration was high enough to reduce yields of potato, beans and poplars. In several locations in U.K., O_3 concentration exceeded 400 mg/m^3 in 1976.

Ozone also reacts with many fibers especially cotton, nylon and polyester, and dyes. The extent of damage appears to be affected by light and humidity. O_3 hardens rubber. A concentration of 0.3 ppm causes nose and throat irritation, 1-3 ppm causes extreme fatigue while a concentration of 9.0 ppm causes severe pulmonary edema.

O_3 is intimately connected with the life-sustaining process. Any depletion of ozone would, therefore, have catastrophic effects on life systems of the earth. Over the last few years, it could be realized that the O_3 concentration of earth's atmosphere is thinning out. What has caused this depletion?

In stratosphere, ozone absorbs UV rays causing the temperature inversion. This temperature inversion limits the vertical mixing of pollutants. However, in spite of this slow vertical mixing, some pollutants enter the stratosphere and remain there for years until they react with ozone and converted to other products. These pollutants thus deplete ozone in the stratosphere. Major pollutants responsible for this depletion are chlorofluorocarbons (CFCs), nitrogen oxides (coming from fertilizers) and hydrocarbons. CFCs are widely used as coolants in air conditioners and refrigerators, cleaning solvents, aerosol propellants and in foam insulation. CFC is also used in fire extinguishing equipment. They escape as aerosol in the stratosphere. Jet engines, motor vehicle, nitrogen fertilizers and other industrial activities are responsible for emission of CFCs, NO_x etc. The supersonics air crafts flying at stratosphere heights cause major disturbances in O_3 levels. The threat to ozone is mainly from CFCs, which are known to deplete O_3 by 14% at the current emission rate. On the other hand NO_x would reduce O_3 by 3.5%. The nitrogen fertilizers release nitrous oxide during de-nitrification. Depletion of O_3 would lead to serious temperature changes on the earth and consequent damage to life support system.

Depletion of ozone in stratosphere causes direct as well as indirect harmful effects. Since the temperature rise in stratosphere is due to heat absorption by ozone, the reduction in ozone would lead to temperature changes and rainfall failures on earth. Moreover one per cent reduction in O_3 increase UV radiation on earth by 2%. A series of harmful effects are caused by an increase in UV radiation. Cancer is the best-established threat to man. When the O_3 layer becomes thinner or has holes, it causes cancers, especially relating to skin like melanoma. A 10% decrease in stratospheric ozone appears likely to lead a 20-30% increase in skin cancer. The other disorders are cataracts, destruction of aquatic life and vegetation and loss of immunity. Nearly 6,000 people die of such cancers in USA each year. A 7% increase in such case has been reported from Australia and New Zealand.

Protecting ozone layer: Scientists throughout the world have shown a great concern over the thinning of ozone layer. This has led to a series of conferences on this issue. The first global conference on the depletion of ozone layer was held in Vienna (Austria) in 1985, the year, scientists discovered hole in South Pole. British team discovered a hole in ozone layer as large as that of the United States. This was followed by Montreal Protocol in 1987, which called for a 50% cut in the use of CFCs by 1998 reducing it to the level of 1986. Many countries including India did not sign the Protocol. India did not see any rationale as its release of CFCs is just 6,000 tones a year, equivalent to one and a half day's of world total. In our country per capita consumption of CFC is 0.02 kg. against 1 Kg. of developed world. CFCs are mainly the problem of developed world, as 95% of CFCs is released by European counties, U. S. A, USSR and Japan. USA alone releases 37% CFCs (producing CFC worth 2 billion dollar). The three-day international conference on Saving the ozone layer was organized jointly in London in March 1989 by the British Government and the UNEP. This conference highlighted the global problem created by the developed world, which in turn, is trying to dictate its terms to the developing countries for CFC pollution. The Montreal Protocol was initially signed by 31 countries.

There was held another international conference on ozone at Helsinki in May 1989 to revise the Montreal protocol. As many as 80 nations agreed to have a total ban on chemicals that cause ozone depletion by 2000 A.D. However, the conference backed away from a plan put forward by Dr. Mostafa Tolba, Executive Director, UNEP to set up an international climate fund. While the developing countries preferred to have the fund, the developed ones, including Japan, USA and UK rejected the plan.

Hydrocarbons

Automobile exhaust contains a variety of hydrocarbons. These are emitted by evaporation of gasoline through carburetors, crankcase etc. The decomposition of organic waste and garbage also produces hydrocarbons like methane. From amongst many hydrocarbons, the chief air pollutants are benzene, benzpyrene and methane. In India, two and three wheelers are the main contributors, and in Delhi and Bangalore, emission form these accounts for about 65% of the total hydrocarbons. If unchecked, this may go up to 80% of the total hydrocarbons of air. About 40% of the vehicular exhaust hydrocarbons are unburned fuel components, the rest are the product of combustion.

They have carcinogenic effects on lung. They combine with NO_x under UV-component of light to form other pollutants like PAN and Ozone (photochemical smog) which cause irritation of eye, nose and throat, and respiratory distress.

Benzene a liquid pollutant is emitted from gasoline. It causes lung cancer. Benzpyrene is most potent cancer inducing hydrocarbon pollutant. It is also present in small amounts in smoke, tobacco, charcoal boiled stakes, and gasoline exhaust. Methane (marsh gas) is a gaseous pollutant, in minute quantity in air, about 0.0002% by volume. In nature this is produced during decay of garbage, aquatic vegetation etc. This is also released due to burning of natural gas and from factories. Higher concentrations may cause explosion. The excess of water seepage in filled up well and pits may lead to excess production of methane, which bursts with high sound and may cause local destruction. At high levels in absence of oxygen, methane may be narcotic on man.

Fluorocarbons

Fluorocarbons, in minute quantities are beneficial, helping prevention of tooth-decay in man but only in very minute amounts. However, higher levels become toxic, In India, there is a problem of fluorosis, as also in other countries as USA, Italy, Holland, France, Germany, Spain, Switzerland, China, Japan and some African and Latin American countries. In our country, it is a public health problem in states of Gujarat, Rajasthan, Punjab, Haryana, Uttar Pradesh, Andhra Pradesh, Tamil Nadu, Karnataka and some areas of Delhi. Fluorides in atmosphere come from industrial processes of phosphate fertilizers, ceramics, aluminum, fluorinated hydrocarbons (refrigerants, aerosol propellants etc.), fluorinated plastic, uranium and other metal. The pollutant is in gaseous or particulate state.

In particulate form it is deposited near the vicinity of emission, whereas in gaseous form it disperses over large areas. On an average fluoride level of air is 0.05 mg/m^3 of air. Higher values may also reach as in some Italian factories as much as 15.14 mg/m^3 of air. Resident of this area inhales about 0.3 mg/m^3 of fluoride daily. In air, fluoride chiefly comes from smoke of industries, volcanic eruptions and insecticide sprays. Fluorides enter leaves of conifers. Fluoride pollution in man and animals is mainly through water.

Metals

The common metals which cause air pollution are mercury, lead, zinc and cadmium. They are released from industries and by human activities in the atmosphere.

Mercury, a liquid volatile metal is present in air as a result of human activities as the use of mercury compounds in production of fungicides, paints, cosmetics, paper pulp etc. It has been reported that inhalation of 1 mg Hg/m^3 of air for three months may lead to death. Nervous system, liver, eyes are damaged. Infants may be deformed. Other symptoms of mercury toxicity, are headache, fatigue, anxiety, lethargy, loss of appetite etc.

Lead is added to gasoline to reduce knocking, and is emitted into the air with the exhausts as volatile lead halides (bromides and chlorides). About 75% of lead burnt in gasoline comes out as lead halides through tail pipe in exhaust gases. Of this about 40% settles immediately on the ground and the rest (60%) gets into air. The WHO prescribed level (2 mg/m^3) in air is already crossed in many countries of world. Lead inhalation causes reduced hemoglobin formation, thus leading to anemia. Lead compounds also damage RBC_s resulting in infection of liver and kidney in man. In automobiles lead accumulation increase emission of hydrocarbons.

Zinc, not a natural component of air, occurs around zinc smelters and scrap zinc refineries. Copper, lead and steel refineries also release some zinc in the air. Zinc in air occurs mostly as white zinc oxide fumes and is toxic to man.

Cadmium occurs in air due to industrial and other human activities. Industries engaged in extraction, refining, electroplating and welding of cadmium containing materials, and those in refining of copper, lead and zinc are the major source of cadmium in air. Production of some pesticides and phosphate fertilizers also emits cadmium to air. This metal is emitted as vapor, and in this state it quickly reacts to form oxide, sulphate or chloride compounds. Cadmium is poisonous at very low levels and is known to accumulate in human liver and kidney. It causes hypertension, emphysema and kidney damages. It may turn to be carcinogenic in mammals.

SOIL POLLUTION : SOURCES AND EFFECTS

Soil which is formed by the weathering of rocks, is a very important resource. Various activities of human beings leading pollution of soil not only in urban and industrial areas but also in rural areas. Dumping of various waste generated in various industries and municipalities causes release of various toxic substances which ultimately find their ways in to the soil and ultimately to the ground water. The use of various types of pesticides, herbicides, insecticides, fertilizers etc. to increase the crop production also leads to the severe contamination of soil. In the soil pollution the different pollutants remain in direct contact of soil for a longer period and enter in the food chain of the nature and also in the air and water.

The important sources of soil pollution are as under:

(i) *Agriculture practices:* The use of large quantity of fertilizers, insecticides, herbicides, weedicides and various soil conditioning agents pollute the soil to a great extent. Similarly excessive amount of plant and animal wastes is also adding to the problem of soil pollution. The fertilizers used to improve the fertility of soil also contaminate it with their impurities. The excessive use of nitrogen, phosphorus and potassium also inhances to this problem.

The increasing use of pesticides to control various pests is causing a stress on the natural environment. During last one decade the number of pesticides has increased manifolds and important among these are organophosphates like malathion, parathion, ethion, trithion etc., and the chlorinated hydrocarbons e.g., BHC, DDT, aldrin, lindane, chlordane and endosulphan. When these pesticides are applied for the contreol of a pest, these are released to the soil and their remanants contaminate to the soil. The herbicides used at the time of seedling remain active for a long time thus add to the soil contamination. Various soil conditioners and fumigants used to increase and protect the soil fertility have several toxic metals which keep on accumulating in the soil.

(ii) *Urban waste:* The large amount of waste being generated in the urban areas contribute to soil pollution. This waste which is normally termed as refuse contains garbage, plastics, metals, fibre, paper, glasses, containers, fuel residues etc. The generation of this waste in huge quantitities has become a problem world over. The capital of India generates approximately 5000 tones of garbage everyday. The soil pollutants ultimately find their way to ground water thus affecting it severely.

(iii) *Industrial waste:* This is one of the most important soil pollutant and its disposal is becoming a serious problem with every passing day. The industrial pollutants are mainly discharged from sugar factories, oil refineries, tanneries, distilleries, fertilizer and pesticide industries and also from chemical and steel factories. The metal processing industries, drugs, cement, petroleum and coal and mineral industries are other important generators of such waste material. Fly ash, which is mainly being generated by the thermal power plants is another important soil pollutant. All the pollutants released by these industries ultimately affect and alter the biological and chemical properties of the soil.

Effects of Soil Pollttants

The various effects of soil pollutants are as under:

(*i*) The beneficial microorganisms such as bacteria etc. are destroyed by metallic contaminents. These contaminents such as Cr, Zn, Pb, Cd, Hg etc. remain in the soil and their accumulation in the soil for a long period is injurious to the living organisms.

(*ii*) Industrial wastes from fertilizers, steel, paper and textile industries are extremely toxic are sometimes very toxic to living beings. These are transeferred to different organisms through the food chain and lead to a variety of harmful effects in living world.

(*iii*) Solid waste which is directly thrown in the open land results into offensive odour and causes a variety of diseases and ground water pollution.

(*iv*) Radioactive pollutants dumped into soil produce great human misearies and are responsible for a number of diseases in human beings.

(*v*) The various volatile materials which are released into the spoil when released into the atmosdphere, contaminate it through the plants they find their way in to human beings causing disruption in the various physiological processes.

(*vi*) Various fertilizers and pesticides addeded in to the soil are responsible for many ill effects in otrher biota.

(*vii*) Many pathogenic bacteria which are present in soil cause serious threats to human health.

WATER POLLUTION

The sources of water on this planet are rain, surface water, the ground water and the sea. Rain water carries the washed out minerals, salts and organic matter from the earth's surface and is stored in ponds, lakes and rivers. It percolates underground and is stored there as ground water. The source of fresh water are ponds, wells, lakes and rivers. Natural water contains numerous organisms like phytoplankton, zooplanktons, fish and so on. Besides it is a good solvent and contains dissolved gases like oxygen. When we say pure water, we mean water free from organisms, particularly microbes, and which usually contains a negligible amount of salts. In India, the ever increasing population, urbanization, agricultural activities and industrialization, accompanied by a greater mechanization in every sector of life, has led to a constant increase in requirements placed upon water. It has been estimated that 70% of available water in India is polluted. The signs of water pollution have been obvious to even the most casual observer. However, water pollution may be defined as "the addition of any substance to water or changing of it's physical and chemical characteristics in any way, which interferes with its use for legitimate purposes". Thus, pollution of natural water implies that it contains a lot of inorganic substances introduced by human activities, which change its quality and are harmful for many living organisms, including man. It is one of the most serious problems in the world, particularly in developing countries. Normally water is never pure in a chemical sense. It contains impurities of various kinds-dissolved as well as suspended. These include dissolved gases (H_2S, CO_2, NH_3, N_2), dissolved minerals (Ca, Mg, Na salt), suspended matter (clay, silt, sand) and even microbes. These are natural impurities derived from atmosphere, catchments areas and the soil. They are in very low amounts and normally do not pollute water and it is potable. Polluted water, however, is turbid, unpleasant, bad smelling, unfit for drinking, bathing, and washing or other purposes. They are harmful and are vehicles of many diseases as cholera, dysentery, typhoid etc.

SOURCES, NATURE AND EFFECTS OF WATER POLLUTANTS

The chief sources of water pollution are: (*i*) Oxygen demanding wastes, (*ii*) industrial effluents, (*iii*) agricultural discharges and (*iv*) industrial wastes from chemical industries, fossil fuel plants (thermal power plants) and nuclear power plants. Each of these sources of pollution carries a variety of pollutants that enter our water bodies. Following are the sources of water pollution and kind of he pollutants carried by them :

1. *Oxygen demanding waste:* Dissolved oxygen has been a fundamental requirement of life in any given body of water. A body of water is classified as polluted when the DO concentration drops below the level necessary for sustaining normal biota for that water. The primary cause of water degradation has been the presence of substances collectively called oxygen demanding wastes. These are primarily organic materials that are oxidized by bacteria to carbon di-oxide and water. Sewage is the waterborne waste derived from home (domestic waste) and animals or food processing plants. Sewage and other oxygen demanding wastes have been classified as water pollutants because their degradation leads to oxygen depletion. This affects the aquatic life, impairs domestic and livestock water supplies by affecting taste, odors and colors. It includes human excreta, paper, cloth, soap, detergents etc. There is uncontrolled dumping of wastes of rural areas, towns and cities into ponds, lakes, stream or rivers. The decomposition of these wastes by aerobic microbes decrease due to higher levels of pollution. The self-purifying ability of the water is lost and water becomes unfit for drinking and other domestic uses. Since decomposition of sewage and other wastes is largely an aerobic process, accumulation of these in water increase its oxygen requirements (BOD).

Phosphates are the major ingredients of most detergents, They favor the luxuriant growth of algae which form water blooms. This extensive algae growth also consumes most of the available oxygen from water. This decrease in level becomes detrimental to growth of other organisms, which produces a foul smell upon decay.

One of the most common primary sources of water pollution is the discharge of untreated or partly treated sewage in water bodies, sometimes due to improper sewage-handling processes of municipal bodies. As oxygen demanding wastes rapidly deplete the DO of water, it is important to estimate the amount of these pollutants in a given body of water. The biochemical oxygen demand (BOD) of water has been a quantity related to the amount of wastes present.

Biological oxygen demand (BOD): In a water sample the BOD indicates the amount of dissolved oxygen used up during the oxidation of oxygen demanding wastes. BOD is the amount of oxygen required for biological oxidation by microbes in any unit volume of water. It could be found out by incubating a sample of water for five days at 20° C. A BOD value generally approximates the amount of oxidisable organic matter, and is, therefore, used as a measure of degree of water pollution and waste level. Thus mostly BOD value is proportional to the amount of organic waste present in water.

BOD values are thus useful in evaluation of self-purification capacity of a water body and for possible control measure of pollution. The quantity of oxygen in water (Dissolved Oxygen–DO) along with BOD is indicated by the kind of organisms present in water. Thus fish become rare at DO value of 4 to 5 ppm of water. Further decrease in DO value may lead to increase in anaerobic bacteria. A BOD of 1 ppm has been characteristic of nearly pure water. Water is regarded as fairly pure with a BOD of 3 ppm, and of doubtful purity when the BOD value reaches 5 ppm.

Eutrophication: In natural conditions relatively small quantities of nutrients and sediments are leached or eroded from the land into water bodies. In turn these are fed by clear rivers and streams, the natural conditions of lakes and esturies is generally *oligotrophic,* that is the water is nutrient poor. This limits the growth of phytoplaktons, but benthis plants (plants that grow attached to or rooted in the bottom) thrive to a depth of 30 feet. Oxygen from the atmosphere is very slow to dissolve and get mixed with water. Benthic plants also help in maintaining the dissolved oxygen level in deeper water because oxygen produced during photosynthesis is directly dissolved into the water. Thus a nutrient poor water body maintains a rich and diverse ecosystem.

With the erosion and leaching of materials, a water body gradually gets filled with sediments and gets enriched with nutrients. The nutrient enrichment promotes the growth of phytoplanktons which in turn make the water more turbid this problem is more compounded by sediments. The oxygen produced by photosynthesis of phytoplanktons supersaturates the upper water and escapes the surface. Phytoplankton has a high turnover rate leading to an unusually high accumulation of detritus. As decomposers mainly bacteria feed on this material, they also consume oxygen in their respiration, thus depleting the dissolved oxygen in the water. When DO is not available the bacteria shift and continue to thrive on fermentation. As a consequence, the DO becomes high at surface level whilebecomes almost zero at lower levels. Thus the lake becoming a eutrophic lake.

Thus eutrophication is nutrient enrichment that promotes the growth of phytoplankton in the water body.

In USA, Lake Erie is an excellent example of eutrophication due to man made problems. In 1965, there were added more than 80 tons of phosphates daily in the lake. Each 400 g of PO_4 encourages about 350 tones of algal slime. Due to this algal growth on the shores of lake appeared as big mounds producing unpleasant odor, clogging pipes and interfering with fishing and navigation. Eutrophication is thus limiting factor in supply of clean water for drinking fishing and navigation etc.

2. Industrial wastes as water pollutants: Many industries, such as steel and paper are situated on the banks of rivers as they require huge amount of water in their manufacturing process. These industries dump their wastes in to rivers. A wide variety of both, inorganic and organic pollutant are present in effluents from breweries, tanneries, dying textiles, paper and pulp mills, steel industries, mining operations etc. The pollutants include oils, greases, plastics, metallic wastes, suspended solids, phenols, toxins, acids, salts, dyes, cyanides, DDT etc., many of which are not readily susceptible to degradation and thus cause serious pollution problems. H_2SO_4 as acid waste from coal mines is a serious pollutant that increase the hardness of water, has disastrous effect on live organisms and corrodes concrete etc. Na, Cu, Cr, Cd, Hg, Pb, etc. are the heavy metal effluents, discharged from industries. Most of the Indian rivers and fresh water streams are seriously polluted by industrial wastes and effluents which come along waste waters of different industries such as petrochemicals, fertilizer factories, oil refineries, pulp, paper textiles, sugar and steel mills, tanneries, distilleries, synthetic material plants for drugs, fibers, rubbers, plastics etc.

3. Agricultural discharges: It includes sediments, fertilizers, pesticides and farm animal wastes. All these pollutants can enter waterways as run off from agricultural lands but farm animal wastes are an especially large problem near the large feed lots on which thousands of animals concentrated. Their discharge reach into the water bodies. As compared to developed nations, India has a relatively low use of chemicals, thus discharge into water are still low. India uses about 16 Kg/ha of fertilizers (chemicals) on an average, whereas the world average is 54 Kg/ha. Thus it is not only the increased use but also escalated production that would enhance pollution.

(a) Artificial fertilizers: Modern agriculture relies heavily on a wide range of synthetic chemicals which include different types of fertilizers and biocides (pesticide, herbicides or weedicides). These chemicals along with wastes are wasted off lands through irrigation, rainfall, drainage etc. reaching into the rivers, lakes, stream etc. where they disturb the natural ecosystem.

How dangerous are they? Are they harmful? Do they benefit? Are they safe? What to use? Which to use? While improving the yield do these chemicals in any manner affect the quality of the food stuffs grown?

Artificial fertilizers crowd out useful minerals naturally present in the topsoil. The microbes (bacteria, fungi, worms etc.) in topsoil enrich the humus and help to produce nutrients to be taken up by the plant and later by animals. But fertilizers enriched soil can not support microbial life and hence there is less humus and less nutrients and the soil can easily become poor and eroded by wind and rain.

Chemical fertilizers are made up of only a few minerals. Thus they impede the uptake of other minerals and imbalance the whole mineral pattern of plant body. Many crops today lack potassium due to excessive use of nitrogenous fertilizer. Excessive potash treatment decreases valuable nutrients in foods, such as ascorbic acid (Vitamin C) and carton. Liming can prevent the release and uptake into the plants of cobalt, nickel, manganese and zinc. Super-phosphate may lead to a copper and zinc deficiency.

Plants also become less resistant to diseases. NO_3 fertilizers increase the total crop yield (carbohydrates) but at the expense of protein. Corn and wheat grown on soil fertilized with N, P and K showed a 20-25% decline in protein content and increase in carbohydrate content. Moreover, subtle balance of amino acid is disturbed within the protein molecule, thus lowering protein quality. Since most of Indians are vegetarians, consumption of low quality protein leads to malnutrition. Fertilizer use produces over-sized fruits and vegetables, which are more prone to insects and other pests.

According to H. H. Koepf, an eminent soil chemist, modern agriculture can honestly claim only two notable crops-*"disease and pests"*. To this we can now add a third-*poison* (as nitrites, nitrates). Nitrate fertilizers used on soil enter our wells and ponds, making their water very rich in nitrates. It not only makes water unfit for drinking but also causes disease. This water when taken by us, the nitrates are converted to nitrites by microbial flora of intestine. These nitrites then combine with the hemoglobin of blood to form methaemoglobin, which interfaces with the O_2-carrying capacity of the blood. The disease produced in called *Methaemoglobinaemia*. This leads to various ailments, damage to respiratory and vascular system, blue coloration of skin and even cancer. A healthy person contains 0.8% of methaemoglobin, whereas in methaemoglobinaemia this level reaches to 10% in the blood. At above 30% concentration there occurs headache, giddiness and above 60%, un-consciousness with stiffness and ocular problem etc takes place. At 80% death occurs. Nitrate poisoning is frequent in Rajasthan due to hard and saline water. Several children have died due to this problem. In 1976, there were cases of NO_3 poisoning of cattle in Nagpur. In Rajasthan NO_3 levels in water area very high, (800 mg/l), which is much beyond the permissible concentration of 45 mg/l by WHO. Consumption of vegetable grown in NO_3 rich soil may also lead to this disease, especially in sick persons and children. Addition of phosphates and NO_3 to water leads to depletion of oxygen due to excessive algal growth. It leads to death of fish and other aquatic life.

(b) Pesticides and biocides: Pesticides are the chemicals used for killing the plant and animals pests. It is a general term that includes bactericides, fungicides, nematicides, insecticides and also the herbicides or weedicides. Since weeds (herbs) are not pests like bacteria, fungi, nematodes, insects, the spectrum of activity of these chemicals is extended beyond the pest; and thus a broader term biocide is used to include also herbicides etc.

A wide range of chemicals is used as biocides. But the most harmful are those, which either do not degrade or degrade very slowly in nature. We prefer to distinguish such chemical substances as *hazardous* substance or *toxicants*. These are highly potent chemicals that enter our food chain and then begin to increase in their concentrations at successive trophic levels in the food chain. Equally hazardous substances are the radionuclides. The hazardous biocides cause considerable harm since their effects are cumulative. Most nations have banned the use of some of these biocides.

The long range effects of such biocides are infact a threat to our ecological security. According to Pearson (1985) pesticide related deaths in developing countries are estimated at 10,000/year and about 1.5-2 million person suffer from acute pesticide poisoning.

Some of the most toxic biocides are DDT (dichloro-diphenyl trichloroethane), BHC (benzene hexachloride), chlordane, heptachlor, methoxychlor, toxaphene, aldrin, endrin an PCBs (polychlorinated biphenyl's). Indiscriminate use of the biocides could make them an integral part of our biological, geological and chemical cycles of the earth. They are everywhere in same form. Measurable amounts of DDT residues may be found in air, soil, and water and at several thousand of Kms. from the point where it had originally entered the ecosystem. For instance if DDT enters a pond, lake, it is taken as such by the plants of the pond, then reaches to zooplankton feeding on plants, then to minnows eating the zooplanktons, then to fish which eats the minnows and finally in the body of birds who eat the fish. Not only DDT as such in its original form keeps on moving form water to different living components of the pond system but more threatening is that–DDT concentration continuously increases in successive trophic levels (various form of living organisms) in a food chain. This phenomenon is known as *biological magnification* or *biological amplification*. This is the reason why our food grains as wheat, rice, vegetables and fruits today contain varying amounts of pesticide residues, which have become their integral part. They can not be removed by washing or other means.

Besides DDT there are also heavy metals like lead, mercury, copper which also show similar behavior in a food chain. Similarly the radionculides as storntium-90 follows biological magnification. We shall present more details of these processes in separate chapter on Toxicology. The outcome of such criminal and indiscriminate use may be acute (immediate) or chronic poisoning. The danger of long term consumption of pesticides residues in food is far more serious that acute poisoning from the point of view of national health. Children born today have to start life with a body burden of pesticides, which increase with age. There is evidence that such chronic accumulation of pesticides played a role in kidney malfunctioning, excess of amino acids in blood and urine, electroencephalogram abnormalities of brain tissue, blood abnormalities etc.

4. Solid waste pollution: Solid waste varies in composition with socioeconomic status of the generating community. The disposal of solid waste poses many problems, depending upon both the types of waste and the disposal method employed. The majority of waste classified as combustible-rubbish, garbage and sewage sludge is disposed off by incineration, using it as land fill or disposal by ocean dumping. Landfill and ocean dumping lead to water pollution.

5. Thermal pollution: Thermal pollution takes place because many electricity generating companies use water in the process of cooling their generators. This heated water is then released into the system from which it was drawn, causing a warming trend of the surface waters. Thermal pollution results when the heated effluent is released into poorly flushed systems. In these cases a permanent temperature increase often results, which tends to decrease the solubility of dissolved oxygen in the waterbody and is thus very injurious to aquatic life.

6. Radioactive waste pollution: The major sources of radioactive wastes have been nuclear explosives, accidents at nuclear power plants, fuel reprocessing plants and research laboratories and hospitals that release these wastes into the atmosphere or into waste water.

Marine Pollution

Discharge of waste substances into the sea resulting in harmful effects to living resources, hazardous to human health, hinderance to fishery and imparement of quality for use of sea water is called as marine pollution. It is associated with the change in physical, chemical and biological conditions of the sea water. All that what is carried by rivers ultimately ends up in the seas. On their way to sea, rivers receive huge amounts of sewage, garbage, agricultural discharge, biocides, including heavy metals. These all are added to sea. Besides these discharges of oils and petroleum products and dumping of radionuclieds waste into sea also cause marine pollution. Huge quantity of plastic is being added to sea and oceans. Over 50 million lb plastic packing material is being dumped in sea of commercial fleets, whereas over 300 million lb entering through inland waterways in USA. Many marine bird ingest plastic that causes gastro-intestinal eggshgel and tissue damage of egg. Radionucilde waste in sea includes Sr-90, Cs-137, Pu-239, Pu-240.

The pollutants in seas may become dispersed by turbulence and ocean currents or concentrated in the food chain. They may sediment at the bottom by processes like adsorption, precipitation and accumulation. Bioaccumulation in food chain may result into loss of species diversity. The pollution in Baltic sea along the coast of Finland, took place largely from sewage and effluents form bottom fauna. There was seen distinct zonation with extent of pollution. In clear or less polluted water there was rich species diversity which tended to decrease with increasing pollution load. In heavily polluted area, macroscopic benthic animals were absent, but chironomid larvae occurred at the bottom.

In marine water the serious pollutant is oil, particularly when afloat on sea. An spill in oil or petroleum product due to accidents or a deliberate discharge of oil polluted waste brings about pollution. About 285 million gallons of oil are spilled each year into ocean, mostly from transport tankers. This is enough to coat a beach 20 feet wide with half and inch oil layer for 8633 miles. About 50,000 to 250,000 birds are killed every year by oil. The oil is soaked in feathers, displacing the air and thus interfere with buoyancy and maintenance of body temperature, Hydrocarbons and benzpyrene accumulate in food chain and consumption of fish by man may cause cancer. Detergents used to clean up the spill are also harmful to marine life.

Mercury Pollution

Mercury enters water naturally as well as through industrial effluents. It is a potent hazardous substance. Both, inorganic and organic forms are highly poisonous. Methyl mercury gives off vapor. Mercury was responsible for the minamata epidemic that caused several deaths, in Japan and Sweden. The tragedy had occurred due to consumption of heavily mercury-contaminated fish (27 to 102 ppm, average 50 ppm) by the villagers. The source of mercury to the bay was a single chloride producing plant, using $HgCl_2$ as a catalyst. In Sweden many rivers and lakes are already polluted due to widespread use of mercury compounds as fungicides and algaecides in paper and pulp industries and in agriculture. Chloral alkali plants seem to be the chief source of mercury containing effluents. Paper and pulp industries of Japan and Canada also cause mercury pollution. Effluents of industries making switches, batteries, thermometers, fluorescent light tubes and high intensity street lamps also contain mercury.

Mercury compounds enter the water body from the effluents and at their bottom these are metabolically converted into methyl mercury compounds by anaerobic microbes. Methyl mercury is highly persistent and thus accumulates in food chain. Methyl mercury is soluble in lipids and thus after being taken by animals it accumulates in fatty tissues. Fish may accumulate the methyl mercury ions directly. There may be nearly 3000 times more mercury in fish than in water. In Minamata bay all the mercury in sea food is as organic methyl mercury compounds. The symptoms of Minamata include malaise, numbness, visual disturbance, dyspepsia, ataxia, mental deterioration, convulsions and final death. Mercury readily penetrated the central nervous system of children born in Minamata causing teratogenic effects. Methyl mercury penetrates through placenta. Swedish fish eaters have high mercury content in blood. In *Drosopial* methyl mercury (0.25 ppm) treatment brought chromosomal disjunction in gametes.

Mercury poisoning is caused due to inactivation of several sulfhydral enzymes by replacement of hydrogen atoms in sulfhydral groups. The antidote, BAL (dimercaprol) is used for mercury poisoning.

Lead Pollution

Lead poisoning is common in adults. The chief sources of lead to water are the effluents of lead and lead processing industries. Lead toys may be chewed by children. Painters also have a risk of lead consumption. In some plastic pipes lead is used as stabilizer. The water may become contaminated in these pipes. Lead is also used in insecticides, food, beverage, ointments and medicinal concoctions for flavoring and sweetening.

Lead pollution causes damage to liver and kidney, reduction in hemoglobin formation, mental retardation and abnormalities in fertility and pregnancy. Chronic lead poisoning may cause three general disease syndromes (*i*) gastroin-testinal disorder (*ii*) neuromuscular effects (leadlapsy)-weakness, fatigue muscular atrophy, and (*iii*) central nervous system effects of CNS Syndrome–that may result to coma and death. Lead poisoning also causes constipation, abdominal pain etc.

Fluoride Pollution

Fluoride is also regularly present in water and soil besides air. The crop plants grown in high-fluoride soils in agricultural, non-industrial areas had a fluoride content as high as 300 ppm. In Haryana and Punjab, consumption of fluoride-rich water from wells caused endemic fluorisis. In Andhra Pradesh also high fluroride content water caused dental fluorisis. On an average, about 20-25 million Indian are affected with fluorisis. In our country this problem has become more severe in Rajasthan. This has already crippled about 3.5 lakh person in state. Fluorisis is prevalent in districts of Jodhpur, Bhilwara, Jaipur, Bikaner, Udazipur, Nagpur, Barmer and Ajmer. Many people in Rajasth have humped back due to high fluoride content in water sources and in arid and grains semi arid zones. In arid and semi-arid soils also fluroide content is very high. Food grains obtained from these soils are also rich in fluorides. Prolonged intake of fluoride containing water stiffens the bone joints, particularly of spinal cord. Fluoride is not absorbed in the blood stream. It has an affinity with calcium and thus gets accumulated in bones, resulting in the mottling of teeth, pain in the bones and joint and outward bending of legs from the knees-knock knee syndrome. Fluoride levels more than 0.5 ppm over a period of 5-10 years results in fluorisis terminating in crippling or paralysis. In water of most villages of Rajasthan fluoride level is higher than permissible limit of 1 mg/liter of water.

Cattle grazing around fluoride sources, as ceramic rocks, phosphate fertilizer plants and aluminum factories often develop fluorisis. The toxic effects are staining, mottling and abrasion of teeth, high fluoride levels in bone and urine, decreased milk production, and lameness. Moreover, the animals also become lethargic.

NOISE POLLUTION

Noise pollution is a direct result of technological development. Noise, with its ever increasing effects on human beings and on the environment, is defined as an acoustic fact which is unpleasant and arouses disturbing feeling or as the totality of unwanted, undesired sounds. The human ear is constantly being assailed by man made sound from all sides, and there remain few places in population areas where relative quiet prevails. What do airplanes, trains, cars, and numatic drills, and radio and television sets have in common? They all produce noise, the most dangerous pollutant of man's environment. Noise has become a permanent part of our lives these days because of the development of machinery, industry and technology. Noise harms the body and mind. Noise not only cause irritation or annoyance but it constricts your arteries, increases the flow of adrenaline and forces your heart to work faster.

The word *noise* (Latin nausea) is usually defined as unwanted or unpleasant sound that causes discomfort. Noise is also defined as "wrong sound, in the wrong place at the wrong time". Noise pollution means, "the unwanted sound dumped into the atmosphere leading to health hazards".

Even if noise is not sufficiently loud to constitute direct threat to human health, continuous exposure to noise shortens human beings sleeping hours and reduces his productivity. The decrease in productivity affects both city dwellers and people who work in factories or in the industrial areas. In China, till the third century BC, noise was used as a method of torture instead of hanging men for dangerous crime. The importance of noise as a pollutant having a deleterious effect on peace of mind and beauty of environment is increasing every day. Formerly noise was limited only to the industry. This too was not much as there were only few industries. These days there has been rapid industrial growth.

Moreover, there has been population explosion, due to which there is heavy traffic, urban crowd and electric equipment (luxury items and entertainment). All these have added to the noise nuisance in environment. In our country, beside these the two other factors are the religious and social functions, which increase the gravity of situation.

Properties

There are two basic properties of sound, (*i*) loudness and (*ii*) frequency. Loudness is the strength of sensation of sound perceived by the individuals. It is measured in terms of decibels. Just sound is about 10 dB, a whisper about 20 dB, library place, 30 dB, normal conversation 35-60 dB, heavy street traffic 60-80 dB, boiler factories 120 dB, jet planes (take off) about 150 dB, rocker engine, about 180 dB. The loudest sound a person can stand without much discomfort is about 80 dB. Sounds beyond 80 dB can be safely regarded as pollutant as its harms hearing system. The WHO has fixed 45 dB as the safe noise level for a city. For international standards a noise level upto 65 dB is considered tolerable. Intensity of some noise sources is as follows:

Sources	Intensity (dB)
Breathing	10
Broadcasting studio	20
Soft whisper	20-30
Trickling clock	30
Library	30-35
Low volume radio	35-40
Normal conversation	35-60
Telephone	60
Office noise	60-80
Alarm clock	70-80
Traffic	50-90
Trunk	90
Motor cycle	105
Lion's roar (12')	105-110
Jet fly (over 1000')	100-110
Train whistle (50')	110
Air craft (100') (Prokeller driven)	110-120
Pneumatic drill	110-120
Commercial jet (air craft (100'))	120-140
Jet take off (300')	120
Space rocket (launching)	170-180

Loudness is also expressed in *sones*. One sone equals the loudness of 40 dB sound pressure at 1000 hz.

Frequency is defined as the number of vibrations per second. It is denoted as *Hertz* (hz). One hz equals to one vibration per second. People can hear sound from 16 (infra-audible) to 20,000 (ultrasonic) hz.

SOURCES AND EFFECTS OF NOISE

Sources of noise are numerous but these may be broadly classified in to two classes: (*i*) Industrial and (*ii*) Non-industrial.

The main contributors to noise are factories and industries, transportation (air, rail and road). The disturbing qualities of noise emitted by industrial premises are generally its loudness, its distinguishing feature such as tonal or impulsive components and its intermitancy and duration.

Among the non-industrial sources, important ones are as follows: (*a*) Loudspeakers, (*b*) automobiles (*c*) aircrafts (*d*) trains (*e*) construction works (*f*) radio, microphone etc. The chief man-made sources in urban areas are automobiles, factories, industries, trains, airplanes. Noise makers are horns, sirens, lawn mover, musical instruments, TV, radio, transistor, telephone, dog, loudspeaker, washing machines, vacuum cleaner, food mixers, pressure cookers, fans, air conditioners, coolers. Ever since the industrial revolution, there has been doubling of environmental noise in every 10 years.

Effects: Noise has been found to interfere with our activities at three levels: (*i*) audiological level (*ii*) biological level, interfering with the biological functioning of the body and (*iii*) behavioral level, affecting the sociological behavior of the subjects.

1. *Auditory effects:* These include auditory fatigue, and deafness. Auditory fatigue appearing the 90 dB and may be associated with side effects as whistling and buzzing in ears. Deafness can be caused due to continuous noise exposure. Temporary deafness occurs at 4000-6000 hz. Permanent loss of hearing occurs at 100 dB.

2. *Non-auditory effects:* These are (*i*) interference with speech communication, (*ii*) annoyance, (*iii*) loss of working and (*iv*) physiological disorders:

(*a*) *Interference with speech communication:* A noise of 50-60 dB commonly interferes with speech; sound of warning (signal) may be misunderstood.

(*b*) *Annoyance:* Balanced person express great annoyance at even low level of noise as crowd, highway, radio etc. The effects are ill temper, bricking.

(*c*) *Loss in working efficiency:* There develop tiredness and those doing mental work may put to deterioration in their efficiency or even complete loss of ability to work.

(*d*) *Physiological disorders:* A number of physiological disorders develop due to imbalance in functioning of the body. These are neurosis, anxiety, insomnia, hypertension, hepatic diseases, behavioural and emotional stress, increase in sweating, giddiness, nausea fatigue etc. Noise also cause visual disturbance, and reduces depth and quality of sleep thus affecting overall mental and physical health. Other effects are, undesirable changes in respiration, circulation of blood in skin and gastrointestinal activity. Noise pollution also causes incidence of peptic ulcers.

Continuous noise causes an increase in cholesterol level resulting in the constriction of blood vessels making you prone to heart attack and strokes. There may be still births and usually low weight children born to mothers living near airports.

Supersonic air planes create a shock wave called *sonic boon*, which produces a startle effect that can be more harmful than a continuous noise. The sonic boon may spread in an area of 10 to 80 miles and when its hits the ground it damages window pans and building structures. This may also fasten the human fetus heart rate. Some of the important health hazards of noise are as follows:

Noise intensity (dB)	Health hazards
80	Annoyance
90	Hearing damage
95	Very annoying
110	Stimulation of reception in skin
120	Pain threshold
130-135	Nausea, vomiting, dizziness
140	Pain in ear
150	Burning of skin
160	Rupture of tympanic membrane
180	Major permanent damage in short time

CONTROL OF NOISE POLLUTION

All noise control problems could fundamentally be denoted as shown in following figure.

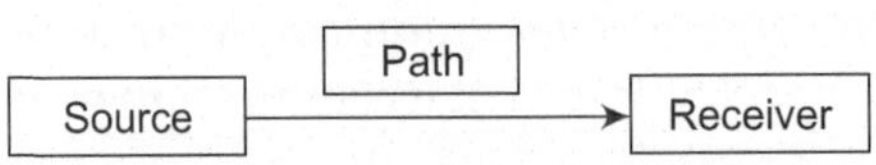

A source or sources produce the noise, and both, direct and indirect paths exist by which the generated noise could be transmitted to one or more receiver. There are following ways to control and reduce the noise menace.

1. *Control at source:* This can be done by (*i*) designing and fabricating silencing devices in air-craft engines, automobiles industrial machines and home appliance and (*ii*) segregating the noisy machines. The proper design of equipment to minimize the noise generation has been

somewhat a complex engineering problem needing a strong background in the fundamentals of vibration, fluid mechanics, dynamics, materials and machine design. It is also important to operate all the equipment at the design conditions. Operating equipment at designed pressure and speed should result in minimum noise generation. It should be apparent that maintenance is an important element in controlling the noise generated by equipment.

2. *Transmission control:* This can be achieved by covering the room walls with sound absorber as acoustic tiles and construction of enclosures around industrial machinery.
3. *To protect exposed person:* The worker exposed to noise can be provided with wearing devices as ear plugs and ear muffs.
4. *To create vegetation cover:* Plants absorb and dissipate sound energy and thus act as buffer zone. Trees should be planted along high ways, streets and other places. Ashok, Neem, Tamarind etc. are good for this purpose.
5. *Control through law:* Silence zones must be created near schools, hospitals and indiscriminate use of loudspeakers at public places must be prevented by laws. Adequate restriction must be put on unnecessary use of horns and vehicles plying with out silencers. There are already such laws in some countries as UK and USA. In India, we have Motors vehicles Act which provides restriction on trucks using double sirens while passing through some localities. But this is not enough. In Delhi and Bombay, there are flights round the clock at airport. Delhi is closely following Bombay in noise pollution and if adequate steps are not taken to reduce sound level, more than 50% of Delhi will be affected in coming years. Restriction may be put on air craft flight at mid-night.
6. *Education:* No doubt we have the technology to control nearly every kind of noise. We know very well about the sources and impact of noise pollution. But the main problem is that the people are not aware that the noise is one of the main environmental problems. Public must be made aware and educated about noise nuisance through adequate news media, lectures and other programs. The movement against noise pollution is very weak in India. The main reasons being that most of us do not consider noise as a pollution but as a part of routine life.

PREVENTION AND CONTROL OF POLLUTION

In our country, the Ministry of Environment and Forests adopted a policy statement for abatement of pollution in 1992, which interalia provides several instruments in the form of regulations, legislation, agreements, fiscal incentives and various other measures to prevent and abate pollution of air, water, noise and land. After the adoption of the Policy Statement, the Ministry and its associated offices have focused various programs and schemes to prevent and control of pollution at the beginning of the pipeline by adoption of cleaner technologies, waste minimization and resource preservation rather than the traditional treatment at the end of the pipe line. The significant benefits in this approach is that when waste is reduced or solvents are revived, it leads to resources conservation of the raw materials used during the various industrial processes and minimize the pollution in the ambient environment.

In our country there have been several legislative measures, even since pre-independence period, both at State and Central Government levels to prevent and control different components of the environment. For instance, the Indian Fisheries Act, 1897, the Indian Ports Act, 1907, Bengal Smoke Nuisance Act, 1905. The Motor Vehicles Act, 1983. The Maharashtra Prevention of Water Pollution Act, 1953; The Orissa River Pollution and Prevention Act, 1954; The Prevention of Food Adulteration Act, 1985; The River Boards Act, 1956; The Atomic Energy Act (Radiation Protection Rules), 1962; The Gujarat Smoke Nuisance Act, 1963 and several other Acts promulgated from time to time.

However, the real awareness about environmental protection at global level was recognized at the United Nations Conference on the Human Environment held at Stockholm (Sweden) in June 1972. This conference was able to focus the attention of international community of environmentalists to tackle environmental problems efficiently. In this conference, our late Prime Minister Mrs. Indira Gandhi took keen interest and initiative to take appropriate steps for the protection and improvement of human environment.

Keeping in view the need for environmental protection, the Indian Parliament passed the Water (Prevention and Control of Pollution) Act, 1974, which became effective from 23 March 1974. The Central Board for Prevention and Control of Water Pollution (CBPCWP) was constituted in Sept. 1974. The Air (Prevention and Control of Pollution) Act, 1981 was promulgated on 16 May, 1981. The Environment (Protection) Act, 1986 was promulgated on 23 May, 1986.

There had already been State Boards to advise the respective State governments on matters related to water and air pollution. The CBPCWP coordinats the activities of the State Pollution Control Boards. While amending the Water (Prevention and Control of Pollution) Act, 1974 in 1988, the Central/State Boards for the Prevent and Control of Pollution were renamed as Central/State Pollution Control Boards as these Boards also deal with air pollution. Consequent to this amendment, there is now a Central Pollution Control Board (CPCB) that makes recommendations and advises the Central Government on pollution matters. The Board advise the Pollution Control Division of the Ministry of Environment and Forests, New Delhi. There are also State Pollution Control Boards (SPCB) to advise respective State governments.

(i) Enforcement of act: The best protection of the environment is not to generate pollutants in the first place, non polluting manufacturing processes

can not be added on to existing units but must be planed from the outset. The Air (Prevention and Control) Act of 1981 was enacted by invoking the Central Governments power under Article 253 to make laws implementing decisions taken at international conferences. The preamble of the Air Act states that the act represents an implementation of the decisions made at United Nations Conference on the Human Environment at Stockholm in 1972. The Air Act has been amended in 1987. The Act enables a magistrate to restrain an air polluter from discharging emissions, and empowers both the central and State boards to give directions to industries, which if not followed, can be enforced by the board closing down the industry or withdrawing its supply of power and water. The penalties have been increased so that the polluter's cost of non compliance is substantial. Finally, citizens can not only sue to enforce the act to gain compliance by the industry, but can also require the board to provide the data needed to build a citizen's case.

The one initiative in formulating national pollution control standards began about 1984, when the central department of environment began to promulgate minimum national standards (MINAS). MINAS have been promulgated both for the water and for air.

(a) The Water (Prevention and Control of Pollution) Act, 1974 represented one of India's first attempt to deal comprehensively with an environmental issue. Parliament adopted minor amendments to the Act in 1978 and revised the Act in 1988 to more closely conform the provisions of the Environment (Protection) Act 1986. The water Act is comprehensive in its coverage, applying to streams, inland waters, subterranean waters, and sea or tidal waters. Standards for the discharge of effluent or the quality of the receiving waters are not specified in the Act itself. Instead, the Act enables the state boards to prescribe these standards. The state boards must maintain and make public a register containing the particulars of the control orders. The Act empowers a state board, upon thirty days notice to a polluter, to execute any work required under a consent order which has not been executed. The board may recover the expenses for such work from the polluter.

(b) The Environment (Protection) Act, 1986: The Act was promulgated to provide for the protection and improvement of environment and matters connected therewith. The Act consists of 26 sections distributed among four chapter, and extends to the whole of India. Section 2 defines the various terms as follows:

"environment" includes water, air and land the interrelationship which exists among and between water, air and land, and human beings, other living creatures, plants, microorganisms and property.

"environmental pollutant" means any solid, liquid or gaseous substance present in such concentration as may be, or tend to be, injurious to environment;

"environmental pollutant" means the presence in the environment of an environmental pollutant;

"hazardous substance" means any substance or preparation which, by reason of its chemical or physio-chemical properties or handling, is liable to cause harm to human beings, other living creature, plants, micro-organisms, property or the environment.

The Act provides general powers to the Central government to take all necessary measures for the purpose of (*i*) protecting and improving the quality of the environment, and (*ii*) preventing, controlling and abating environmental pollution. Besides other powers, the Central government shall have power for (*i*) planning and execution of a nation-wide programme for the prevention, control and abatement of environmental pollution, (*ii*) laying down standards for the quality of environment in its various aspects, (*iii*) laying down standards for emission or discharge of environmental pollutants from various sources whatsoever, (*iv*) restriction of areas in which industry, operations or processes shall not be carried out or shall be carried out subject to certain safeguards, (*v*) laying down procedures and safeguards for prevention of accidents which may cause environmental pollution, (*vi*) laying down procedure for handling of hazardous substances, (*vii*) examination of such manufacturing processes, materials and substances as are likely to cause environmental pollution, (*viii*) carrying out and sponsoring investigations and research relating to problems of environmental pollution, (*ix*) collection and dissemination of information on environmental pollution and (*x*) preparation of manuals, codes or guides relating to the prevention, and abatement of environmental pollution.

The Air (Prevention and Control of Pollution) Act, 1981 was amended in 1987 to remove the difficulties encountered during implementation, to confer more powers on the implementing agencies and to impose more stringent penalties of the provisions of the Act. The main point was also to amend the definition of air pollutants to include noise also. There is thus also the Air (Pollution and Control of Pollution) Amendment Act, 1987.

The Water (Prevention and Control of Pollution) Act, 1974 was also amended in 1988. An important amendment was to rename the Central/State Boards for Prevention and Control of Water Pollution as Central/State Pollution Control Boards as Boards also deal with air pollution. Some more powers were given to CPCB. The Boards have been given power to close or stop supply of water and electricity to offending establishments. The citizens may file criminal complaints against offenders after 60 days notice to Boards. Even at the time of establishment of industry the person will have to take consent of the Board. There is thus also the Water (Prevention and Control of Pollution) Amendment Act, 1988.

(c) The Motor Vehicles Act, 1988: This Act has come into forces from Ist July 1989. The salient features of the provisions of the Act, besides other things also

include the requirements to be observed in matter of vehicles fitness. Some of the features are as follows:

1. For registration of a new vehicle, the vehicle is to be produced before the registering authority for inspection to satisfy that the vehicle is fit for registration. The certificate of fitness is to be issued for a new vehicle for a period of two years. Thereafter, the renewal shall be for a period of one year till the vehicle attains the age of 10 years.
2. Regarding construction, equipment and maintenance of motor vehicles, from1.10.1989 every motor vehicle shall comply with the emission standards.

Method of Test	Maximum smoke density		
	Light ml	Bosch unit	Hartidge
Absorption Coefficient: (i) Full load at a speed of 60% to 70% of maximum engine rate speed declared by the manufacturer	3.1	5.2	75
(ii) Free acceleration	2.3	—	65

3. Transportation of goods of dangerous or hazardous nature to human life has been regulated under the Act. The vehicle carrying such goods should have prescribed labels indicating the nature of hazardous goods. The packages should also bear such labels. The driver should know the fundamentals in case of the vehicle is involved in accident. Driver should have minimum X standard qualification.
4. Every vehicle is required to meet the safety standards of components. Every vehicles manufacturer shall have to certify that every part used in the vehicle complies with the standards reliable to such components laid down by Bureau of Indian Standards.
5. A prototype of the vehicle to the manufactured by the manufacturer will have to be tested by VRDE, Ahmadnagar, ARAI, Pune or CMTTI, Budni or any other agency specified by the Central Government.
6. The horn to be used is to be in accordance with the approved specifications of Bureau of Indian Standards.
7. New items are included for offences and penalties in the Act. Amounts for different types of offences have been specified.

To help the owners of car, scooter maintain the prescribed level of exhaust emissions, the Directorate of Transport in Delhi has established Free Pollution Checking Centers at each of its offices in Delhi. Besides this, mobile teams are also covering different parts of the city. Delhi Administration has also been providing free facilities at different Petrol Stations all over the city since November 1987 for checking exhaust carbon monoxide levels from cars and scooters.

(ii) To check vehicular pollution: Motor vehicles are one of the most important sources of air pollution. Pollution of air environment can be minimised by controlling the emissions from the vehicles. This can be achieved by: (*i*) using proper proportion proportion of gasoline and air, (*ii*) more exact timing of fuel feeding, (*iii*) using gas additives to improve combustion, (*iv*) by injecting air into the exhaust to convert exhaust compounds to less toxic materials, and by (*v*) updating of engine design and/or install abatement equipment to improve combustion with the existing engine design. Carbon monoxide results from low air content of the fuel mixture, whereas NO_x production is promoted by high combustion temperatures. A hydrocarbon follows more or less the pattern of CO. The complete elimination of these three pollutants may be achieved by either updating the present design of engines or by making appropriate changes in devices for improving combustion.

Some gas vapours escape between walls and the piston which enter the crankcase and the discharge into atmosphere. Hydrocarbons (about 25%) are released in this way. Thus use of filters that capture and recycle these escaped gases in the engine should help control the emission of these hydrocarbons.

(iii) Lead free petrol: Lead free petrol must be available at a cheaper rate so that vehicle users can be motivated towards toxic free fuel.

(iv) Industrial pollution: To check air pollution by industrial and power plant chimney wastes, we must device measures for removal of the particulate mater and gaseous pollutants from the wastes. Removal of particulate mater involves their collection under the influence of different forces, thereby moving them continuously out of the gas stream. The equipment used for their removal are: (*i*) cyclone collector, and (*ii*) electrostatic precipitators (ESPs). Thus we have to generate the control technology. At present there are few power plants and industries that have installed the requisite ESPs. In cyclone collectors the waste gas containing particles is subjected to centrifugation. The suspended particles move towards the wall of cyclone body, and then to its bottom and finally discharged out. The cyclone collectors remove about 70% of the particles. Electrostatic precipitators (ESPs) are used to remove the particles from gas stream. Suspended particles become charged or ionized, and they are attracted to charged electrodes and removed. ESPs can remove 99% of the particulate pollutants from chimney exhaust. ESPs work very well in power plants, paper mills, cement mills, carbon block plants etc.

(v) Alternative sources of energy: The alternative sources of energy such as wind, solar and water may be taken into account in the consideration of various solutions to air pollution problems.

(vii) Plantation of trees: Plantation of trees, specially, broad leafed plants help in retaining most of the gases and dust in their leaves, twigs and stems.

(viii) Major activities: The other major activities to control through include:

(a) *Taj protection mission:* Consequence upon the Supreme Court orders dated 4-9-96 in the writ petition no. 13381/84, the Planning Commission estimated an amount of Rs. 600 crores on a 50:50 percent (Center-State) matching basis to implement various schemes related to protection of the Taj Mahal. A Mission Management Board under the chairmanship of the Chief Secretary, UP has been constituted for overseeing the implementation, monitoring and reviewing of various programs/ schemes formulated for the protection of Taj Mahal.

(b) *Air quality monitoring:* There is no scientific and proper monitoring of various environmental pollutants in the country. This could be undertaken only very recently and information could become available for some areas. A National network of ambient air quality monitoring stations was initiated in 1984. Till to date (1989) under this network a total of 140 stations have been sanctioned. Of these 103 stations are operational covering about 24 cities/towns. Ten more station, 5 each for Bombay and Calcutta are likely to be sanctioned soon. Three automatic ambient air quality monitoring stations (2 stationary, 1 mobile) were established at Delhi in 1988 under the Indo-EEC bilateral program. The parameters to be measured are SO_2, CO, NO_x, SPM, temperature, humidity, wind speed and directions.

(c) *Assessment of water quality:* Under the National water quality monitoring programme, the water quality monitoring of rivers being done. Till 1987 this network had 200 monitoring stations on rivers all over the country. In 1988, there were added 106 station to the network. Thus at present there are 306 monitoring stations and 27 station on the Ganga under the Ganga Action Plain.

(d) *Assessment of coastal water quality:* The CPCB in collaboration with the Dept. of Ocean Development has identified 173 monitoring station all along the Indian Coast to assess to water quality. Four SPCB have also been involved. Data on 25 parameters are being processed to schemes to control and monitor pollution of the coastal waters.

(e) *Preparation of environmental standards:* Based on the standards prepared by the CPCB and the Bureau of Indian Standards (BIS), effluent and emission standards for different kinds of industries including thermal power plants have been notified under the Environment (Protection) Act, 1986. The industries covered are, caustic soda, man made fiber, oil refinery, sugar, thermal power plants, cotton, textiles, composite woolen mills, dyes, electroplating, cement, stone crushing, coke ovens natural rubber, synthetic rubber, small pulp and paper, fermentation, tanneries, fertilizers, aluminum, copper, lead and smelting, calcium carbide, carbon black, nitric acid, sulphuric acid, iron and steel. The work on prescription of standards for emissions from vehicular pollution in 12 metro cities is in progress.

(f) *Enforcement of standards:* This is very helpful to control pollution at source. Minimum National Standards (MINAS) and air emission standards are being evolved by the CPCB for major categories of water and air polluting industries respectively. These standards refer to the maximum limit of effluents and emission that an industry may discharge into any water body or the atmosphere. The SPCBs can stipulate the same or more stringent standards for effluents and emission discharges.

National and Zonal Task Forces have been set up to implement the standards in fertilizer industries, iron and steel, cement, pulp and paper (small) and thermal power. The progress in set up of effluent treatment plants (ETPs) in different industries is also evaluated for preparation of standards along with MINAS and air emission standards. Effluent standards, prescribed by pollution control board is given as under:

Parameters	Tolerance Limit
1. pH	5.52 to 9.0
2. Suspended Solids (mg/l.)	100.00
3. Temperature max. (°C)	40°C
4. Oil and Grease (mg/l)	10
5. Ammonical nitrogen as (mg/l) N	50
6. BOD at 20 C (mg/l)	30
7. COD (mg/l)	250
8. Arsenic (mg/l)	0.2
9. Mercury (mg/l)	0.01
10. Lead (mg/l)	0.1
11. Cadmium (mg/l)	2.0
12. Flexavalent chromium (mg/l)	0.1
13. Copper (mg/l)	3.0
14. Nickel (mg/l)	3.0
15. Selinium (mg/l)	0.05
16. Zink (mg/l)	5.0
17. Dissolved phosphate (mg/l)	5.0
18. Dissolved fluoride (mg/l)	10.0

Emission standards for vehicular exhausts as prescribed by WHO is given as under:

Pollutants	Light Vehicle	Heavy duty Petrol vehicles	Heavy duty Diesel vehicles	Motorcycle
Particulate matter	.33	.045	.75	.2
SO_2	.68	.39	1.5	.02
NO_x	3.2	0.99	21.0	0.07
CO	40.0	.21	2.1	10.0
HC	6.0	11.0	12.7	17.0

(*g*) *Ganga action plan:* The Ganga is regarded as the cradle of Indian civilization. It has been sinking and stinking by the tones of dangerous chemical and organic wastes emptied into it daily. The govt. of India announced an ambitious new plan in 1985 for cleaning up the Ganga river. There is a separate Ganga Project Directorate (GPD) in the Ministry of Environment and Forests for regeneration and development work on this major river basin of country. The Authority, under the Chairmanship of the Prime Minister reviews the overall progress of Ganga Action Plan at regular intervals and provides guidance. The Monitoring Committee and the Steering Committee of the Action Plan also review the progress from time to time. The three State Government of U.P., Bihar and W. Bengal are involved in the plan. A number of schemes (262) necessary for plan have already been sanctioned to these three states costing Rs. 258.44 crores. The major objective of the Action Plan is the immediate reduction of pollution load on the river and the establishment of self sustaining treatment plant system. Keeping in these views, following components have been identified as the components of the action plan:

1. Sewer system renovation.
2. Diversion of sewer from/ through interception.
3. Renovation and construction of new and old sewage treatment plant, pumping stations etc.
4. Appropriate arrangement for sewer and waste utilization.
5. Diversion of sewer lines to nearest treatment plants for treatment.
6. Prevention of pollution through river bank communities and cattle population.
7. Launching of low cost sanitation to reduce pollution load.
8. Application of various biological methods for stream purification.
9. Establishment of pilot projects for resource energy recovery.
10. Control dead body disposal in the river.

The action plan also laid down in detail the names of cities and towns situated on the Ganga, their population, quantity of sewage generated, cost of installation, maintenance and operation of sewage pumping and treatment plants and revenues to be generated from resources recycling units.

Evaluation of ganga action plan: A comprehensive evaluation of GANGA Action Plan by independent agencies was undertaken in April 1995. A cost benefit analysis was under taken with the assistance of the Department of for International Development of UK. The conclusions and recommendations of these studies are being used to bring about improvement in the subsquent Ganga Action Plan Phase-II and the National River Conservation Plan.

(h) *National river conservation plan including Ganga action plan phase-II:* Through a Government Resolution dated 5-12-1996 GAP Phase-II has been merged with the National River Conservation Plan (NCP). Thus the expended NRCP covers 141 towns located along 22 inter-State rivers in 14 States. The total cost of the scheme is Rs. 2013.40 crores. During the 8th Five year Plan, NRCD and GAP Phase-II were Centrally Sponsored Schemes with 50:50 cost sharing between the central government and the concerned State governments. The NRCA at its IX meeting held on 12-07-97 decided to convert NRCP in to 100% funded Centrally Sponsered Scheme. The Cabinet Committee on Economic affairs approved the 1000% funding pattern in 1998.

(i) *Yamuna action plan:* Under this action plan, pollution abatement works ar being taken up in 21 towns. Of these 12 are in Haryna, 8 in Uttar Pradesh desides Delhi. So far 31 schemes have been completed. Out of the project outlay of 496.45 crore the expenditure incurred totals to 390.84 crore. External assistance of Yen 17.77 billion is being provided by OECF, Japan to partly finance the Yamuna Action Plan.

(j) *Gomti action plan:* Under this component, pollution abatement works ae being taken up in Lucknow, Sultanpur and Jaunpur in Uttar Pradesh. About 269 mld of sewage is targeted to be intercepted, diverted and treated under this action plan.

(k) *Damodar action plan:* Under this Action Plan, pollution abatement works are being taken up in 12 towns. Of these 8 are in Bihar and 4 are in West Bengal. However, due to low priority given by West Bengal government and problems of operation and maintenance of GAP I assets in Bihar, work on DHP has not progressed.

(l) *Control of hazardous substances:* The Environmental (Protection) Act, 1986 specifically defines the hazardous substances in Indian legal environment. These substances may have the property to produce toxic effects, are highly reactive and flammable in nature. Due to such nature, special attention is required during handling, transportation etc. The common methods include:

1. Substitution i.e. changing to less hazardous substances from chronic substance.
2. Change/modification in production/manufacturing/handling processes.
3. Isolation of the system.
4. Use of wet processes instead dry processes.
5. Efficient use of ventilation/exhaust etc. with proper arrangement of exhaust vents etc.
6. Dilution method.
7. Application of personal safety devices/equipments.
8. Personal hygienic habits.
9. Good house keeping and their maintenance.
10. Disposal of waste material.
11. Special control procedures.
12. Periodic medical examinations and control.
13. Training and education of the personnel concerned to the process/ handling etc.

(m) Notification on uniform consent procedure to be followed by state pollution control boards and pollution control committees: A notification containing Draft Rules to provide for uniform consent procedure to be followed by the SPCBs and PCCs has been prepared and notified on 20th December 1999 under the Environment (Protection) Act, 1986. The objective of the notification is to bring out rationalization in the consent management practices being followed by the Pollution Control Boards in the State and Union Territories for the purpose of Water (Prevention and Control) Act, 1974, the Air (Prevention and Control of Pollution) Act, 1981 and Authorization Under the Hazardous Waste (Management and Handling) Rules 1989.

REFERENCES

Pollution - Definition from the Merriam-Webster Online Dictionary". Merriam-webster.com. 2010-08-13. Retrieved 2010-08-26.

Spengler, John D.; Sexton, K. A. (1983). "Indoor Air Pollution: A Public Health Perspective". Science 221 (4605): 9–17 [p. 9]. doi:10.1126/science.6857273.

Hong, Sungmin; *et al.*, (1996). "History of Ancient Copper Smelting Pollution During Roman and Medieval Times Recorded in Greenland Ice". Science 272 (5259): 246–249 [p. 248]. doi:10.1126/science.272.5259.246.

David Urbinato (Summer 1994). "London's Historic "Pea-Soupers"". United States Environmental Protection Agency. Retrieved 2006-08-02.

Deadly Smog". PBS. 2003-01-17. Retrieved 2006-08-02.

Lee Jackson, Dirty Old London: The Victorian Fight Against Filth (2014).

Cited in David Clay Large, Berlin (2000) pp. 17-18.

Hugh Chisholm (1910). The Encyclopaedia Britannica: A Dictionary of Arts, Sciences, Literature and General Information. Encyclopaedia Britannica, 11th edition. p. 786.

Patrick Allitt, A Climate of Crisis: America in the Age of Environmentalism (2014) p. 206.

Jeffry M. Diefendorf; Kurkpatrick Dorsey (2009). City, Country, Empire: Landscapes in Environmental History. University of Pittsburgh Press, pp. 44–49.

James R. Fleming; Bethany R. Knorr of Colby College. "History of the Clean Air Act". American Meteorological Society. Retrieved 2006-02-14.

Patrick Allitt, A Climate of Crisis: America in the Age of Environmentalism (2014) pp. 15-21

1952: London fog clears after days of chaos (BBC News).

John Tarantino. "Environmental Issues". The Environmental Blog. Retrieved 2011-12-10.

Judith A. Layzer, "Love Canal: hazardous waste and politics of fear" in Layzer, The Environmental Case (CQ Press, 2012) pp. 56-82.

Lenssen, "Nuclear Waste: The Problem that Won't Go Away", Worldwatch Institute, Washington, D.C., 1991: 15.

Sharon M. Friedman, "Three Mile Island, Chernobyl, and Fukushima: An Analysis of Traditional and New Media Coverage of Nuclear Accidents and Radiation." Bulletin of the Atomic Scientists 67.5 (2011): 55-65.

Jonathan Medalia, Comprehensive Nuclear-Test-Ban Treaty: Background and Current Developments (DIANE Publishing, 2013.)

Falchi, Fabio; Cinzano, Pierantonio; Duriscoe, Dan; Kyba, Christopher C. M.; Elvidge, Christopher D.; Baugh, Kimberly; Portnov, Boris A.; Rybnikova, Nataliya A.; Furgoni, Riccardo (2016-06-01). "The New World Atlas of Artificial Night Sky Brightness". Science Advances 2 (6): e1600377. doi:10.1126/sciadv.1600377. ISSN 2375-2548.

Concerns about MTBE from U.S. EPA website.

Declaration of the United Nations Conference on the Human Environment, 1972.

Environmental Performance Report 2001 (Transport, Canada website page).

State of the Environment, Issue: Air Quality (Australian Government website page).

Pollution and Society Marisa Buchanan and Carl Horwitz, University of Michigan.

http://cdiac.ornl.gov/trends/emis/tre_tp20.html.

Beychok, Milton R. (1967). Aqueous Wastes from Petroleum and Petrochemical Plants (1st ed.). John Wiley & Sons. ISBN 0-471-07189-7. LCCN 67019834.

Silent Spring, R Carlson, 1962.

Beychok, Milton R. (January 1987). "A Data Base for Dioxin and Furan Emissions from Refuse Incinerators". Atmospheric Environment 21 (1): 29–36. doi:10.1016/0004-6981(87)90267-8.

World Resources Institute: August 2008 Monthly Update: Air Pollution's Causes, Consequences and Solutions Submitted by Matt Kallman on Wed, 2008-08-20 18:22. Retrieved on April 17, 2009.

Isalkar, Umesh (29 July 2014). "Over 1,500 Lives Lost to Diarrhoea in 2013, Delay in Treatment Blamed". The Times of India. Indiatimes. Retrieved 29 July 2014.

David, Michael, and Caroline. "Air Pollution – Effects". Library.thinkquest.org. Retrieved 2010-08-26.

American Petroleum Institute (API) (February 1990). Management of Water Discharges: Design and Operations of Oil-Water Separators (1st ed.). American Petroleum Institute.

Land Reclamation, Soil Quality and Agriculture
Edited by: Dr. Pawan Kumar 'Bharti' and Alka Chauhan
ISBN: 978-93-5056-882-8
Edition: 2017
Published by: Discovery Publishing House Pvt. Ltd., New Delhi (India)

9 Recent Techniques in Bio-composting of Solid Wastes

[1]M. Pavithra, [2]Ashoka Reddy Yerva and [3]M. A. Anila

INTRODUCTION

Any material that is thrown away or discarded as useless and unwanted is considered as solid waste. At first glance, the disposal of solid waste may appear to be a very simple and mundane problem. In this age of lasers, microcomputers, and space flight, it hardly seems possible that garbage disposal should present any great challenge. But many factors make solid waste disposal a complex problem of huge proportions for a modern industrial society.

Classification of Solid Wastes

Domestic and municipal wastes: These include garbage and rubbish, like waste paper, plastic, cloth from households, office, hostel and market.

Industrial wastes: The two general categories are process and non-process wastes. The non-process wastes are common to all industries such as packaging, office and cafeteria wastes. Process wastes are more complex and specific to the industrial plants. Their composition depends on type of products produced.

Agricultural wastes: These include cereal and millet straw, paddy husk, sugarcane trash and other crop residues.

Special wastes: The waste materials which endanger public health and welfare and seriously affect environment are:

(*a*) Radioactive wastes from atomic power stations, labs and hospitals.
(*b*) Toxic wastes such as pesticides, heavy metals, pharmaceuticals.
(*c*) Biological products such as antibiotics, enzymes, pathogens.

Technologies in Solid Waste Management

Solid waste management is a difficult process because it involves many disciplines. These include, technologies associated with the control of generation, storage, collection, transfer and transportation, processing, marketing, incineration and disposal of solid wastes. All of these processes

[1] Ph.D Scholar (Agronomy), TNAU, Coimbatore, Tamil Nadu, India.
[2] Ph.D Scholar (Agronomy), TNAU, Coimbatore, Tamil Nadu, India.
[3] Ph.D Scholar (Agronomy), TNAU, Coimbatore, Tamil Nadu, India.

have to be carried out within existing legal and social guidelines that protect the public health and environment and are aesthetically acceptable. They must be responsive to public attitudes and the disciplines included in the disposal process include administrative, financial, legal, architectural, planning and engineering functions. For successful integrated solid waste management plant, it is necessary that all these disciplines communicate and interact with each other in a positive interdisciplinary relationship. The various techniques employed in solid waste management include:

1. Composting
2. Sanitary land filling (Controlled tipping)
3. Thermal process (Incineration and pyrolysis)
4. Recycling and reuse

Composting

Composting is a process in which the organic portion of solid waste is allowed to decompose under carefully controlled conditions. It is a biological rather than a chemical or mechanical process; decomposition and transformation of the waste material are accomplished by the action of bacteria, fungi, and other microorganisms.

Role of Microbes in Composting

Mostly indigenous organism populations are used for the composting process; microbial inoculants are utilized only under certain conditions. The process of composting straw for 200 days under optimum conditions of temperature and moisture. In the mesophilic stage metabolism of the labile-C-rich substrates increases rapidly, generating heat. At this point there is a mixture of bacteria, actinomycetes, and fungi contributing to the decomposition process. As the temperature reaches 40°C the system turns from a mesophilic to a thermophilicstage, favoring mainly thermophilic bacteria and actinomycetes, with *Bacillus* being the dominant genus. Common *Bacillus* species found at this stage, and accounting for 10% of the decomposition, are *brevis, circulans, coagulans, licheniformis,* and *subtilis*. The actinomycetes, such as the *Norcardia* spp., *Streptomyces thermofuscus,* and *S. thermoviolaceus*are important in this phase when humic materials are formed from decomposition and condensation reactions. The actinomycetes are estimated to account for 15 to 30% of the decomposition of composted material. The compost produced from this process is lower in C than the initial material, has a lower C:N and a higher pH, and can contain considerable NO_3. The end product of composting depends on the original substrate, any added nutrients, degree of maturity, and composting method.

The normal time taken for compost preparation in most methods is rather long, ranging from 100-180 days. Considerable research has therefore been done to accelerate the composting process.

This is possible by the introduction of suitable microorganisms with demonstrate efficiency in the rate of organic matter decomposition. This process of composting by introduction of suitable microorganisms is known as *bio-composing.*

Using microbial inoculants enables for fast decomposition of biodegradable material and suppression of foul odor.

Vermicomposting

The key role of earthworms in improving the soil fertility is well known for a longer period. Earthworms feed on any organic wastes, consume three to five times their body weight and after using 5 to 10 per cent of the organic wastes for their growth, excrete the mucus coated undigested matter as worm casts. Worm casts consist of organic matter that has undergone physical and chemical breakdown through the activity of the muscular gizzard, that grinds the material to a particle size of 1-2 micron. The nutrients present in the worm casts are readily soluble in water for the uptake of plants. Vermicastings are rich sources of macro and micronutrients, vitamins, enzymes, antibiotics, growth hormones and immobilized micro flora.

Vermicompost refers to organic manure produced by earthworms. It is a mixture of worm castings, including humus, live earthworms, their cocoons and other micro organisms. Vermicomposting is an appropriate method for disposal of non-toxic solid and liquid organic wastes. It helps in cost effective and efficient recycling of animal wastes (Poultry droppings, horse, piggery excreta and cattle dung), agricultural residues and industrial wastes using low energy.

Types of Earthworms

Several types of earthworms are found in our soils. Earthworms can be divided into the following two categories:

1. Epigeic–the surface living worms
2. Endogeic–the burrowing worms

Epigeic: These worms are found on the surface and are reddish brown in colour. They do not process the soil but are efficient in composting of organic wastes. They enhance the rate of organic manure production through biodegradation or mineralization.

eg. *Lampitomauritii, Octochaetonaserrata, Perionyxexcavatus*

Endogeic: These species burrow and mix the soil, from different horizons in the profile. They ingest organic and mineral fraction of soil, thus promoting the formation of organo mineral complexes. Organo–mineral crumbs are brought from deeper parts of the soil profile to the surface. Different species of earthworms show specificity to soil types, moisture content and temperature.

Method of Vermicomposting

- *Selection of earthworm:* Earthworm that is native to the local soil may be used.
- *Size of pit:* Any convenient dimension such as 2 m × 1 m × 1 m may be prepared.
- *Preparation of vermibed:* A layer, 15-20 cm thick of good loamy soil above a thin layer of (5 cms) broken bricks and sand should be made.
- *Inoculation of earthworms:* About one hundred earthworms are introduced as an optimum inoculating density into a compost pit of about 2 m × 1 m × 1 m, provided with vermibed.
- *Organic layering:* It is done on the vermibed with fresh cattle dung. The compost pit is then layered to about 5 cm with dry leaves or hay or organic wastes. Moisture content of the pit is maintained by the addition of water.
- *Wet organic layering:* It is done after four weeks with moist green organic waste, which can be spread over it to a thickness of 5 cm. This practice can be repeated every 4 days. Mixing of wastes periodically without disturbing the vermibed ensures proper vermicomposting. Wet layering with organic wastes can be repeated till the compost pit is nearly full.

Harvesting of compost: At maturation (after 120 days), the moisture content is brought down, by stopping the addition of water. This ensures drying of compost and migration of worms in to the vermibed. The mature compost, a fine loose granular mass (about 1500 kg), is removed from the pit, sieved, dried and packed. Matured vermicompost is rich in nutrient (table 10.1) and recommended @ 50 t ha-1.

Vermibed for the Preparation of Vermicompost

Table 10.1: Nutrient Status of Vermicompost Prepared by Perionyxexcavatus

Macronutrients		
1.	Total nitrogen %	0.66
2.	Total P_2O_5%	1.93
3.	Total K_2O%	0.42
Micro nutrients		
1.	Fe (ppm)	19.8
2.	Zn (ppm)	0.90
3.	Mn (ppm)	16.50
4.	Cu (ppm)	2.30
General characters of vermicompost		
1.	pH	7.00
2.	EC dsm^{-1}	1.20
3.	Organic carbon% 30.50	

PHOSPHO-SULPHO-NITRO-COMPOST (PSNC)

In this method, use of suitable minerals, fertilizers and microbial cultures to fortify the compost so that the end product contains more nutrients per unit volume or weight. It also makes use of compost accelerating culture and biofertilisers for further nutrient enrichment.

Like conventional compost, PSNC can be prepared by the heap or pit method for which a bright sunny site is selected. For the heap method, the floor should be temporarily cemented about 1.5 feet above the floor so that nutrients will not leak in to the soil. About 1000 kg of wastes can be accommodated in a 12′ × 7.5′ × 3.5′ (Lx Wx H) heap.

Method of Preparation

30 kg of wastes (dry wt. basis) are spread on the floor followed by 30 kg of cow dung (fresh cow dung), 660 g urea (0.5% N basis) is then added. For this, dissolve urea in 20 liter water and spray a part of solution of urea over the layer. 17 kg Mussouri rock phosphate or MRP (5% PO basis) is spread over the layer. As 25 MRP not now mined, another suitable rock phosphate can be used. Then 6 kg of pyrites (22% S content) is added at the rate of 10% on materials dry weight basis. A portion of finely powdered soil is then spread at the rate of 5% on materials dry weight basis. Water is sprayed over the layer to attain 60-70% moisture. All above steps are repeated in the stated sequence until the heap is 3-4 feet high.

To accelerate the decomposition process, fungal culture is added at the rate of 500 g mycelial mat/tonne of material 8 where as bacterial culture having 10 viable cells/ml is added (50 ml/kg of material). To further accelerate the process, the multi-bio-inoculum containing cellulose decomposers (*Paecilomycesfusisporus*and *Aspergillusawamori*), P-solubilizers (*Bacillus polymyxa*and *Pseudomonas striata*) and N-fixer (*Azotobacterchroococcum*) etc. were added at 5 and 30 days of decomposition @500 g mycelial mat/1000 kg material on dry weight basis. After 3-4 weeks of decomposition, the first turning is done which is followed by a second turning two weeks later. Moisture is to be maintained at 60-70% of materials on dry weight basis.

Finally, the upper side and all boundaries of the heap are covered with cow dung slurry to maintain optimum moisture content inside the heap. To avoid rain, wind, and to maintain the moisture and temperature the heap should be covered with a polythene sheet. Fungal bioinoculum treated wastes decomposed faster and attained maximum maturity criteria (C:N ratio, lignin/cellulose ratio and CEC/TOC ratio) in four months as compared to the usual six months in compost prepared from vegetable waste, soybean straw and wheat straw. However, cotton stalk and sugarcane trash may need more time to attain maturity criteria for good quality of compost production. For faster decomposition of cotton stalk and pigeonpea woody tissue, the size of the materials would be reduced to 3-4 cm.

INSTITUTE OF BIOLOGICAL SCIENCES (IBS) RAPID COMPOSTING TECHNOLOGY

This technology involves inoculating the plant substrates with cultures of a cellulose decomposing fungus (*Trichodermaharzianum*), for composting. Sawdust mixed with the leaves of *subabul* (*Leucaenaleucocephala*), a leguminous tree, is used as the medium of growth for compost fungus activator. The composting time, using this procedure, ranges from 21 to 45 days, depending on the plant substrates used. The procedure consists of two parts: the production of the compost fungus activator and the composting process.

Preparation of Substrates

Substrates such as rice straw, weeds and grasses should be chopped as this helpsspeed up decomposition by increasing the surface area available for microbial action, and providing better aeration.

If large quantities of substrates are to be used (several tons), a forage cutter/ chopper is needed. Substrates should be moistened with water. If a large volume of substrates are to be composted, a sprinkler is more convenient. Carbonaceous substrates should be mixed with nitrogenous ones at a ratio of 4:1 or less, but never lower than 1:1 (on a dry weight basis). Some possible combinations are:

- 3 parts rice straw: 1 part *subabul*
- 4 parts rice straw: 1 part chicken manure
- 4 parts grasses: 1 part legume materials + 1 part manure
- 4 parts grasses: 1 part *Chromolaenaodorata*or *Mikaniacordata*(weeds) + 1 part animal manure

Composting Procedure

The substrates should be piled loosely to provide better aeration within the heap. Compost heaps should be located in shady areas such as under big trees. The platform should be raised about 30 cm from the ground, to provide adequate aeration at the bottom. Alternatively, aeration can be provided by placingperforated bamboo trunks horizontally and vertically at regular intervals, to carry air through the compost heap. The compost fungus activator is broadcasted onto the substrates during piling. The amount of CFA used is usually 1% of the total weight of the substrates (i.e. about 1 kg compost fungus activator/100 kg substrate).

The heap should be completely covered with white plastic sheets or plastic sacks. This maintains the heat of decomposition, and minimizes water evaporation and ammonia volatilization. The compost heap usually heats up in 24-48 hours. Temperature should be maintained at or above 50°C, and the heap should be turned over every 5-7 days for the first two weeks, and thereafter once every two weeks.

Decomposition will continue until the substrate is finely fragmented, so that the finished product has a powdery texture. Once decomposition is complete, the compost should be sun dried again until its moisture content is 10-20%. If mature compost is needed at once, it should be sun dried for one day, or as soon as its temperature drops to 30°C. Drying removes excess moisture, and makes the compost much easier to handle.

EFFECTIVE MICROORGANISMS (EM) BASED PRODUCTION PROCESS

The concept of Effective Microorganisms (EM) was developed in Japan. EMs consists of mixed cultures of beneficial and naturally-occurring microorganisms that can be applied as inoculants to increase the microbial diversity of soils and plants. EM contains selected species of microorganisms including predominant populations of lactic acid bacteria and yeasts, and smaller numbers of photosynthetic bacteria, actinomycetes and other types of organisms. All of these are mutually compatible with one another and can co-exist in liquid culture.

Input Required

The following methods and ingredients were used in pit method by the group in Myanmar. A unit pitconsists of 6′ × 4′ x 3′ (Lx Bx H), enclosed by low walls and covered with roof. The raw materials for organic fertilizerproduction are cow dung 2 portions, rice husk 1 portion, rice husk/charcoal 1 portion, rice bran (milled) 1 portionand compost accelerator (33 litres of EM solution or *Trichoderma*sps. solution/ pit).

Preparation of EM Solution (accelerator)

Firstly one litre of 'instant solution' is made by mixing 10 mL EM, 40 Ml molasses and 950 mL water and leaving it for five to seven days, depending on temperature. Then the solution is added to one litre of molasses and 98 litres of water to obtain 100 litres of ready-to-use EM solution. This amount is enough for three pits. The EM solution functioning as accelerator reduces the composting period from three months to one month.

Procedure: Firstly, mix all the ingredients, except accelerator. Then make 0.5 ft layer of mixture in the pit and sprinkle accelerator over it. Repeat the same procedure until the pit is full. Cover with plastic sheet. Two or three weeks later, mix the whole pit to boost aerobic decomposition. The compost/organic fertilizer is ready to use a couple of weeks later.

A pit turns out 900 kg of final product per batch, which are usually packed in 30 kg plastic bags. Assuming that it takes 30 days on average to produce a batch and only 8 pits may be used for technical reasons, the annual potential production capacity works out to 86.4 tons (0.9 t × 8 pits × 12 months). Research has shown that the inoculation of EM cultures to the soil/plant ecosystem can improve soil health, and the growth, yield, and quality of crops.

MICROBIALLY ENRICHED COMPOST FOR RECYCLING OF MUNICIPAL SOLID WASTE

Method of Preparation

This methodology was developed at Indian Institute of Soil Science. Compost was prepared by pit method. The pit should be concrete made so that the nutrients may not percolate in to the soil. About 2000 kg of wastes can be accommodated for decomposition in a pit (10 ft length × 5 ft width and 3 ft deep) method.

Ingredient Required

Waste materials (segregated material is preferable), fresh cow dung, urea, water, bioinoculum and polythene sheets. 200 kg of fresh waste is spread on the floor followed by 40 kg of fresh cow dung (on dry weight basis). 2.64 kg urea (0.5% N basis) is dissolved in 20 liter water and is sprayed over the layer. Bioinoculum is added in the form of slurry on the layer (8 layers). These steps are repeated till the heap attains 3-4 feet high. Fungal culture is added at 500 g mycelial mat/tonne of material. Initially, at 1-5 days, bioinoculum such as *Aspergillusheteromorphus, Aspergillusterrus, Aspergillusflavus*and *Rhizomucorpusillus*is added and owing to a high initial temperature (55 to 70°C) at the thermophilic stage, the bioinoculum is again added after 30 days of decomposition.

Finally, the upper side of the pit is covered with cow dung slurry. To avoid rain, wind and to maintain the moisture and temperature, one-polythene sheet must be used to cover the heap. After 3-4 weeks of decomposition, the first turning of heap must be done. Maintain the moisture content at 60-70% of materials on dry weight basis. Compost will be ready after 2.5 months. For 1000 kg microbial enriched compost production, the total quantity of fresh waste material, cow dung, urea required will be 1600, 320 and 21 kg, respectively .

COIR PITH COMPOST

Large quantity of coir waste of about 7.5 million tonnes is available annually from coir industries of India. Coir fibre isusually used in rope making industries which generates bulk amount of dusty materials called coir dust/coir pith.

Composting of coir pith reduces its bulkiness, C:N ratio, lignin and cellulose contents and increases its manorial value.Coir pith composting is an aerobic composting. Thus, a heap of 4′ × 3′ × 4′ (L×W×H) is made. Initially coir pith shouldbe put upto 3″ height and thoroughly moistened. Then nitrogenous source may be added in the form of urea @5 kg/tor fresh poultry litter @200 kg/t. Microbial inoculum namely *Pleurotus*spps. was added. For maintaining aerobic condition either turning (once in 10 days) is done or inserting perforated unused PVC or iron pipe both vertically andhorizontally. Sixty per cent moisture is to be maintained at the time of composting. The matured compost is ready touse within 60 days.

Nutritive Value of Raw and Composted Coir Pith

S.No.	Parameters	Raw Coir pith (%)	Composted Coir Pith (%)
1.	Nitrogen (N)	0.26	1.24
2.	Phosphorus (P)	0.01	0.06
3.	Potassium (K)	0.78	1.20
4.	Lignin	30.00	4.80
5.	Cellulose	26.52	10.10
6.	C:N ratio	112:1	24:1

SUGARCANE TRASH COMPOST

Sugarcane produces about 10 to 12 tonnes of dry leaves per hectare per crop. Its trash contains 28.6% organiccarbon, 0.35 to 0.42% nitrogen, 0.04 to 0.15% phosphorus and 0.50 to 0.42% potassium. Sugarcane trash can beeasily composted by using the fungi like *Trichurus, Aspergillus, Penicillium*and *Trichoderma.*

For one ton of sugarcane trash 50 kg fresh dung is recommended. The dung can be mixed with 100 litres of waterand thoroughly mixed with sugarcane trash. Rock phosphate @ 5 kg/ton of waste and inoculums @ 2 kg/ton can beadded. After mixing all the inputs with sugarcane trash, heap should be formed with a minimum height of 4′. Thisheight is required to generate more heat in the composting process, and the generated heat will be retained long timeinside the material. The composted material should be turned periodically once in 15 days for better aeration.

Nutritive Value of Sugarcane Trash Compost

S.No.	Nutrient Elements	%
1.	Nitrogen (N)	0.5
2.	Phosphorus (P)	0.2
3.	Potassium (K)	1.1

PRESSMUD COMPOST

Pressmud is a by-product obtained from sugar industry. About 3% of pressmud is obtained for the total quantity ofcane crushed.

Pressmud is spread in the compost yard to form a heap of 9′ × 10.5′ × 4.5′ (L × W × H). Distillery effluent is sprayed on theheaps to a moisture level of 60% and the pressmud heap is allowed overnight to absorb the effluent. Bacterial culturewas diluted with water (1:10) and added @ 10 L/t. after 3 days. Depending on the moisture content of heap, theeffluent should be sprayed once or twice in a week. This should be repeated for 8 weeks so that the pressmud andeffluent proportion reaches an optimum ratio of 1:3. The heaps are then allowed for one month curing.

The bioinoculants such as *Azotobacter* can be added to enrich the compost for nitrogen and the introduction ofphosphorus solubilizing microorganisms like *Aspergillusawamori*or *Bacillus polymyxa* will improve the availablephosphorus content in the manure.

Nutritive Value of Pressumud Compost

S.No.	Nutrient Elements	Raw Pressumed	Composted Pressmud
1.	Nitrogen (N)%	1.0-1.5	2.7-3.5
2.	Phosphorus (P)%	1.4-2.5	3.0-4.0
3.	Potassium (K)%	0.5-2.0	3.0-3.5
4.	C:N ratio	25-36	10-11.4

POULTRY WASTE COMPOST

Using paddy straw: Fresh poultry droppings are mixed thoroughly with chopped paddy straw (< 2 cm size) @ 1:1.25 ratio. *Pleurotussajor-caju*is inoculated @ 5 packets (250 g each) per tonne of substrate. Periodical watering should be done once in 15 days and turning should be given on 21, 35 and 42 day of composting (avoid turning during first 3 weeks of composting). Materials are converted to matured compost within a period of 50 days.

Nutritive Value of Poultry Waste Compost using Paddy Straw

S.No.	Nutrient Elements	%
1.	Nitrogen (N)%	1.89
2.	Phosphorus (P)%	1.83
3.	Potassium (K)	1.34
4.	C:N ratio	12.20

Using coir pith

Poultry waste collected either from caged system or deep litter system along with coir pith (1:1.25 ratio) is inoculated with *Pleurotussajor-caju*@ 2 packets per tonne of waste. The moisture content of the heap should be maintained at 50 to 60 %. Periodical turning must be given on 21, 28 and 35 days of composting. Another two packets of bioinoculum is to be added during turning given on the 28 day of composting. Good quality compost will be attained after 45 day of composting.

Nutrive Value of Poultry Waste Compost Using Coir Pith

S.No.	Nutrient Elements	Caged system manure	Deep litter system manure
1.	Nitrogen (N)%	2.08	2.13
2.	Phosphorus (P)%	2.61	2.40
3.	Potassium (K)%	2.94	2.03
4.	C:N ratio	13:1	14:1

PAPER MILL SLUDGE COMPOST

The paper industry is one of the major industries in India that contributes to water and soil pollution. The level ofpaper consumption in India is 4.2 mt that generates 0.5 mt of sludge.

Paperboard mill sludge (400 kg), fly ash (200 kg), coir pith (200 kg), FYM (200 kg), urea (5 kg) and rock phosphate (5 kg) along with bacterial culture *Bacillus spheroticus* (5 litres) and *Pleurotussajorcaju* (20 bottles) are mixedthoroughly to ensure maximum contact of substrate with organism. Treated board mill effluent is sprinkledsufficiently to bring the moisture content to 60%. To enhance aeration in compost heaps, turning is given atfortnightly intervals. Enough cow dung slurry (25-50 kg) and moisture are added during turnings and reheaping isdone every time till the compost reaches maturity stage. The final compost is ready for soil application within 90 days of composting.

Nutritive Value of Paperboard Mill Sludge Compost @ 5 t/ha

S.No.	Nutrient Elements	Caged system manure	Deep litter system manure
1.	Nitrogen (N)%	0.34	1.34
2.	Phosphorus (P)%	0.05	0.58
3.	Potassium (K)%	0.42	1.12
4.	C:N ratio	83.0	19.0

REFERENCES

Waksman, A. Selman, 1927. Principles of Soil Microbiology, The Williams & Wilkins Company, USA.

Eldor A. Paul 2007. Soil Microbiology, Ecology and Biochemistry. 3rd edition, Academic Press is an Imprint of Elsevier, UK.

Subba Rao, N.S. 2002. Soil Microbiology. 4th Edition. Oxford and IBH Publishing House Co. Pvt. Ltd. New Delhi.

Manna, M.C. and Asha Sahu, 2013. Rapid Composting Methods, Indian Institute of Soil Science, Bhopal.

Land Reclamation, Soil Quality and Agriculture
Edited by: Dr. Pawan Kumar 'Bharti' and Alka Chauhan
ISBN: 978-93-5056-882-8
Edition: 2017
Published by: Discovery Publishing House Pvt. Ltd., New Delhi (India)

10

Heavy Metal Pollution in Our Environment

Remediation Through Plants

[1]Jamshed Zaidi, [1]Gunjan Sharma and [1]Amit Pal

ABSTRACT

Phytoremediation has emerged as the most desirable technology which uses plants for removal or transformation of environmental pollutants to make them harmless. Many living organisms can accumulate certain toxicants inside the body in much higher concentration than present in their environments. Thus, the use of plants for the decontamination of heavy metals is growing attention because of several problems associated with pollutant removal using conventional methods. The present article highlights the significance of Phytoremediation which have been proposed as an attractive alternative owing to their low cost and high efficiency. The plants used in the phytoremediation technique must have a considerable capacity of metal absorption, its accumulation and reducing the time of decontamination in an ecosystem. It is an eco-friendly and cost effective technique for removal of toxicant from the environment.

Keywords: Heavy metal, phytoremediation, toxicants.

INTRODUCTION

In general the term 'heavy metals' refers to any metallic element, which has a relatively high density and is toxic or poisonous even at low concentration to any organism (Lenntech, 2004). These are the group of metals and metalloids with atomic density greater than 4 g/cm^3, or 5 times or more, greater than water (Nriagu, 1989; Garbarino *et al.*, 1995, Hawkes, 1997).

Heavy metals are natural components of the Earth's crust. They cannot be degraded or destroyed. To a small extent they enter our bodies via food, drinking water and air. As trace elements, some heavy metals (e.g. copper, selenium, zinc) are essential to maintain the metabolism of the human body. However, at higher concentrations they can lead to poisoning. Heavy metal poisoning could result, for instance, from drinking-water contamination (e.g. lead pipes), high ambient air concentrations near emission sources, or intake via the food chain. Heavy

[1] Institute of Environment & Development Studies, Bundelkhand University, JHANSI–284 128, INDIA

metals are dangerous because they tend to bioaccumulate. Bioaccumulation means an increase in the concentration of a chemical in a biological organism over time, compared to the chemical's concentration in the environment. Compounds accumulate in living things any time they are taken up and stored faster than they are broken down (metabolized) or excreted.

Source of Heavy Metals

Heavy metals occur as natural constituents of the earth crust, and are persistent environmental contaminants since they cannot be degraded or destroyed. To a small extent, they enter the body system through food, air, and water and bio-accumulate over a period of time (Lenntech, 2004; UNEP/GPA, 2004). In rocks, they exist as their ores in different chemical forms, from which they are recovered as minerals. Heavy metal ores include sulphides, such as iron, arsenic, lead, lead-zinc, cobalt, gold silver and nickel sulphides; oxides such as aluminium, manganese, gold, selenium and antimony. Some exist and can be recovered as both sulphide and oxide ores such as iron, copper and cobalt. Ore minerals tend to occur in families whereby metals that exist naturally as sulphides would mostly occur together, likewise for oxides. Therefore, sulphides of lead, cadmium, arsenic and mercury would naturally be found occurring together with sulphides of iron (pyrite, FeS_2) and copper (chalcopyrite, $CuFeS_2$) as minors, which are obtained as by-products of various hydrometallurgical processes or as part of exhaust fumes in pyrometallurgical and other processes that follow after mining to recover them. During mining processes, some metals are left behind as tailings scattered in open and partially covered pits; some are transported through wind and flood, creating various environmental problems (Habashi, 1992). Heavy metals are basically recovered from their ores by mineral processing operations (Peplow, 1999; Lenntech, 2004; UNEP/GPA, 2004).

There are different sources of heavy metals in the environment such as: (*i*) natural sources, (*ii*) agricultural sources, (*iii*) industrial sources, (*iv*) domestic effluent, (*v*) atmospheric sources and (*vi*) other sources. Heavy metal pollution can originate from both natural and anthropogenic sources. Activities such as mining and smelting operations and agriculture have contaminated extensive areas of world such as Japan, Indonesia and China mostly by heavy metals such as Cd, Cu and Zn (Herawati *et al.*, 2000), Cu, Cd and Pb in North Greece (Zanthopolous *et al.*, 1999) in Albania (Shallari *et al.*, 1998) .

(i) Natural sources: World wide data on emission of heavy metals from natural sources are particularly scanty, but a summary of literature survey has been prepared (Pacyna, 1986). Wind-blown dusts and volcanic eruptions are of particulate relevance to ecosystem inventories and budgets of heavy metals. Wind dust, which arises from desert region such as Sahara, has high levels of Fe and lesser amounts of Mn, Zn, Cr, Ni and Pb (Ross, 1994). Marine aerosols and forest fires also exert a major influence in the transport of some heavy metals

in many environments. While the long range transport of dusts, particularly from the Sahara, has received considerable recent attention (SCOPE, 1974), the transport of dusts originating in Asia and elsewhere to the Pacific, Arctic and Antarctic has also been investigated (Davidson *et al.*, 1985). Some major eruptions have more far-reaching range of heavy metal concentrations (ppm) in ignéous and sedimentary rocks (Cannon *et al.*, 1978). The contribution to ecosystem of elements from sea sprays and mists often transported many kilometers inland is widely recognized. Cu and Mn from such marine sources have been detected in rain water input to terrestrial environments (Vermette and Bingham, 1986). The natural process of 'bubble bursts' is a source of airborne Cd, Cu, Ni, Pb and Zn via sea salt particles (Pacyna, 1986). Airborne emissions of heavy metals originate from forest and prairie fires (Ross, 1994). Volatile heavy metals such as Hg and Se are part of carbonaceous matter produced during the fire. Natural vegetation emits heavy metals into the soil and atmosphere through leaching from leaves and stems, decomposition and volatilization. Many heavy metals have been detected in inland coastal areas due to sea sprays and aerosols produced in oceanic activities.

(ii) Agricultural sources: The inorganic and organic are the most important sources of heavy metals to agricultural soil include liming, sewage sludge, irrigation waters and pesticides. Others, particularly fungicides, inorganic fertilizers and phosphate fertilizers have variable levels of Cd, Cr, Ni, Pb and Zn depending on their sources. Cadmium is of particular concern in plants since it accumulates in leaves at very high levels, which may be consumed by animals or human being. Cadmium enrichment also occurs due to the application of sewage sludge, manure and limes (Nriagu, 1988; Yanqun *et al.*, 2005). Although the levels of heavy metals in agricultural soil are very small, but repeated use of phosphate fertilizer and the long persistence time for metals, there may be dangerously high accumulation of some metals (Verkleji, 1993). Animal manure enriches the soil by the addition of Mn, Zn, Cu and Co and sewage sludge by Zn, Cr, Pb, Ni, Cd and Cu (Verkleji, 1993). The increase in heavy metal contamination of agricultural soil depends on the rate of application of the contributors with its elemental concentration and soil characteristics to which it is applied. Heavy metal accumulation in soil is also due to application of soil amendments such as compost refusing and nitrate fertilizers (Ross, 1994). The orchards where these compounds have been used frequently resulted into contamination of orchard soil with high levels of heavy metals such as Cu, As, Pb, Zn,Fe, Mn and Hg. Pesticides such as lead arsenate were used in Canadian orchards for more than six decades and were found to be enriched with Pb, As and Zn having greater consequences for food contamination. Continued irrigation of agricultural soil can lead to accumulation of heavy metals such as Pb and Cd. The contamination of soil by heavy metals may also be from irrigation water sources such as deep wells, rivers, lakes or irrigation canals (Ross, 1994).

Fertilizers: Huge amounts of fertilizers are frequently applied to soils in concentrated farming systems to deliver suitable N, K and P for crop growth. The complexes used to offer these elements comprise rare quantity of heavy metals (for example Cadmium and Lead) as contaminations, that, after continual fertilizer application may meaningfully proliferate their quantity in the soil (Jones and Jarvis, 1981). Certain phosphatic fertilizer applications unintentionally add Cd and other possibly dangerous elements for the soil, including F, Pb and Hg (Raven *et al.*, 1998). Long term use of phosphate based fertilizers, dust from smelters, sewage sludge application, industrial waste and bad watering practices in agricultural lands contaminate agricultural soil (Passariello *et al.*, 2002; Schwartz *et al.*, 2001). Phosphatic fertilizers are made from rocks containing phosphates. It is found as sedimentary, igneous and metamorphic rock in the earth's crust. Sedimentary rocks contain high concentration of Uranium, Thorium and rare earth elements (Hurst, 1989).

Pesticides L: Numerous known insecticides used widely in agriculture in the past contained considerable amounts of metals. As in the recent past, near 10% of the chemicals have permitted for use as pesticides and in UK fungicides were based on complexes which comprise Cu, Hg, Pb, Mn or Zn. For Example, such pesticides that are fungicidal spray that contained copper like copper oxychloride and Bordeaux mixture that consists of copper sulphate (Jones and Jarvis, 1981). Lead arsenate was applied in fruit orchards for several years to regulate some parasitic pests. Compounds that consist of arsenic were applied widely to control livestock ticks and for the control of insects in banana in New Zealand and Australia, wood has been well-preserved with preparations of Copper, Chromium and Arsenic (CCA). Linked with fertilizers, the application of these ingredients has been more restricted, being localized to special sites or crops (McLaughlin *et al.*, 2000).

Bio solids and manures: The supply of various bio solids viz., composts, cattle's manure and municipal sewage sludge (MSS) to land unconsciously points towards the build-up of heavy metals like Arsenic, Cadmium, Chromium, Copper, Lead as well as Hg, Se, Ni, Mo, Zn, Sb, in the soil (Basta *et al.*, 2005). Some animal wastes like livestock, poultry and pig manures created in agriculture are usually supplied to crops and meadows either in the form of solids or semi solids (Sumner, 2000). Though most compost can be seen as valued fertilizers, in the poultry and pig industry, the Cu and Zn are included in foods as growth enhancers and As presence in poultry fitness products may have the ability to cause metal pollution of the soil (Sumner, 2000; Chaney and Oliver, 1996). The manures that are created from animals as a result of these diets possess greater amounts of Cu, As and Zn and if continually supplied to prohibited areas of land, can result in reasonable accumulation of these metals in the longer period of time in these soils. Bio solids (including sewage sludge) are basically solid products organic in nature, formed by treatment processes of wastewater that can be usefully recycled. Heavy metals most usually established in bio solids include Ni, Pb, Cd, Cu, Cr and Zn and the metal amounts are ruled by nature and the strength of the industrial processes, as well as the sort of activity worked during the treatment of bio solids (Mattigod and Page, 1983). Under specific situations, metals supplied to soils by applying bio solids can be percolated downwards by the soil horizons and may have the ability to pollute groundwater (McLaren *et al.*, 2005). Latest researches on some soils of New Zealand applied with bio solids have resulted in increased amounts of Ni, Cd and Zn in drainage percolates (Keller *et al.*, 2002; McLaren *et al.*, 2004).

(iii) Industrial sources: High temperature processing of metals such as smelting and castings emit metals in particulate and vapor forms. Vapor form of heavy metals such as As, Cd, Cu, Pb, Sn and Zn combine with water in the atmosphere to form aerosols. These maybe either dispersed by wind (dry deposition) or precipitated in rainfall (wet deposition) causing contamination of soil or water bodies. Contamination of soil and water bodies can also occur through runoff from erosion of mine wastes, dusts produced during the transport of crude ores, corrosion of metals and leaching of heavy metals to soil and ground water. Soil contamination of heavy metals occurs due to different types of processing in refineries. Energy supplying power stations such as coal burning power plants, petroleum combustion, nuclear power stations and high tension lines contribute many heavy metals such as Se, B, Cd, Cu, Zn, Cs and Ni to the environment. Other industrial sources include processing of plastics, textiles, microelectronics, wood preservation and paper processing. Contamination of plants growing beneath the power line with high concentration of Cu is reported to be toxic to the grazing animals (Kraal and Ernst, 1976).

Mining: Withdrawal and milling of metal minerals joined with industries have bequeathed various countries, the bequest of extensive circulation of metal pollutants in soil. Through withdrawal, tailings (larger particles settled at the end of the flotation cell while mining) are straight discharged in naturally occurring depressions, as well as onsite wetlands resulting in high amounts (DeVolder, 2003). Widely Pb and Zn mineral withdrawal and smelting have resulted in pollution of soil that causes danger to human and environmental health. Many retrieval methods that are used for these places are prolonged and costly and may not result in restoration of soil efficiency. Assimilation routes encompass the incorporation of plant material that is grown in contaminated soils (food chain), or the ingestion of contaminated soils directly (Basta and Gradwohl, 1998). Extra materials are produced by a variation of industries such as tanning, textile, petrochemicals from unintentional oil spills or consumption of petroleum-based products, insecticides and pharmaceutical industries and are extremely variable in configuration. Although certain products are disposed of on soil, some have assistances for agriculture and forestry. Copper in ecosystem is due to industrial and mining activities. Farmable land has increased concentration of mercury that leads to the contamination of food chain. Presence of lead in soil is also due to mining and smelting activities. Moreover cobalt is also a part of earth crust's and exists in the form of cobaltite, erythrite and smaltite. High level of nickel is being present in soil due to increased mining activities (Gimeno-García *et al.*, 1996).

Domestic sources

Domestic wastes may consist of (*i*) Untreated or solely mechanically treated waste waters; (*ii*) Substances which have passed through the filters of biological treatment plants and (*iii*) Waste substances passed over sewage outfalls and discharged to receiving water bodies often end up into the sea from coastal residential areas. The use of detergents creates a possible pollution hazard, since common house hold detergent products can affect the water quality. Most enzyme detergents contained trace amounts of the elements Fe, Mn, Cr, Co, Zn, Sr and B (Angino *et al.*, 1970). With regard to pollution resulting from urbanized areas, there is an increasing awareness that urban runoff presents a serious problem of heavy metal contamination. Studies by (Bolter *et al.*, 1974) indicate that lead is leached by humic and other acids, thus increasing its availability for runoff rather than seepage into the upper soil layer.

Waste water

The supply of wastewater coming from industrial land municipal sources and associated wastes to soil dates back 400 years and is a usual practice now in different parts of the globe (Reed *et al.*, 1995). Internationally, it is projected that 20 million hectares (mha) of arable land are watered with some sort of waste water. In various African and Asian cities, studies propose that agriculture relied on watering with wastewater contributes for 50% of the vegetable source to urban areas (Bjuhr, 2007). Farmers usually are not worried about environmental welfares or dangers and are principally concerned with maximizing their productions and profits. Though the metal amounts in wastewater discharges are comparatively low, long-term watering of land with such wastewater can finally cause heavy metal build-up in the soil.

(iv) Atmospheric source: Natural and man-made processes have been shown to result in metal containing airborne particulates. Depending on prevailing climatic conditions, these particulates may become wind-blown over great distances; nonetheless, they are subjected to the fate that they are ultimately returned to the lithosphere as precipitations by rain or snowfall. Additional sources of atmospheric metal enrichment, such as the high temperature anthropogenic sources, are of special importance on a global scale. Geothermal sources, such as volcanic eruptions, have caused significant atmospheric pollution (Eshleman *et al.*, 1971).

Air borne sources

Aerial source of metals that include chimney or duct releases of air, vapor streams or gas and brief discharge like dust from storage places and waste piles. Metals that are from airborne sources are usually discharged as particulates consist on the gas stream. Some metals like Cd, As and Pb can similarly volatilize by high temperature activities. These metals will change to oxides and shrink as smaller particulates until a reducing air is upheld. Emissions from chimney may be circulated over an extensive area by natural air flow still dry and/ or wet precipitation actions eliminate them from the gas tributary. Another chief source of soil pollution is the floating release of Pb from the burning of petrol having tetraethyl lead; this enhances considerably the part of Pb in soils of urban areas and in those next to main roads. Zinc and Cadmium can also be applied to soils next to roads; the sources include tyres and lubricant oils (USEPA, 1996).

Automobile sources

Automobile emission is directly related to metal contamination at the neighboring roadside ecosystem. Metal contaminants like Pb, Cd, Zn and Cu are mobile in nature and are found in engines, tiers and petrol of vehicles. Toxic metals are accumulated in top soils and vegetation near the road ecosystem (Jamal *et al.*, 2013).

Table 10.1: Different Sources of Heavy Metals (Lone et al., 2008)

S.No.	Heavy metals	Sources
1	As	Semiconductors, petroleum refining, wood preservatives, animal feed additives, coal power plants, herbicides, volcanoes, mining and smelting
2	Cu	Electroplating industry, smelting and refining, mining, biosolids
3	Cd	Geogenic sources anthropogenic activities metal smelting and refining, fossil fuel burning, application of phosphate fertilizers, sewage sludge
4	Cr	Electroplating industry, sludge, solid waste, tanneries
5	Pb	Mining and smelting of metalliferous ores, burning of leaded gasoline, municipal sewage, industrial wastes enriched in Pb, paints
6	Hg	Volcano eruptions, forest fire, emissions from industries producing caustic soda, coal, peat and wood burning
7	Se	Coal mining, oil refining, combustion of fossil fuels, glass manufacturing industry, chemical synthesis (e.g., varnish, pigment formulation)
8	Ni	Volcanic eruptions, land fill, forest fire, bubble bursting and gas exchange in ocean, weathering of soils and geological materials
9	Zn	Electroplating industry, smelting and refining, mining, biosolids

(vi) Other sources: Other sources of heavy metals include refuse incineration, landfills and transportation (automobiles, diesel-powered vehicles and aircraft). Two main anthropogenic sources that contaminate the soil are fly ash produced

due to coal burning and the corrosion of commercial waste products, which add Cr, Cu, Pb and galvanized metals (primarily Zn) into the environment (Al-Hiyaly *et al.,* 1988). Coal burning adds heavy metals such as Cd, Hg, Mn, Ni, Al, Fe and Ti into the soils. Oil burning contributes V, Fe, Pb and Ni to the environment. Metal emission during the transportation of vehicles includes Ni and Zn from tires, Al from catalyst, Cd and Cu primarily from diesel engines and Ni and Zn from aerosol emissions. Lubricants, which are anti-wear protectants for vehicles, emit Cd, Cr, Hg, Ni, Pb and Zn, particularly in case of inefficient engines. The burning of leaded gasoline has been an important source of Pb in the environment. Incinerations of municipal wastes generate significant concentrations of Zn, Pb, Al, Sn, Fe and Cu.

Some Heavy Metals and their Effects

Khair (2009) showed that heavy metals contamination as a grave issue of our environment and are major contaminating agents of our food supply. Microorganisms, plants and animals all are affected by the presence of heavy metals (Igweet *et al.,* 2005). Toxic heavy metals affecting microorganisms are involved in impairment of biochemical systems of plants and animals. As the contaminants are released into water channels that are used for the irrigation purpose are observed to contaminate the plants as well as their products. Occupational workers and consumers both are at risk of exposure to such activities. Certain metals like cadmium, arsenic, and zinc are harmful contaminants once they enter the soil and water (Jamal *et al.,* 2013). Like all living organisms, plants are often sensitive both to the deficiency and to the excess availability of some heavy metal ions as essential micronutrient, while the same at higher concentrations and even more ions such as Cd, Hg, As are strongly poisonous to the metabolic activities. Worked have been conducted throughout the world to determine the effects of toxic heavy metals on plants (Reeves and Baker, 2000). Contamination of agricultural soil by heavy metals has become a critical environmental concern due to their potential adverse ecological effects. Such toxic elements are considered as soil pollutants due to their widespread occurrence and their acute and chronic toxic effect on plants grown of such soils.

Effects of arsenic

Occurring naturally in the environment, arsenic can be released in larger quantities through volcanic activity, erosion of rocks, forest fires, and also by human activities. The wood preserving industry uses about 90% of the industrial arsenic in the U.S. Arsenic is also found in paints, dyes, metals, drugs, soaps and semi-conductors. Animal feeding operations and certain fertilizers and pesticides can release high amounts of arsenic to the environment as can industry practices such as copper or lead smelting, mining, and coal burning (Martin, 2009).

Arsenate (As) is an analog of phosphate (P) and competes for the same uptake carriers in the root plasmalemma of plants. As tolerance has been identified by several workers in a number of plant species (Meharg, 1994; Sharples *et al.*, 2000). The As tolerance in grasses results from suppression of a high-affinity P/ As uptake system (Meharg and Macnair, 1992). This suppression reduces As influx to a level at which plant can easily detoxify it, presumably by constitutive mechanisms (Meharg, 1994). As tolerance is achieved by a single-gene encoding for the suppressed P/As transport (Meharg and Macnair, 1992). Despite this clear understanding of the process controlling decrease in As uptake, tolerant grasses still assimilate As, albeit at much lower rate compared with non-tolerant. Nevertheless, assimilation over the life history of plants growing on contaminated soil can results in a very high As concentration, e.g. 3470 mg/g As in *Agrostis tenuis* and 560 mg/g As in *Holcus lanatus* (Porter and Peterson, 1975). The As also undergoes transformation within plant cells to other less phytotoxic As species (Meharg, 1994). In phytoplankton and macroalgae As is converted to arsenite, dimethyl arsinic acid (DMA), and monomethyl arsinic acid (MMA). Such methylated forms of As are then metabolized to organophospho lipids and arseno sugars (Phillips, 1990). Previously, terrestrial plants have been documented only for the presence of arsenate and arsenite (Meharg, 1994; Van den Broeck *et al.*, 1998).

Effect of cadmium

The regulatory limit of cadmium (Cd) in agricultural soil is 100 mg/kg soil (Salt *et al.*, 1995). But this threshold is continuously exceeding because of several human activities. Plants exposed to high levels of Cd causes reduction in photosynthesis, water uptake, and nutrient uptake. Plants grown in soil containing high levels of Cd show visible symptoms of injury reflected in terms of chlorosis, growth inhibition, browning of root tips and finally death (Wójcik and Tukiendorf, 2004; Mohanpuria *et al.*, 2007).

Effect of cobalt

Cobalt (Co) naturally occurs in the earth's crust as cobaltite [CoAsS], erythrite [$CO_3(AsO_4)_2$] and smaltite [$CoAs_2$]. Increase in Co concentration of soils can be caused by deposition from the burning of fossil fuels, wearing of Co containing alloys and spreading of sewage sludge and manure (Barceloux, 1999). However, environmental risks of Co are managed through the establishment of environmental quality criteria and standards. Plants can accumulate small amount of Co from the soil. The uptake and distribution of Co in plants is species-dependent and controlled by different mechanisms (Kukier *et al.*, 2004; Li *et al.*, 2004; Bakkaus *et al.*, 2005). Very little information is available regarding the phytotoxic effect of excess Co. Phytotoxicity study of Co in barley (Hordeum vulgare L.), oilseed rape (Brassica napus L.) and tomato (Lycopersicon esculentum L.) has recently shown the adverse effect on shoot growth and biomass (Li *et al.*, 2009). In addition to biomass, excess of Co restricted the concentration of Fe, chlorophyll, protein and catalase activity in leaves of cauliflower. Further, high level of Co also affected the translocation of P, S, Mn, Zn and Cu from roots to tops in cauliflower. In contrast to excess Cu or Cr, Co significantly decreased water potential and transpiration rate. While diffusive resistance and relative water content increased in leaves of cauliflower upon exposure to excess Co (Chatterjee and Chatterjee, 2000).

Effect of chromium

Chromium (Cr) is a heavy metal that causes serious environmental contamination in soil, sediments, and groundwater (Shanker *et al.*, 2005). The tanning industry is one of the major consumers of water and most of it is discharged as wastewater, which contains high amount of Cr (1.07– 7.80 mg/l). Worldwide anthropogenic discharge of Cr in fresh water bodies has been estimated to be 3550 mt (Nriagu, 1990). Cr (VI) is a very toxic, powerful epithelial irritant and a proven human carcinogen established by International Agency for Research on Cancer (IARC), the Environmental Protection Agency (EPA) and the World Health Organization (WHO). Toxicity of Cr has been studied in many plants. Excess of Cr causes inhibition of plant growth, chlorosis in young leaves, nutrient imbalance, wilting of tops, and root injury (Chatterjee and Chatterjee, 2000; Dixit *et al.*, 2002; Sharma *et al.*, 2003; Scoccianti *et al.*, 2006). Inhibition of chlorophyll biosynthesis has also been reported in terrestrial plants (Vajpayee *et al.*, 2000). For example, barley seedlings grown in 100 μM Cr showed 40% inhibition of growth (Skeffington *et al.*, 1976). Toxic effects of Cr on plant growth and development include alterations in the germination process as well as in the growth of roots, stems and leaves. Hence, exposure to high level of Cr affected total dry matter production and yield of plants (Shanker *et al.*, 2005). Cr also causes deleterious effects on plant physiological processes such as photosynthesis, water relations and mineral nutrition. Metabolic alterations by Cr exposure have also been described in plants either by a direct effect on enzymes and metabolites or by its ability to generate ROS (Shanker *et al.*, 2005).

Effect of Copper

Copper (Cu) is considered as a micronutrient for plants (Thomas *et al.*, 1998) and plays important role in CO_2 assimilation and ATP synthesis. Cu is also an essential component of various proteins like plastocyanin of photosynthetic system and cytochrome oxidase of respiratory electron transport chain (Demirevska-Kepova *et al.*, 2004). But enhanced industrial and mining activities have contributed to the increasing occurrence of Cu in ecosystems. Cu is also added to soils from different human activities including mining and smelting of Cu-containing ores. Mining activities generate a large amount of waste rocks and tailings, which get deposited at the surface. Excess of Cu in soil plays a cytotoxic role, induces stress and causes injury to plants. This leads to plant growth retardation and leaf chlorosis (Lewis *et al.*, 2001). Exposure of plants to excess Cu generates oxidative stress and ROS (Stadtman and Oliver, 1991). Oxidative stress causes disturbance of metabolic pathways and damage to macromolecules (Hegedus *et al.*, 2001).

Effect of lead

Lead (Pb) is one of the ubiquitously distributed most abundant toxic elements in the soil. The toxic level of Pb in soil results from disposal of municipal sewage sludge, mining and smelting activities, Pb containing paints, paper and pulp, gasoline and explosives. It exerts adverse effect on morphology, growth and photosynthetic processes of plants. High level of Pb also causes inhibition of enzyme activities, water imbalance, alterations in membrane permeability and disturbs mineral nutrition (Sharma and Dubey, 2005). Pb inhibits the activity of enzymes at cellular level by reacting with their sulfhydril groups. High Pb concentration also induces oxidative stress by increasing the production of ROS in plants (Reddy *et al.*, 2005).

Effects of manganese

Accumulation of excessive manganese (Mn) in leaves causes a reduction of photosynthetic rate (Kitao *et al.*, 1997a,b). Mn is readily transported from root to shoot through the transpiration stream, but not readily remobilized through phloem to other organs after reaching the leaves. Necrotic brown spotting on leaves, petioles and stems is a common symptom of Mn toxicity (Wu, 1994). With time, the speckles can increase in both number and size resulting in necrotic lesions, leaf browning and death (Elamin and Wilcox, 1986a,b). General leaf bronzing and shortening of internodes has been documented in *Cucumis sativus* (Crawford *et al.*, 1989). Another common symptom is known as "crinkle leaf", and it occurs in the youngest leaf, stem and petiole tissue. It is also associated with chlorosis and browning of these tissues (Wu, 1994; Bachman and Miller, 1995). Roots exhibiting Mn toxicity are commonly brown in color (Le Bot *et al.*, 1990; Foy *et al.*, 1995) and sometimes crack (Foy *et al.*, 1995). Chlorosis in younger leaves by Mn toxicity is thought to be caused through Mn induced Fe deficiency. Manganese toxicity in some species starts with chlorosis of older leaves moving toward the younger leaves with time (Bachman and Miller, 1995).

Effect of mercury

The large input of mercury (Hg) into the arable lands has resulted in the widespread occurrence of mercury-contamination in the entire food chain. Hg is a unique metal due to its existence in different forms e.g. HgS, Hg^{2+}, Hg° and methyl-Hg. However in agricultural soil, ionic form (Hg^{2+}) is predominant (Han *et al.*, 2006). Hg released to the soil mainly remains in solid phase through adsorption onto sulfides, clay particles and organic matters. Increasing evidence has shown that Hg^{2+} can readily accumulate in higher and aquatic plants

(Kamal *et al.,* 2004; Wang and Greger, 2004; Israr *et al.,* 2006). High level of Hg^{2+} is strongly phytotoxic to plant cells. Toxic level of Hg^{2+} can induce visible injuries and physiological disorders in plants (Zhou *et al.,* 2007). For example, Hg^{2+} can bind towater channel proteins, thus inducing leaf stomata to close and physical obstruction of water flow in plants (Zhang and Tyerman, 1999). High level of Hg^{2+} interfere the mitochondrial activity and induces oxidative stress by triggering the generation of ROS. This leads to the disruption of biomembrane lipids and cellular metabolism in plants (Messer *et al.,* 2005; Israr and Sahi, 2006; Cargnelutti *et al.,* 2006).

Effect of nickel

Nickel (Ni) is a transition metal and found in natural soils at trace concentrations except in ultramafic or serpentinic soils. However, Ni^{2+} concentration is increasing in certain areas by human activities such as mining works, emission of smelters, burning of coal and oil, sewage, phosphate fertilizers and pesticides (Gimeno-García *et al.,* 1996). Ni^{2+} concentration in polluted soil may reach 20- to 30-fold (200–26,000 mg/kg) higher than the overall range (10–1000 mg/kg) found in natural soil (Izosimova, 2005). Excess of Ni^{2+} in soil causes various physiological alterations and diverse toxicity symptoms such as chlorosis and necrosis in different plant species (Zornoza *et al.,* 1999; Pandey and Sharma, 2002; Rahman *et al.,* 2005), including rice (Samantaray *et al.,* 1997). Plants grown in high Ni^{2+} containing soil showed impairment of nutrient balance and resulted in disorder of cell membrane functions. Thus, Ni^{2+} affected the lipid composition and H-ATPase activity of the plasma membrane as reported in Oryza sativa shoots (Ros *et al.,* 1992). Exposure of wheat to high level of Ni^{2+} enhanced MDA concentration (Pandolfini *et al.,* 1992). Moreover, Gonnelli *et al.,* (2001) reported an increase in MDA concentration of Ni^{2+} sensitive plants compared to a Ni^{2+} tolerant Silene. Such changes might disturb membrane functionality and ion balance in the cytoplasm, particularly of K^+, the most mobile ion across plant cell membrane. Other symptoms observed in Ni^{2+}-treated plants were related with changes in water balance. High uptake of Ni^{2+} induced a decline in water content of dicot and monocot plant species. The decrease inwater uptake is used as an indicator of the progression of Ni^{2+} toxicity in plants (Pandey and Sharma, 2002; Gajewska *et al.,* 2006).

Effects of zinc

Soil is also contaminated with zinc (Zn) in addition to Cd by the sewage sludge or urban composts, fertilizers, emissions from municipal waste incinerators, residues from metalliferous mining, the metal smelting industry, and other human activities. Zn is an essential nutrient for living organisms, while Cd is nonessential and potentially toxic for higher plants, animals and humans. Concentrations of Zn found in contaminated soils frequently exceed to those required as nutrients and may cause phytotoxicity. Zn concentrations in the range of 150 to 300 mg/kg have been measured in polluted soils (de Vries *et al.*, 2002; Warne *et al.*, 2008). High levels of Zn in soil inhibit many plant metabolic functions; result in retarded growth and cause senescence. Zinc toxicity in plants limited the growth of both root and shoot (Choi *et al.*, 1996; Ebbs and Kochian, 1997; Fontes and Cox, 1998). Zinc toxicity also causes chlorosis in the younger leaves, which can extend to older leaves after prolonged exposure to high soil Zn levels (Ebbs and Kochian, 1997). The chlorosis may arise partly from an induced iron (Fe) deficiency as hydrated Zn^{+2} and Fe^{+2} ions have similar radii (Marschner, 1986). Excess Zn can also give rise to manganese (Mn) and copper (Cu) deficiencies in plant shoots. Such deficiencies have been ascribed to a hindered transfer of these micronutrients from root to shoot. This hindrance is based on the fact that the Fe and Mn concentrations in plants grown in Zn-rich media are greater in the root than the shoot (Ebbs and Kochian, 1997). Another typical effect of Zn toxicity is the appearance of a purplish-red color in leaves, which is ascribed to phosphorus (P) deficiency.

Plant Response to Heavy Metals

Metal excluders

They prevent metal from entering their aerial parts or maintain low and constant metal concentration over a broad range of metal concentration in soil, they mainly restrict metal in their roots. The plant may alter its membrane permeability, change metal binding capacity of cell walls or exude more chelating substances (Cunningham, 1995).

Metal indicators

Species which actively accumulate metal in their aerial tissues and generally reflect metal level in the soil may be considered as metal indicators. They tolerate the existing concentration level of metals by producing intracellular metal binding compounds (chelators), or alter metal compartmentalisation pattern by storing metals in non-sensitive parts (Ghosh and Singh, 2005).

Metal accumulator plant species

They can concentrate metal in their aerial parts, to levels far exceeding than soil. Hyperaccumulators are plants that can absorb high levels of contaminants concentrated either in their roots, shoots and/or leaves (Raskin *et al.*, 1994; Cunningham and Ow, 1996; Baker *et al.*, 1994). Baker and Brooks have defined metal hyperaccumulator as plants that contain more than or up to 0.1% i.e. more than (1000 mg/g) of copper, cadmium, chromium, lead, nickel cobalt or 1% (>10,000 mg/g) of zinc or manganese in the dry matter. For cadmium and other rare metals, it is > 0.01% by dry weight. Researchers have identified hyperaccumulator species by collecting plants from the areas where soil contains greater than usual amount of metals as in case of polluted areas or geographically rich in a particular element (Gleba *et al.*, 1999). Approximately 400 hyperaccumulator species from 22 families have been identified. The *Brassicaceae* family contains a large number of hyperaccumulating species with widest range of metals; these include 87 species from 11 genera (Baker and Brooks, 1989).

Role of Plants in Phytoremediation Process

There are several ways in which plants are used to clean up, or remediate, contaminated sites. To remove pollutants from soil, sediment and/or water, plants can break down, or degrade, organic pollutants or contain and stabilize metal contaminants by acting as filters or traps The uptake of contaminants in plants occurs primarily through the root system, in which the principal mechanisms for preventing contaminant toxicity are found. The root system provides an enormous surface area that absorbs and accumulates the water and nutrients essential for growth, as well as other non-essential contaminants. Researchers are finding that the use of trees (rather than smaller plants) is effective in treating deeper contamination because tree roots penetrate more deeply into the ground. In addition, deep-lying contaminated ground water can be treated by pumping the water out of the ground and using plants to treat the contamination.

Plant roots also cause changes at the soil-root interface as they release inorganic and organic compounds (root exudates) in the rhizosphere. These root exudates affect the number and activity of the microorganisms, the aggregation and stability of the soil particles around the root, and the availability of the contaminants. Root exudates, by themselves can increase (mobilise) or decrease (immobilise) directly or indirectly the availability of the contaminants in the root zone (rhizosphere) of the plant through changes in soil characteristics, release of organic substances, changes in chemical composition, and/or increase in plant-assisted microbial activity.

Phytoremediation is an alternative or complimentary technology that can be used along with or, in some cases in place of mechanical conventional clean-up technologies that often require high capital inputs and are labour and energy intensive. Phytoremediation is an in situ remediation technology that utilises the inherent abilities of living plants. It is also an ecologically friendly, solar-energy driven clean-up technology, based on the concept of using nature to cleanse nature.

Phytoremediation Processes

Depending on the underlying processes, applicability, and type of contaminant, phyto-remediation can be broadly categorised as:

- *Phytodegradation*: use of plants to uptake, store and degrade contaminants within its tissue.
- *Phytostimulation or rhizodegradation*: use of rhizospheric associations between plants and symbiotic soil microbes to degrade contaminants.

- *Phytovolatilisation:* use of a plant's ability to uptake contaminants from the growth matrix and subsequently transform and volatilise contaminants into the atmosphere.
- *Phytoextraction:* use plants to absorb, translocate and store toxic contaminants from a soil matrix into their root and shoot tissue.
- *Rhizofiltration:* use of roots to uptake also store contaminants from an aqueous growth matrix.

Phytostabilisation

Plant-mediated immobilisation or binding of contaminants into the soil matrix, thereby reducing their bioavailability.

Depending on the contaminants, the site conditions, the level of clean-up required, and the types of plants, phytoremediation technology can be used for containment (phytoimmobilization and phytostabilization) or removal (phytoextraction and phytovolatilization) purposes. The four different plant-based technologies of phytoremediation, each having a different mechanism of action for remediating metal-polluted soil, sediment, or water: (1) phytostabilization, where plants stabilize, rather than remove contaminants by plant roots metal retention; (2) phytofiltration, involving plants to clean various aquatic environments; (3) phytovolatilization, utilizing plants to extract certain metals from soil and then release them into the atmosphere by volatilization; and (4) phytoextraction, in which plants absorb metals from soil and translocate them to harvestable shoots where they accumulate. Ecological issues also need to be evaluated when developing a phytoremediation strategy for a polluted site. In particular, one has to consider how the phytoremediation efforts might affect local ecological relationships, especially those involving other crops. Since the phytoremediation plants will be grown under contaminated soil/water conditions, where other crops may not thrive because of contaminant toxicities, the competition problem is unlikely to arise.

Phytostabilization

Phytostabilization uses certain plant species to immobilize contaminants in soil, through absorption and accumulation by roots, adsorption onto roots or precipitation within the root zone and physical stabilization of soils. This process reduces the mobility of contaminants and prevents migration to groundwater or air. This can re-establish a vegetative cover at sites where natural vegetation is lacking due to high metal concentrations (Tordoff *et al.*, 2000). Thorough planning is essential for successful revegetation, including physical and chemical analyses, bioassays and field trials. The main approaches to revegetation are summarized in Table 10.2. Metal-tolerant species may be used to restore vegetation to such sites, thereby decreasing the potential migration of contaminants through wind, transport of exposed surface soils, leaching of soil and contamination of groundwater (Stoltz and Greger, 2002). Unlike other phytoremediative techniques, phytostabilization is not intended to remove metal contaminants from a site, but rather to stabilize them by accumulation in roots or precipitation within root zones, reducing the risk to human health and the environment. It is applied in situations where there are potential human health impacts, and exposure to substances of concern can be reduced to acceptable levels by containment. The disruption to site activities may be less than with more intrusive soil remediation technologies. Phytostabilization is most effective for fine-textured soils with high organic-matter content, but it is suitable for treating a wide range of sites where large areas are subject to surface contamination (Cunningham *et al.,* 1997; Berti and Cunningham 2000). However, some highly contaminated sites are not suitable for phytostabilization, because plant growth and survival is impossible (Berti and Cunningham 2000). Phytostabilization has advantages over other soil-remediation practices in that it is less expensive, easier to implement, and preferable aesthetically (Berti and Cunningham 2000; Schnoor 2000). When decontamination strategies are impractical because of the extent of the contaminated area or the lack of adequate funding, phytostabilization is advantageous (Berti and Cunningham 2000). It may also serve as an interim strategy to reduce risk at sites where complications delay the selection of the most appropriate technique.

Characteristics of plants appropriate for phytostabilization at a particular site include: tolerance to high levels of the contaminant(s) of concern; high production of root biomass able to immobilize these contaminants through uptake, precipitation, or reduction; and retention of applicable contaminants in roots, as opposed to transfer to shoots, to avoid special handling and disposal of shoots. Yoon *et al.,* (2006) evaluated the potential of 36 plants (17 species) growing on a contaminated site and found that plants with a high bio-concentration factor (BCF, metal concentration ratio of plant roots to soil) and low translocation factor (TF, metal concentration ratio of plant shoots to roots) have the potential for phytostabilization . The lack of appreciable metals in shoot tissue also eliminates the necessity to treat harvested shoot residue as a hazardous waste (Flathman and Lanza 1998). In a field study, mine wastes containing copper, lead, and zinc were stabilized by grasses (Agrostis tenuis cv. Goginan for acid lead and zinc mine wastes, Agrostis tenuis cv. Parys for copper mine wastes, and Festuca rubra cv. Merlin for calcareous lead and zinc mine wastes) (Smith and Bradshaw 1992). The research of Smith and Bradshaw (1992) led to the development of two cultivars of Agrostis tenuis Sibth and one of Festuca rubra L which are now commercially available for phytostabilizing Pb-, Zn-, and Cu-contaminated soils. Stabilization also involves soil amendments to promote the formation of insoluble metal complexes that reduce biological availability and plant uptake, thus preventing metals from entering the food chain (Adriano *et al.,* 2004; Berti and Cunningham 2000; Cunningham *et al.,* 1997).

One way to facilitate such immobilisation is by altering the physicochemical properties of the metal-soil complex by introducing a multipurpose anion, such as phosphate, that enhances metal adsorption via. anion-induced negative charge and metal precipitation (Bolan *et al.*, 2003). Addition of humified organic matter (O.M.) such as compost, together with lime to raise soil pH (Kuo *et al.*, 1985), is a common practice for immobilizing heavy metals and improving soil conditions, to facilitate re-vegetation of contaminated soils (Williamson and Johnson, 1981). Soil acidification, due to the oxidation of metallic sulphides in the soil, increases heavy metal bioavailability; but liming can control soil acidification; also, organic materials generally promoted fixation of heavy metals in non-available soil fractions, with Cu bioavailability being particularly affected by organic treatments (Clemente *et al.*, 2003). The production of sulphate by sulphide oxidation increased solubility of Zn and Mn, and therefore their concentrations in plant-available (DTPA-extractable) fractions. However, the bioavailability of Cu did not decrease with either soil pH increase or with lime, indicating that the organic treatments might have had a significant effect. Revegetation of mine tailings usually requires amendments of phosphorus, even though phosphate addition can mobilize arsenic (As) from the tailings. Leachates and uptakes of As were found to be higher with an organic fertilizer amendment than superphosphate, particularly in combination with barley (Mains *et al.*, 2006b). Active phytoremediation followed by natural attenuation, was effective for remediation of the pyrite-polluted soil (Clemente *et al.*, 2006). The Met PAD IM bio test was used to assess the extent of metal accumulation by plants in mining areas. Plants were identified as hyper tolerant which can be used for phytostabilization (Boularbah *et al.*, 2006). Two plant species, Hyparrhenia hirta and Zygophyllum fabago, that have naturally colonized some parts of mine tailings in South-East Spain, have been reported to tolerate high metal concentrations in their rhizospheres. These plant species do not take up high concentrations of metals, providing a good tool to achieve surface stabilization of tailings with low risk of affecting the food chain (Conesa *et al.*, 2006). Phytostabilization efforts in the Mediterranean region have been found to be improved by using mixtures including local metallicolous legume and grass species (Frérot *et al.*, 2006). It is better to identify the plants spontaneously colonizing the contaminated site, since they are more ecologically adapted than introduced species.

Phytofiltration

Phytofiltration is the use of plant roots (rhizofiltration) or seedlings (blasto-filtration) to absorb or adsorb pollutants, mainly metals, from water and aqueouswaste streams (Prasad and Freitas 2003). Plant roots or seedlings grown in aerated water absorb, precipitate and concentrate toxic metals from polluted effluents (Dushenkov and Kapulnik 2000; Elless *et al.*, 2005). Mechanisms involved in biosorption include chemisorption, complexation, ion exchange, micro precipitation, hydroxide condensation onto the biosurface, and surface adsorption (Gardea-Torresdey *et al.*, 2004). Rhizofiltration uses terrestrial plants instead of aquatic plants because the former feature much larger fibrous root systems covered with root hairs with extremely large surface areas. Metal pollutants in industrial-process water and in groundwater are most commonly removed by precipitation or flocculation, followed by sedimentation and disposal of the resulting sludge (Ensley 2000). The process involves raising plants hydroponically and transplanting them into metal-polluted waters where plants absorb andconcentrate the metals in their roots and shoots (Dushenkov *et al.*, 1995; Salt *et al.*, 1995; Flathman and Lanza 1998; Zhu *et al.*, 1999). Root exudates and changes in rhizosphere pH may also cause metals to precipitate onto root surfaces. As they become saturated with the metal contaminants, roots or whole plants are harvested for disposal (Flathman and Lanza 1998; Zhu *et al.*, 1999). Dushenkov *et al.*, (1995), Salt *et al.*, (1995), and Flathman and Lanza (1998) contend that plants for phytoremediation should accumulate metals only in the roots. Dushenkov *et al.*, (1995) explain that the translocation of metals to shoots would decrease the efficiency of rhizofiltration by increasing the amount of contaminated plant residue needing disposal. However, Zhu *et al.*, (1999) suggest that the efficiency of the process can be increased by using plants with a heightened ability to absorb and translocate metals. Several aquatic species have the ability to remove heavy metals from water, including water hyacinth (Eichhornia crassipes, Kay *et al.*, 1984; Zhu *et al.*, 1999), pennywort (Hydrocotyle umbellata L., Dierberg *et al.*, 1987), and duckweed (Lemna minor L., Mo *et al.*, 1989). However, these plants have limited potential for rhizofiltration because they are not efficient in removing metals as a result of their small, slowgrowing roots (Dushenkov *et al.*, 1995). The high water content of aquatic plants complicates their drying, composting, or incineration. In spite of limitations, Zhu *et al.*, (1999) indicated that water hyacinth is effective in removing trace elements in waste streams. Sunflower (Helianthus annus L.) and Indian mustard (Brassica juncea Czern.) are the most promising terrestrial candidates for removing metals from water. The roots of Indian mustard are effective in capturing Cd, Cr, Cu, Ni, Pb, and Zn (Dushenkov *et al.*, 1995), whereas sunflower removes Pb (Dushenkov *et al.*, 1995), U (Dushenkov *et al.*, 1997a), 137Cs, and 90Sr (Dushenkov *et al.*, 1997b) from hydroponic solutions. A novel phytofiltration technology has been proposed by Sekhar *et al.*, (2004) for removal and recovery of lead (Pb) from wastewaters. This technology uses plantbased biomaterial from the bark of the plant commonly called Indian sarsaparilla (*Hemidesmus indicus*). The target of their research was polluted surface water and groundwater at industrially contaminated sites. Cassava waste biomass was also effective in removing two divalent metal ions, Cd (II) and Zn (II), from aqueous solutions (Horsfall and Abia 2003). Modification of thecassava waste biomass by treating it with thioglycollic acid resulted in increased adsorption rates for Cd, Cu, and

Zn (Abia *et al.*, 2003). Several species of Sargassum biomass (non living brown algae) were effective biosorbents for heavy metals such as Cd and Cu (Davis *et al.*, 2000). Plants used for phytofiltration should be able to accumulate and tolerate significant amounts of the target metals, in conjunction with easy handling, low maintenance costs, and a minimum of secondary waste requiring disposal. It is also desirable for plants to produce significant amounts of root biomass or root surface area (Dushenkov and Kapulnik 2000).

Phytovolatilization

Phytovolatilization Some metal contaminants such as As, Hg, and Se may exist as gaseous species in the environment. In recent years, researchers have sought naturally-occurring or genetically-modified plants capable of absorbing elemental forms of these metals from the soil, biologically converting them to gaseous species within the plant, and releasing them into the atmosphere. This process is called phytovolatilization.

Volatilization of Se from plant tissues may provide a mechanism of selenium detoxification. As early as 1894, Hofmeister proposed that selenium in animals is detoxified by releasing volatile dimethyl selenide from the lungs, based on the fact that the odour of dimethyl telluride was detected in the breath of dogs injected with sodium tellurite. Using the same logic, it was suggested that the garlicky odour of plants that accumulate selenium may indicate release of volatile selenium compounds. This is the most controversial of phytoremediation technologies. Hg and Se are toxic (Suszcynsky and Shann 1995), and there is doubt about whether the volatilization of these elements into the atmosphere is desirable or safe. The volatile selenium compound released from the selenium accumulator Astragalus racemosus was identified as dimethyl diselenide (Evans *et al.*, 1968). Selenium released from alfalfa, a selenium nonaccumulator, was different from the accumulator species and was identified as dimethyl selenide. Lewis *et al.*, (1966) showed that both selenium nonaccumulator and accumulator species volatilize selenium. Selenium phytovolatilization has received the most attention to date (Lewis *et al.*, 1966; Terry *et al.*, 1992; Banuelos *et al.*, 1993; McGrath 1998) because this element is a serious problem in many parts of the world where there are Se-rich soil (Brooks 1998). According to Brooks (1998), the release of volatile Se compounds from higher plants was first reported by Lewis *et al.*, (1966). Terry *et al.*, (1992) report that members of the Brassicaceae are capable of releasing up to 40 g Se ha^{-1} day –1 as various gaseous compounds. Some aquatic plants, such as cattail (Typha latifolia L.), have potential for Se phytoremediation (Pilon-Smits *et al.*, 1999). Volatile Se compounds such as dimethylselenide are 1/600 to 1/500 as toxic as inorganic forms of Se found in soil (DeSouza *et al.*, 2000). The volatilization of Se and Hg is also a permanent site solution, because the inorganic forms of these elements are removed, and gaseous species are not likely to redeposit at or near the site (Atkinson *et al.*,

1990; Heaton *et al.,* 1998). Furthermore, sites that utilize this technique may not require much management after the original planting. This remediation method has the added benefits of minimal site disturbance, less erosion, and no need to dispose of contaminated plant material (Heaton *et al.,* 1998). Heaton *et al.,* (1998) suggest that the transfer of Hg (O) to the atmosphere would not contribute significantly to the atmospheric pool. This technique appears to be a promising tool for remediating Se- and Hg-contaminated soils. Volatilization of arsenic as dimethylarsenite has also been postulated as a resistance mechanism in marine algae. However, it is not known whether terrestrial plants also volatilize arsenic in significant quantities. Studies on arsenic uptake and distribution in higher plants indicate that arsenic predominantly accumulates in roots and that only small quantities are transported to shoots. However, plants may enhance the biotransformation of arsenic by rhizospheric bacteria, thus increasing the rates of volatilization (Salt *et al.,* 1998). Unlike other remediation techniques, once contaminants have been removed via volatilization, there is a loss of control over their migration to other areas. Some authors suggest that the addition to atmospheric levels through phytovolatilization would not contribute significantly to the atmospheric pool, since the contaminants are likely to be subject to more effective or rapid natural degradation processes such as photo-degradation (Azaizeh *et al.,* 1997). However, phytovolatilization should be avoided for sites near population centres and at places with unique meteorological conditions that promote the rapid deposition of volatile compounds (Heaton *et al.,* 1998). Hence the consequences of releasing the metals to the atmosphere need to be considered carefully before adopting this method as a remediation tool.

Phytoextraction

Phytoextraction, also called phytoaccumulation, refers to the uptake and translocation of metal contaminants in the soil by plant roots into above-ground components of the plants. The terms phytoremediation and phytoextraction are sometimes incorrectly used as synonyms, but phytoremediation is a concept, whereas phytoextraction is a specific clean-up technology (Prasad and Freitas 2003). Certain plants, called hyperaccumulators, absorb unusually large amounts of metals compared to other plants and the ambient metals concentration. Natural metal hyperaccumulators are plants that can accumulate and tolerate greater metal concentrations in shoots than those usually found in non-accumulators, without visible symptoms. According to Baker and Brooks (1989), hyperaccumulators should have a metal accumulation exceeding a threshold value of shoot metal concentration of 1% (Zn, Mn), 0.1% (Ni, Co, Cr, Cu, Pb and Al), 0.01% (Cd and Se) or 0.001% (Hg) of the dry weight shoot biomass. Over 400 hyperaccumulator plants have been reported, including members of the Asteraceae, Brassicaceae, Caryophyllaceae, Cyperaceae, Cunouniaceae, Fabaceae, Flacourtiaceae, Lamiaceae, Poaceae, Violaceae, and Euphobiaceae. Recently Environment Canada has released a database "Phytorem" which contains a worldwide inventory of more than 750 terrestrial and aquatic plants, both wild and cultivated species and varieties, of potential value for phytoremediation. These plants are selected and planted at a site based on the metals present and site conditions. After they have grown for several weeks or months, the plants are harvested. Planting and harvesting may be repeated to reduce contaminant levels to allowable limits (Kumar *et al.*, 1995). The time required for remediation depends on the type and extent of metal contamination, the duration of the growing season, and the efficiency of metal removal by plants, but it normally ranges from 1 to 20 years (Kumar *et al.*, 1995; Blaylock and Huang 2000). This technique is suitable for remediating large areas of land contaminated at shallow depths with low to moderate levels of metal-contaminants (Kumar *et al.*, 1995; Blaylock and Huang 2000) Types of Phytoextraction Two basic strategies of phytoextraction are being developed: chelate-assisted phytoextraction, which we term induced phytoextraction; and long-term continuous phytoextraction. If metal availability is not adequate for sufficient plant uptake, chelates or acidifying agents may be added to the soil to liberate them (Cunningham and Ow 1996; Huang *et al.*, 1997; Lasat *et al.*, 1998). However, side effects of the addition of chelate to the soil microbial community are usually neglected. It has been reported (Wu *et al.*, 1999) that many synthetic chelators capable of inducing phytoextraction might form chemically and microbiologically stable complexes with heavy metals, threatening soil quality and groundwater contamination. Several chelating agents, such as EDTA (ethylene diamine tetra acetic acid), EGTA (ethylene glycol-O,O2-bis-[2-amino-ethyl]-N,N, N2, N2,-tetra acetic acid), EDDHA (ethylenediamine di o-hyroxyphenylacetic acid), EDDS (ethylene diamine disuccinate) and citric acid, have been found to enhance phytoextraction by mobilizing metals and increasing metal accumulation (Tandy *et al.*, 2006; Cooper *et al.*, 1999). The increase in the phytoextraction of Pb by shoots of *Z. mays* L. was more pronounced than the increase of Pb in the soil solution with combined application of EDTA and EDDS (Luo *et al.*, 2006). Although EDTA was, in general, more effective in soil metal solubilization, EDDS, less harmful to the environment, was more efficient in inducing metal accumulation in *B. decumbens* shoots (Santos *et al.*, 2006). However, there is a potential risk of leaching of metals to groundwater, and a lack of reported detailed studies regarding the persistence of metal-chelating agent complexes in contaminated soils (Lombi *et al.*, 2001a,b). Effective phytoextraction requires both plant genetic ability and the development of optimal agronomic practices, including (1) soil management practices to improve the efficiency of phytoextraction, and (2) crop management practices to develop a commercial cropping system. Ebbs *et al.*, (1997) reported that *B. juncea*, while having one-third the concentration of Zn in its tissue, is more effective at removing Zn from soil than *Thlaspi caerulescens*, a known hyperaccumulator of Zn. The advantage is due primarily to the fact that *B. juncea* produces ten-times more biomass than *T. caerulescens*. Plants for phytoextraction should be able to grow outside their area of collection, have profuse root systems and be able to transport metals to their shoots.

Application of Phytoremediation

Phytoremediation has been successfully tested in many locations, but full-scale applications are still limited. At a U.S. Army testing facility in Maryland, hybrid poplar trees have been planted in a one-acre site over a shallow groundwater plume contaminated with organics from several toxic disposal pits. The poplar trees act as hydraulic pumps to prevent the spread of contaminants to a nearby marsh. In addition to hydraulic control, researchers have determined that phytovolatilisation and rhizofiltration are other mechanisms by which the system is treating the contaminated plume. After the second growing season, the trees successfully contained the contaminated groundwater plume with rates estimated at 2-10 gallons of water per day for each tree. Results have also indicated that the poplar trees are degrading the contaminants in the groundwater plume.

In Canada, Environment Canada is working with the company that operates the world's largest smelter to treat landfill leachate using constructed wetlands. Also, at the Milan Ammunition Plant in Tennessee, U.S.A., a constructed wetland design deployed submersed and emergent plants in surface and subsurface flow systems to degrade TNT, RDX and other explosives contaminants found in groundwater onsite. By testing ten species of aquatic plants in growth chambers and hydroponic solutions, researchers were able to select a number of species for the lagoon (surface flow) unit of the wetland system. The species recommended were elodea *(Elodea Michx), sago pondweed (Stuckenia pectinatus) and water grass (Luziola fluitans).*

The use of plants and soil as a vegetative cap for landfill sites is another effective phytoremediation technique. Vegetative covers serve as a form of hydraulic control by maximising the available storage capacity of soil, as well as the evaporation rates and transpiration processes of plants, thereby minimising water infiltration. They can also assist in the degradation of wastes and contaminants contained within the landfill or on land. In Slovenia, one landfill is covered with poplar trees to prevent creation of landfill leachate that could harm groundwater and surface water.

In Kazakhstan, a program has begun to remediate pesticide contamination through the use of planted systems. International oil companies have also begun using phyto-degradation at many sites, with over sixty sites planted or in the planning stages.

In the United Arab Emirates, a study has been carried out examining the growth characteristics and performance of mangroves, halophytes and other plants in soil irrigated with saline water. Salinity is a serious threat for crop production in arid regions, where the high rate of evaporation, combined with the demand for scarce water reserves, causes salt build-up during the cultivation process. The study showed that some plants have the necessary physiological mechanisms and capacities to accumulate significant concentrations of iron, manganese and magnesium, calcium, sodium and chloride ions, thereby reducing the overall salinity of the soil system and potential related effects on crop physiological and growth performance. Based on this work, it has been suggested that by introducing highly salt-tolerant species (i.e., *Conocarpus erectus, Atriplex lentiformis,* etc.) that can be irrigated with saline water, higher plant and agricultural production levels in arid regions can be achieved.

One of the promising aspects of phytotechnologies is the possibility of deriving additional benefit from the planted system during or after the prevention or clean-up of pollution. Trees planted as a riparian corridor that protect streams from agricultural pollution may be managed to provide forest products like nuts, fruits, lumber or fibre. Trees can be selected that do not move toxins from roots to above ground, thus allowing for a safe harvest while roots clean up groundwater. In addition, contaminated urban sites may be planted to clean up soil and groundwater while at the same time providing recreation and park use.

Various plants have been employed in the treatment of wastewaters. Biddlestone *et al.,* used reed (Phragmites australis) bed systems to reduce dairy waste with a BOD5 value of 1,006 mg/L, down to 57 mg/L (Biddlestone, *et al.,* 1991). Sub-surface constructed wetlands with Phragmites australis for wastewater treatment have been intensively studied in the Czech Republic, for several decades (Vymazal, 2002). The size of these wetlands was in the range of 18 ~ 4,500 m^2, and the treatment efficiency was found to be excellent (i.e. 88% reduction in BOD5, and 84% for suspended solids). Similar results were also obtained with Typha latifolia and Salix atrocinerea in Spain, for municipal wastewater treatment (Ansola, *et al.,* 2003). In addition, a comparative study of Cyperus papyrus (papyrus) and Miscanthidium violaceum-planted wetlands for wastewater treatment in Uganda revealed that papyrus was the more efficient for removing nutrients (ammonium-nitrogen and total reactive phosphorus) (Kyambadde, 2004). Bodini *et al.,* (2011) showed that *Cupressus sempervirens* and *Quercusilex* proved tolerant to six month olive mill wastewater, followed by six-month water irrigation. The olive mill wastewater is characterized by low pH, high BOD5 and COD loads, and phytotoxic levels of phenolic compounds, and thus has been a waste management problem in olive oil producing countries. It is interesting to note that phytoremediation of textile effluent with *Glandularia pulchella* was tested to decolorize structurally different dyes. Differential patterns of enzyme induction, with respect to time, were obtained for lignin peroxidase, tyrosinase and dichloro phenol in do phenol reductase, during the decolorization of dye mixture (Kabra, *et al.*, 2012).

Microbial bioremediation has been successful, to some extent, in the degradation of certain organic contaminants. However, it is ineffective for toxic metal contaminants. In general, organic molecules can be degraded, but toxic metals can only be remediated by removal from soil (Raskin, *et al.*, 1997). Removal of toxic heavy metals is one of the major targets for phytoremediation (Raskin, *et al.*, 1997; Salt, *et al.*, 1998). Phytoextraction, together with rhizofiltration, are the best-developed subgroups of toxic metal phytoremediation. All plants have an ability to accumulate heavy metals, which are essential for their growth and development (Salt, *et al.*, 1995). These metals include Fe, Mn, Zn, Cu, Mg, Mo, and Ni. On the other hand, certain plants also have the ability to accumulate other heavy metals (e.g. Cd, Cr, Pb, Co, Ag, Se, and Hg), which have no known biological function (Salt, *et al.*, 1995). Inorganics are usually present as charged cations or anions, and thus are hydrophilic (Pilon-Smits, 2005). Some plants are capable of accumulating exceptionally high concentrations of phytotoxic metals, such as Zn, Ni, Cd, Mn, Cu, and Co, in their harvestable biomass (Cunningham and Ow, 1996). For example, a number of the Brassicacae family, *Thlaspi caerulescens*, can accumulate up to 4% zinc in its tissue, without apparent damage (Cunningham, *et al.*, 1995). Another example of Ni hyper-accumulator is *Alyssum bertolonii*, which has been successfully used for phytoremediation in practice (Pilon-Smits, 2005). The ecological role of metal hyper-accumulation is still not clear, but it has been suggested that metal accumulation provides protection against fungal and insect attack (Raskin, *et al.*, 1997; Salt, *et al.*, 1998). Table 10.1 includes some applications of phytoextraction for toxic elemental pollutants. Examples of well-known hyperaccumulators are Pteris vittata and Indian mustard (Brassica juncea), which accumulate arsenic and lead, respectively. Mercury has been removed from soils by transgenic plants expressing a modified bacterial gene. It was reported that Thlaspicaerulescens has a high resistance to the toxic effects of both Zn and Ni in its shoots (Salt, *et al.*, 1995).

Organic pollutants in the environment are mostly manmade, and xenobiotic to the plant. Organic pollutants are released into the environment via spill (fuel, solvents), military activities (explosives, chemical weapons), agriculture (pesticides, herbicides), industry (chemical, petrochemical), wood treatment, etc. (Pilon-Smits, 2005). Unlike inorganic pollutants, organic pollutants can be degraded to stable intermediates, or even mineralized to inorganic compounds (e.g. CO_2, H_2O, and Cl_2) by some plants and their associated enzymes. This process is called phytodegradation. Several plant degradative enzymes (e.g. dehalogenase, peroxidase, nitroreductase, laccase, and nitrilase) have been identified in previous studies (Schnoor, *et al.*, 1995; Morikawa and Erkin 2003). Until now, soil amendments that can induce the uptake and accumulation of organics in plants are mostly not known. Plants can facilitate biodegradation of organic pollutants by microbes in their rhizosphere (root-soil interface). This is called phytostimulation, or rhizodegradation (Pilon-Smits, 2005). Phyto mulation is used for hydrophobic organics (e.g. PCBs, PAHs and other hydrocarbons, log Kow > 3.0) that cannot be taken up by plants, but that can be degraded by microbes. Plants release organic compounds in the rhizosphere, which can serve as carbon sources for bacteria and fungi. Densities of microbes in the rhizosphere can be as much as two to four orders of magnitude greater than populations in the surrounding soils, and these microbes are able to degrade a number of recalcitrant xenobiotics, such as polychlorinated biphenyls (PCBs), and polycyclic aromatic hydrocarbons (PAHs) (Salt, *et al.*, 1998). Organic pollutants removed by phytodegradation include explosives, such as 2,4,6-trinitrotoluene (TNT) (Rylott and Bruce, 2009; French, *et al.*, 1999), and solvents, such as trichloroethylene (TCE). The removal of TNT from contaminated wetlands, and TCE from ground water using poplar trees, has been successfully applied in America. While nitroreductase and laccase break down TNT, dehalogenase helps reduce chlorinated solvents, such as TCE, to chloride ion, carbon dioxide, and water (Schnoor, *et al.*, 1995). Others examples include pesticides (Olette, *et al.*, 2008), as well as herbicides (Dosnon-Olette, *et al.*, 2010). In contrast, phytostimulation works particularly well for some organics. Examples are polychlorinated biphenyls (PCBs) (Ehsan, *et al.*, 2007; Shen, *et al.*, 2009), polycyclic aromatic hydrocarbons (PAHs), such as naphthalene [Peng, *et al.*, 2011; Didier *et al.*, 2012), and petroleum hydrocarbons, such as diesel (Palmroth, *et al.*, 2002; Lin and Mendelssohn, 1998), and ethylene glycol (Teamkao and Thiravetyan, 2010).

Radionuclide contamination represents another major opportunity for phytoremediation (Salt, *et al.*, 1995). Contamination of soil and water by radionuclides occurs due to natural processes, nuclear weapon testing, discharges from nuclear installations, disposal of nuclear waste, and occasional nuclear accidents, such as Chernobyl in 1986, and Fukushima in 2011 (Eapen, *et al.*, 2006). After the Chernobyl nuclear accident in the Ukraine, the so-called Chernobyl sunflower project began in 1994 (Adler, 1996). The sunflower (Helianthus annuus) preferentially absorbed cesium (137Cs) and strontium (90Sr) from a mixture of metals. The plants did not metabolize the radionuclides, but the cesium stayed in the roots, and most of the strontium moved to the shoots. It was reported that Brassica juncea also was able to accumulate 90Sr (Salt, *et al.*, 1995). Similar results were obtained using a giant milky weed (Caltropis gigantean), and the plant was found to be a potential candidate plant for phytoremediation of 137Cs and 90Sr (Eapen, *et al.*, 2006)]. It seems that the same plant-driven approach can also be applied to decontaminating the Fukushima nuclear accident that occurred in Japan. On the other hand, it was found that a common reed (Phragmites australis), grown in uranium-contaminated soils, accumulated uranium (238U) in the roots, and translocated to the shoots, in limited amounts (Cerne, *et al.*, 2011). The plant could be useful for phytoremediation of mine waters in uranium mining areas. In addition, Saleh investigated water hyacinth (Eichhornia crassipes) for phytoremediation of cesium (137Cs) and cobalt (60Co) (Saleh, 2012). Cesium (137Cs) and cobalt (60Co) are known to be dominant radionuclides among fission products, and release of these radionulides may arise from low-level radioactive disposal facilities. Table 10.2 shows various radionuclides, which were removed from radionuclide-contaminated soil and water by using plants, such as birch and sunflower (Helianthus annuus). It appears that rhizofiltration is a practical way to treat radionuclide-contaminated water, and will become an important process for environmental management of large areas contaminated with radionuclides .

Limitations of Phytoremediation

The application of phytoremediation for pollution control has several limitations that require further intensive research on plants and site-specific soil conditions. It is generally slower than most other treatment viz., chemical, physical and microbiological plants with low biomass yields and reduced root systems do not support efficient phytoremediation and most likely do not prevent the leaching of contaminants into aquatic system. Environmental conditions also determine the efficiency of phytoremediation as the survival and growth of plants are adversely affected by extreme environmental conditions, toxicity and the general conditions of soil in contaminated lands. In phytoremediation technology, multiple metals contaminated soil and water requires specific metal hyperaccumulator species and therefore requires a wide range of research prior to the applications. Though the phytoremediation is cost effective environment friendly, ability to reclaim heavy metals contaminated site, several limitations also create trouble in implementing the strategy, e.g., metal must be in bio-available form to plants; if metals is tightly bound to the organic portions of the soil, some time it may not be available to plants. Furthermore, if the metals are water soluble, in nature it will pass by the root system without accumulation.

The phytoremediation of mixed heavy metals contaminated soil have conformant with some problem e.g., The cadmium/zinc model hyperaccumulator *Thlaspi caerulescens* is sensitive toward copper (Cu) toxicity, which is a problem in remediation of Cd/Zn from soils in the presence of Cu by application of this species. In *T. caerulescens* Cu induced inhibition of photosynthesis followed the sun reaction type of damage, with inhibition of the photosystem II reaction center charge separation and the water-splitting complex. Despite some limitations, present day phytoremediation technology are using worldwide and various research laboratories are at present engaged to overcome the limitations.

Table 10.2: Examples of Hyperaccumulators and their Accumulation Characteristics

Plant species	Metal	Results	Reference
Alyssum bertolonii	Ni	10900 (mg kg^{-1})	Li *et al.* (2003)
Alyssum caricum	Ni	12500 (mg kg^{-1})	Li *et al.* (2003)
Alyssum corsicum	Ni	18100 (mg kg^{-1})	Li *et al.* (2003)
Alyssum heldreichii	Ni	11800 (mg kg^{-1})	Bani *et al.* (2010)
Alyssum markgrafii	Ni	19100 (mg kg^{-1})	Bani *et al.* (2010)
Alyssum murale	Ni	4730–2010 (mg kg^{-1})15000 (mg kg^{-1})	Bani *et al.* (2010)Li *et al.* (2003)
Alyssum pterocarpum	Ni	13500 (mg kg^{-1})	Li *et al.* (2003)
Alyssum serpyllifolium	Ni	10000 (mg kg^{-1})	Prasad (2005)
Alyssum sps.	Ni	Majority of Ni is stored either in the leaf epidermal cell vacuoles, or in the basal portions of the numerous stellate trichomes. The metal concentration in the trichome basal compartment was the highest ever reported for healthy vascular plant tissue, approximately 15–20% dry weigh	Broadhurst *et al.* (2004)
Arabis gemmifera	Cd and Zn	Hyperaccumulator of Cd and Zn, with phytoextraction capacities almost equal to *I. caerulescens*	Kubota and Takenaka (2003)
Austromyrtus bidwilli. P. acinosa Roxb	Mn	Australian native hyperaccumulator of Mn, grows rapidly, has substantial biomass, wide distribution and a broad ecological amplitude	Bidwell *et al.* (2002); Xue *et al.* (2004)
H. annuus	Pb	Pb concentrated in the leaf and stem indicating the prerequisites of a hyperaccumulator plant	Boonyapookana *et al.* (2005)
H. indicus	Pb	Heavy metal mainly accumulated in roots and shoots	Chandra Sekhar *et al.* (2005)
Isatis pinnatiloba	Ni	1441 (mg kg^{-1})	Altinozlu *et al.* (2012)
Lemna gibba	As	A preliminary bioindicator for As transfer from substrate to plants. Used for As phytoremediation of mine tailing waters because of its high accumulation capacity	Mkandawire and Dudel, (2005)

P. vittata, P. cretica, P. longifolia and *P. umbrosa*	As	Suitable for phytoremediation in the moderately contaminated soils	Caille *et al.* (2004)
Pistia stratiotes	Ag, Cd, Cr, Cu, Hg, Ni, Pb and Zn	—	Odjegba and Fasidi (2004)
Pteris vittata	AS, Cr	8331 (mg kg^{-1})20675 (mg kg^{-1})	Kalve *et al.*, (2011) Baldwin and Butcher (2007)
Rorippa globosa	Cd	>100 (mg kg^{-1})	Wei *et al.* (2008)
Schima superba	Mn	62412.3 (mg kg^{-1})	Yang *et al.* (2008)
Sedum alfredii Hance	Cd	Mined ecotype had a greater ability to tolerate, transport, and accumulate Cd, compared to non-mined ecotype	Xiong *et al.* (2004)
Sesbania drummondii	Pb	Pb accumulated as lead acetate in roots and leaves. Lead nitrate in the nutrient solution biotransformed to lead acetate and sulfate in its tissues.	Sharma *et al.* (2004)
Solanum nigrum and *C. canadensis*	Cd	High concentration of Cd accumulated. Tolerant to combined action of Cd, Pb, Cu and Zn	Wei *et al.* (2004)
Spartina plants	Hg	Organic Hg was absorbed and transformed into an inorganic form (Hg^{+}, Hg^{2+}) and accumulated in roots	Tian *et al.* (2004)
Stanleya pinnata	Se	Adapted to semi-arid western U. S. soils and environments. Uptake, metabolism and volatilization of Se	Parker *et al.* (2003)
Thlaspi caerulescens	Cd	High Cd-accumulating capability, acquiring Cd from the same soil pools as non-accumulating species	Schwartz *et al.* (2003)
Thlaspi caerulescens	Cd	263 (mg kg^{-1})	Lombi *et al.* (2001)

REFERENCES

Abia AA, Horsfall M, Didi O (2003) The Use of Chemically Modified and Unmodified Cassava Waste for the Removal of Cd, Cu and Zn Ions from Aqueous Solution. Bioresource Technol 90: 345–348.

Adler, T. (1996) Botanical Cleanup Crews: Using Plants to Tackle polluted Water and Soil (Phytoremediation). Sci. News 150: 42-43.

Adriano, D.C., Wenzel, W.W., Vangronsveld, J., & Bolan, N.S. (2004). Role of Assisted Natural Remediationin Environmen-Tal Cleanup. Geoderma, 122, 121–142.

Al-Hiyaly SA, McNeilly T, Bradshaw AD (1988) The Effect of Zinc Concentration from Electricity Pylons-evolution in Replicated Situation. New Phytol 110:571–580.

Altinozlu H, Karagoz a, Polat T, Unver I., (2012). Nickel Hyperaccumulation by Natural Plants in Turkish Serpentine Soils. *Turk J Bot*, 36:269-280.

Angino EE, Magnuson LM, Waugh TC, Galle OK, and Bredfeldt J (1970) Arsenic in Detergents-Possible Danger and Pollution Hazard. Science 168:389–392.

Ansola, G., Gonzalez, J. M., Cortijo, R., Luis, E.d, 2003. Experimenta Land Full Scale Pilot Plant Constructed Wetlands for Municipal Wastewater Treatment. Ecolog-ical Engineering 21,43e52.

Atkinson, R., Aschmann, S.M., Hasegawa, D., Eagle-Thompson, E.T., & Frankenberger, J.R. (1990). Kinetics of the Atmospherically Importantre Actions of Dimethylselenide. Environmental Science and Technology, 24,1326–1332.

Azaizeh, H.A., Gowthaman, S., &Terry, N. (1997). Microbial Selenium Volatilization in Rhizosphere and Bulk Soils from A Constructed Wetland. J. Environ. Qual., 26(3),666–672.

Bachman GR, Miller WB (1995) Iron Chelate Inducible Iron/Manganese Toxicity in Zonal Geranium. J Plant Nutri 18:1917–1929.

Baker AJM, Brooks RR (1989) Terrestrial Higher Plants which Hyperaccumulate Metallic Elements. A Review of their Distribution. Ecol. Phytochem. Biorecov. 1:81-126.

Baker AJM, McGrath SP, Sidoli CMD, Reeves RD (1994) The Possibility of in Situ Heavy Metal Decontamination of Polluted Soils using Crops of Metal-accumulating Plants. Resour Conserv Recyc. 11:41-49.

Baker, A.J.M., & Brooks, R.R. (1989). Terrestrial Higher Plants which Hyperaccumulate Metallic Elements – Review of their Distribution, Ecology and Phytochemistry. Biorecovery,1,81–126.

Bakkaus, E., Gouget, B., Gallien, J.P., Khodja, H., Carrot, H., Morel, J.L., Collins, R., 2005. Concentration and Distribution of Cobalt in Higher Plants: the use of Micro PIXE Spectroscopy. Nuclear Instruments and Methods B231, 350–356.

Bani, A, Pavlova, D, Echevarria, G, Mullaj, A, Reeves, RD., Morel, JL, Sulçe, S (2010). Nickel Hyperaccumulaion by the Species Alyssum and Thlaspi (Brassicaceae) from the Ultramafic Soils of the Balkans. Bot Serbica. 34, 3-14.

Banuelos, G. S., Cardon, G., Mackey, B., Ben-Asher, J., Wu, L P., Beuselinck, P., *et al.*, (1993). Boron and Selenium Removalin B-laden Soils by Four Sprinkler Irrigated Plants Pecies.

Barceloux, D.G., 1999. Cobalt. Journal of Toxicology. Clinical Toxicology 37, 201–206.

Basta NT, Gradwohl R (1998) Remediation of Heavy Metal Contaminated Soil using Rock Phosphate. Better Crops 82(4) : 29–31.

Basta NT, Ryan JA, Chaney RL (2005) Trace Element Chemistry in Residual-treated Soil: Key Concepts and Metal Bioavailability. J Environ Qual 34(1) : 49–63.

Battarbee R, Anderson N, Appleby P, Flower RJ, Fritz S, Haworth E, Higgit S, Jones V, Kreiser A, Munro MA, Natkanski J, Oldfield F, Patrick ST, Richardson N, Rippey B, Stevenson AC (1988) Lake Acidification in The United Kingdom, ENSIS, London.

Berti WR, Cunningham SD (2000) Phytostabilization of Metals. In Raskin I, Ensley BD (eds) Phytoremediation of Toxic Metals-using Plants to Clean-up the Environment. John Wiley & Sons, Inc., New York. pp. 71-88.

Biddle Stone, A. J., Gray, K. R., Job, G.D., 1991. Treatment of Dairy Farm Waste Waters in Bidwell SD, Woodrow, IE., Batianoff, GN, Sommer-Knudsen, J (2002). Hyperaccumulation of Manganese in the Rainforest Tree Austromyrtus Bidwillii (Myrtaceae) from Queensland, Australia. Functional Plant Biology, 29, 899–905.

Bjuhr, J. (2007) Trace Metals in Soils Irrigated with Waste Water in a Periurban Area Downstream Hanoi City, Vietnam, Seminar Paper, Institution en för mark Vetenskap, Sveriges Lantbruks Universitet (SLU), *Uppsala*, Sweden.

Blaylock, M. J., & Huang, J. W. (2000). Phytoextraction of Metals. InI. Raskin & B.D. Ensley (Eds.), Phytoreme-diationo Toxic Metals: Using Plants to Clean-up the Environment (pp.53–70). New York: Wiley.

Blaylock, M. J., D. E. Salt, S. Dushenkov, O. Zakharova, C.Gussman, Y. Kapulnik, B. D. Ensley, and I. Raskin (1997) Enhanced Accumulation of Pb in Indian Mustard by Soil-Applied Chelating Agents. Environ. Sci. Technol. 31: 860-865.

Blaylock, M.J., Salt, D.E., Dushenkov, S., Zakharova, O., Gussman, C., Kapulnik, Y., *et al.*, (1997). Enhanced Accumulation Pb in Indian Mustard by Soil-applied Chelating Agents. Environ. Sci. Technol., 31(3),860–865.

Bodini, S. F., A. R. Cicalini, and F. Santori (2011) Rhizospheredynamics During Phytoremediation of Olive Mill Wastewater. Bioresour. Technol. 102: 4383-4389.

Bolan NS, Adriano DC, Naidu R (2003) Role of Phosphorus in (im) Mobilization and Bioavailability of Heavy Metals in the Soil-plant System. Rev Environ Contam Toxicol 177 : 1–44.

Bolter E, Wixson BG, Butherus DL, Jennett JC (1974) Distribution of Heavy Metals in Soils Near an Active Lead Smelter. In: Fed Kenheuer PJ (ed) Issue Confronting Min. Ind. Ann. Meet. Sect. Aime 47th. Department of Cond. Cont. Ext. University of Minneapolis. Minneapolis, 73.

Boonyapookana, B, Parkplan, P, Techapinyawat, S, DeLaune, RD, Jugsujinda, A. (2005). Phytoaccumulation of Lead by Sunflower (Helianthus annuus), Tobacco (Nicotiana tabacum), and Vetiver (Vetiveria zizanioides). Journal of Environmental Science and Health A, 40, 117-137.

Boularbah A, Schwartz C, Bitton G, Aboudrar W, Ouhammou A, Morel JL (2006) Heavy Metal Contamination from Mining Sites in South Morocco: 2. Assessment of Metal Accumulation and Toxicity in Plants. Chemosphere 63(5) : 811–817.

Broadhurst, CL, Chaney, RL, Angle, JS, Maugel, TK., Erbe, EF, Murphy, CA (2004). Simultaneous Hyperaccumulation of Nickel, Manganese and Calcium in Alyssum Leaf Trichomes. Environmental Science & Tech- nology, 38, 5797–5802.

Brooks, R.R. (ed) (1998). Plants that Hyperaccumulate Heavymetals (p.384). Walling Ford: CAB International.

Caille, N, Swanwick, S., Zhao, F J, McGrath, S P (2004). Arsenic Hyperaccumulation by Pteris Vittata from Arsenic Contaminated Soils and the Effect of Liming and Phosphate Fertilisation. Environmental Pollution, 132, 113-120.

Cannon HL, Connally GG, Epstein JB, Parker JG, Thornton I, Wixson G (1978) Rocks: Geological Sources of Most Trace Elements. In: Report to the Workshop at South Scas Plantation Captiva Island, FL, US. Geochem Environ 3 : 17–31.

Cargnelutti D, Tabaldi LA, Spanevello RM, Jucoski GO, Battisti V, Redin M, Linares CEB, Dressler VL, Flores MM, Nicoloso FT, Morsch VM, Schetinger MRC (2006) Mercury Toxicity Induces Oxidative Stress in Growing Cucumber Seedlings. Chemosphere 65 : 999–1006.

Cerne, M., B. Smodiš, and M. Štrok (2011) Uptake of Radionu-clides by a Common Reed (Phragmites australia (Cav.) Trin. exSteud.) Grown in the Vicinity of the Former Uranium Mine at Žirovski vrh. Nucl. Eng. Des. 241: 1282-1286.

Chandra Sekhar, K, Kamala, CT, Chary, N S, Balaram, V, Garcia, G (2005). Potential of Hemidesmus Indicus for Phytoextraction of Lead from Industrially Contaminated Soils. Chemosphere, 58, 507–514.

Chaney RL, Oliver DP (1996) Sources, Potential Adverse Effects and Remediation of Agricultural Soil Contaminants. In: Naidu R (eds) Contaminants and the Soil Environments in the Australia-Pacific Region. Kluwer Academic Publishers, Dordrecht, The Netherlands. pp. 323–359.

Chatterjee J, Chatterjee C (2000) Phytotoxicity of Cobalt, Chromium and Copper in Cauliûower. Environ Pollut 109 : 69–74.

Choi JM, Pak CH, Lee CW (1996) Micronutrient Toxicity in French Marigold. J Plant Nutri 19 : 901–916.

Clemente R, Almela C, Bernal PM (2006) A Remediation Strategy Based on Active Phytoremediation Followed by Natural Attenuation in a Soil Contaminated by Pyrite Waste. Environ Pollut 143(3) : 397–406.

Clemente R, Walker JD, Roig A, Bernal PM (2003) Heavy Metal Bioavailability in a Soil Affected by Mineral Sulphides Contamination Following the Mine Spillage at Aznalc′ollar (Spain). Biodegradation 14: 199–205.

Conesa MH, Faz A, Arnaldos R (2006) Initial Studies for the Phytostabilization of a Mine Tailing from the Cartagena–La Union Mining District (SE Spain). Chemosphere 66(1) : 38–44.

Conesa, M.H., Faz, A., & Arnaldos, R. (2006). Initial Studies for the Phytostabilization of Amine Tailing from the Cartagena–La Union Mining District(SESpain). Chemosphere, 66(1), 38–44.

Crawford TW, Stroehlein JL, Kuehl RO (1989) Manganese and Rates of Growth and Mineral Accumulation in Cucumber. J Am Soc Horti Sci 114 : 300–306.

Cunningham SD, Anderson TA, Schwab PA, Hsu FC (1996). Phytoremediation of Soils Contaminated with Organic Pollutants. Adv Agron 56: 55-114.

Cunningham SD, Berti WR, Huang JW (1995) Phytoremediation of Contaminated Soils. Trends Biotechnol 13 : 393-397.

Cunningham SD, Ow DW (1996) Promises and Prospects of Phytoremediation. Plant Physiol 110(3) : 715-719.

Cunningham SD, Shann JR, Crowley DE, Anderson TA (1997) Phytoremediation of Contaminated Water and Soil. In : E.L. Kruger, T., A. Anderson and J., R. Coats (eds) Phytoremediation of Soil and Water Contaminants. ACS Symposium Series 664. American Chemical Society, Washington DC. pp. 2-19.

Cunningham, S.D., & Ow, D.W. (1996). Promises and Prospect so Phytoremediation. Plant Physiology, 110(3),715–719.

Davidson CI, Santhanam S, Fortmann RC, Olson MP (1985) Atmospheric Transport and Deposition of Trace Elements onto the Greenland Ice Sheet. Atmos Environ 19 : 2065–2082.

Davis TA, Volesky B, Vieira RHSF (2000) Sargassum Seaweed as Biosorbent for Heavy Metals. Water Research 34 : 4270–4278.

Demirevska-kepova K, Simova-Stoilova L, Stoyanova Z, Holzer R, Feller U (2004) Biochemical Changes in Barely Plants After Excessive Supply of Copper and Manganese. Environ Exp Bot 52 : 253–266.

Desouza, M.P., Pilon-Smits, E.A.H., & Terry, N. (2000). The Physiology and Biochemistry of Selenium Volatilization by Plants. InI. Raskin, & B.D. Ensley (Eds.), Phytoremediation of Toxicmetals: Using Plants to Clean-up Theenvironment (pp.171–190). New York: Wiley.

DeVolder PS, Brown SL, Hesterberg D, Pandya K (2003) Metal Bioavailability and Speciation in a Wetland Tailings Repository Amended with Bio Solids Compost, Wood Ash and Sulfate. J Environ Qual 32(3) : 851–864.

Devries W, Lofts S, Tipping E, Meili M, Groenenberg JE, Schutze G (2002) Impact of Soil Properties on Critical Concentrations of Cadmium, Lead, Copper, Zinc and Mercury in Soil and Soil Solution in view of Eco Toxicological Effects. Rev Environ Contam Toxicol 191: 47–89.

Didier, P., L. G. Philippe, H. Sonia, B. Amar, M. C. Claudia, D.Marielle, and F. Jairo (2012) Prospects of Miscanthus x Giganteusfor PAH Phytoremediation: A Microcosm Study. Ind. Crop. Prod.36: 276-281.

Dierberg, F.E., Débuts, T.A., & Goulet,J.R.N.A. (1987). Removal of Copper and Lead using at hin-ilmtechnique. In K.R. Reddy & W.H. Smith(Eds.), Aquatic Plants for Water Treatment and Resourcere Covery Magnolia, 497–504.

Dixit V, Pandey V, Shyam R (2002) Chromium Ions Inactivate Electron Transport and Enhance Superoxide Generation in vivo in pea (*Pisum sativum* L.cv. Azad) Root Mitochondria. Plant Cell Environ 25 : 687–693.

Dosnon-Olette, R., P. Trotel-Aziz, M. Couderchet and P. Eullaf-froy (2010) Fungicides and Herbicide Removal in Scenedesmuscell Suspension. Chemosphere 79: 117-123.

Dushenkov S, Kapulnik Y (2000) Phytofilitration of Metals. In : Raskin I, Ensley BD (eds) Phytoremediation of Toxic Metals: Using Plants to Clean- up the Environment. Wiley, New York. 89–106.

Dushenkov S, Vasudev D, Kapulnik Y, Gleba D, Fleisher D, Ting KC (1997a) Removal of Uranium from Water using Terrestrial Plants. Environ Sci Technol 31(12) : 3468–3474.

Dushenkov S, Vasudev D, Kapulnik Y, Gleba D, Fleisher D, Ting KC (1997b) Phytoremediation: A Novel Approach to an Old Problem. In : D. L. Wise (eds), Global Environmental Biotechnology, Elsevier, Amsterdam. 563–572.

Dushenkov V, Kumar PBAN, Motto H, Raskin I (1995) Rhizofiltration: The Use of Plants to Remove Heavy Metals from Aqueous Streams. Environ. Sci. Technol., 29 : 1239–1245.

Eapen, S., S. Singh, V. Thorat, C. P. Kaushik, K. Raj and S. F.D'Souza (2006) Phytoremediation of Radiostrontium (90Sr) Andradiocesium (137Cs) using Giant Milky Weed (Calotropis gigantean R.Br.) Plants. Chemosphere 65: 2071-2073.

Ebbs SD, Kochian LV (1997) Toxicity of Zinc and Copper to Brassica Species: Implications for Phytoremediation. J Environ Qua. 26 : 776–781.

Ebbs, S. D., Lasat, M. M., Brandy, D. J., Cornish, J., Gordon, R., & Kochian, L.V.(1997). Heavy Metals in the Environment: Phytoextraction of Cadmium and Zinc from a Contaminated soil. Journal of Environmental Quality, 26, 1424–1430.

Ehsan, S., S. O. Prasher and W. D. Marshall (2007) Simulta-neous Mobilization of Heavy Metals and Polychlorinated Biphenyl (PCB) Compounds from Soil with Cyclodextrin and EDTA in Admixture. Chemosphere 68: 150-158.

Elamin OM, Wilcox GE (1986a) Effect of Magnesium and Manganese Nutrition on Muskmelon Growth and Manganese Toxicity. J Am Soc Horti Sc. 111 : 582–587.

Elamin OM, Wilcox GE (1986b) Effect of Magnesium and Manganese Nutrition on Watermelon Growth and Manganese Toxicity. J Am Soc Horti Sci 111 : 588–593.

Elless PM, Poynton YC, Williams AC, Doyle PM, Lopez CA, Sokkary AD (2005) Pilot-scale Demonstration of Phytofiltration for Drinking Arsenic in New Mexico Drinking Water. Water Research 39(16) : 3863–3872.

Engineered Reed Bed Systems. Process Biochemistry 26,265 e268.

Ensley BD (2000) Rational for Use of Phytoremediation. In: Raskin I, Ensley BD (eds) Phytoremediation of Toxic Metals: Using Plants to Clean-up the Environment. John Wiley & Sons Inc, New York. pp. 3-12.

Ensley, B., D. (2000). Rationale for Use of Phytoremediation. In : Raskin I, Ensley BD (eds) Phytoremediation of Toxic Metals: Using Plants to Clean-up the Environment. Wiley, New York. pp. 3–12.

Eshleman A, Siegel SM, Siegel BZ (1971) Is Mercury from Hawaiian Volcanoes a Natural Source of Pollution? Nature 223 : 471–475.

Evans CS, Asher C, Johnson CM (1968) Isolation of Dimethyl Diselenide and Other Volatile Selenium Compounds from *Astragalus racemosus* (Pursh.) Aust. J Biol Sci 21 : 13–20.

Flathman PE, Lanza GR (1998) Phytoremediation: Current Views on an Emerging Green Technology. J Soil Contam 7(4) : 415–432.

Fontes RLS, Cox FR (1998) Zinc Toxicity in Soybean Grown at High Iron Concentration in Nutrient Solution. J Plant Nutri 21 : 1723–1730.

Foy CD, Weil RR, Coradetti CA (1995) Differential Manganese Tolerances of Cotton Genotypes in Nutrient Solution. J Plant Nutri 18 : 685–706.

French, C. E., S. J. Rosser, G. J. Davies, S. Nicklin, and N. C.Bruce (1999) Biodegradation of Explosives by Transgenic Plants Expressing Pentaerythritol Tetranitrate Reductase. Nat. Biotechnol.17: 491-494.

Frérot H, Lefèbvre C, Gruber W, Collin C, Dos Santos A, Escarre J (2006) Specific Interactions between Local Metallicolous Plants Improve the Phytostabilization of Mine Soils. Plant Soil 282 : 53–65.

Gajewska E, Sklodowska M, Slaba M, Mazur J (2006) Effect of Nickel on Antioxidative Enzyme Activities, Proline and Chlorophyll Contents in Wheat Shoots. Biologia Plantarum 50 : 653–659.

Garbarino JR, Hayes H, Roth D, Antweider R, Brinton TI, Taylor H (1995) Contaminants in the Mississippi River. U. S. Geological Survey Circular, 1133, Virginia, USA.

Gardea-Torresdey JL, de la Rosa G, Peralta-Videa JR (2004) Use of Phytofiltration Technologies in the Removal of Heavy Metals: A Review. Pure Applied Chem 76(4) : 801–813.

Ghosh M, Singh SP (2005) A Comparative Study of Cadmium Phytoextraction by Accumulator and Weed Species. Environ Pollut 133 : 365-371.

Gimeno-Garcia E, Andreu V, Boluda R (1996) Heavy Metals Incidence in the Application of Inorganic Fertilizers and Pesticides to Rice Farming Soils. Environ Pollut 92 : 19–25.

Gleba D, Borisjuk NV, Borisjuk LG, Kneer R, Poulev A, Skarzhinskaya M, Dushenkov S, Logendra S, Gleba YY, Raskin I (1999) Use of Plant Root for Phytoremediation and Molecular Farming. Proc Natl Acad Sci USA. 96, 5973-5977.

Gonnelli C, Galardi F, Gabbrielli R (2001) Nickel and Copper Tolerance in Three Tuscan Populations of Silene Paradoxa. Physiologia Plantarum 113: 507–514.

Habashi F (1992) Environmental Issues in the Metallurgical Industry – Progress and Problems, Environmental Issues and Waste Management in Energy and Mineral Production. Balkam Rotherdam 1143-1153.

Han FX, Su Y, Monts DL, Waggoner AC, Plodinec, J M (2006) Binding, Distribution and Plant Uptake of Mercury in a Soil from Oak Ridge, Tennessee, USA. Sci Total Environ 368: 753–768.

Hawkes J S (1997) Heavy Metals. J Chem Edu 74(11): 1374.

Heaton, A.C.P., Rugh, C.L., Wang, N., & Meagher, R.B. (1998). Phytoremediation of Mercury- and Methylmercury-Polluted Soils using Genetically Engineered Plants. Journal of Soil Contamination,74,497–510.

Hegedus, A., Erdei, S. and Horvath, G. (2001). Comparative Studies of H_2O_2 Detoxifying Enzymes in Green and Greening Barley Seedlings under Cadmium Stress. *Plant Science,* 160, 1085–1093.

Herawati N, Suzuki S, Hayashi K, Rivai IF, Koyoma H (2000) Cadmium, Copper and Zinc Levels in Rice and Soil of Japan, Indonesia and China by Soil Type. Bull Environ Contam Toxicol 64 : 33 39.

Horsfall M, Abia AA (2003) Sorption of Cadmium (II) and Zinc (II) Ions from Aqueous Solutions by Cassava Waste Biomass (Manihot Sculenta Cranz). Water Research 37: 4913–4923.

Huang, J.W., Chen, J., Berti, W.R., & Cunningham, S.D. (1997). Phytoremediation of Lead Contaminated Soil: Role of Synthetic Chelate Sin Lead Phytoextraction. Environ. Sci. Technol., 31(3),800–805.

Hurst FJ (1989) The Recovery of Uranium from Phosphoric Acid, IAEA, Vienna IAEATECDOC: 553.

Hutton M, Symon C (1986) The Quantities of Cadmium, Lead, Mercury and Arsenic Entering the U.K. Environment from Human Activities. Sci Total Environ 57: 129-150.

Igweet J C, Nnorom IC, Gbaruko BCG (2005) Kinetics of Radionuclides and Heavy Metals Behaviour in Soils: Implications for Plant Growth. African J Biotechnol 4: 1541-1547.

Interstate Technology and Regulatory Cooperation - Phytotechnologies Technical and Regulatory Document and the Phytotechnologies Decision Tree. Retrieved from http://www.itrcweb.org

Israr M, Sahi S (2006) Antioxidative Responses to Mercury in the Cell Cultures of *Sesbania drummondii.* Plant Physiol Biochem 44: 590–595.

Israr M, Sahi S, Datta R, Sarkar D (2006). Bioaccumulation and Physiological Effects of Mercury in Sesbania Drummondii. Chemosphere 65: 591–598.

Izosimova A (2005) Modelling the Interaction between Calcium and Nickel in the Soil-plant System. FAL Agric Res 288:99.

Jamal Q , Palwasha D, Kamran K, Shahzad M, Saadat Hu, Kiran, Munir, Anees M (2013) Heavy Metals Accumulation and their Toxic Effects: Review. Journal of Bio-Molecular Sciences (JBMS). 1(1-2): 27-36.

Jones LHP, Jarvis SC (1981) The Fate of Heavy Metals. in : Green DJ, Hayes MHB (eds.) The Chemistry of Soil Processes, John Wiley & Sons, New York, NY, USA, 593.

Journal of Environmental Quality, 22(4), 786–797.

Kabra, A. N., R. V. Khandare, T. R. Waghmode and S. P. Govin-dwar (2012) Phytoremediation of Textile Effluent and Mixture of Structurally Different Dyes by Glandularia Pulchella (Sweet) tronc. Chemosphere 87: 265-272.

Kamal M, Ghaly AE, Mahmoud N, Cote R (2004) Phytoaccumulation of Heavy Metals by Aquatic Plants. Environ Inter 29: 1029–1039.

Kay SH, Haller WT, Garrard LA (1984) Effect of Heavy Metals on Water Hyacinths [Eichhornia Crassipes (Mart.) Solms]. Aquatic Toxicology 5: 117–128.

Keller C, McGrath SP, Dunham SJ (2002) Trace Metal Leaching Through a Soil Grassland System After Sewage Sludge Application. J Environ Qual 31(5):1550–1560.

Khair, M. H. (2009) Toxicity and Accumulation of Copper in Nanno Chloro Psisoculata (Eustigmatophycea, Heterokont). *World Applied Sciences Journal,* 6, 378–384.

Kitao M, Lei TT, Koike T (1997a) Effects of Manganese Toxicity on Photosynthesis of White Birch (Betula Platyphylla var. Japonica) Seedlings. Physiol Planta 101: 249–256.

Kitao M, Lei TT, Koike T (1997b) Effects of Manganese in Solution Culture on the Growth of ûve Deciduous Broad-leaved Tree Species with Different Successional Characters from Northern Japan. Photosyn 36 : 31–40.

Koch I, Wang L, Ollson CA, Cullen WR, Reimer KJ (2000) The Predominance of Inorganic Arsenic Species in Plants from Yellowknife, Northwest Territories, Canada. Environ Sci Technol 34: 22–26.

Kraal H, Ernst W (1976) Inûuence of Copper High Tension Lines on Plants and Soil. Environ Pollut 11: 131–135.

Kubota, H, Takenaka, C. (2003). Arabis Gemmifera is a Hyperaccumulator of Cd and Zn. International Journal of Phytoremediation, 5, 197–120.

Kukier U, Peters CA, Chaney RL, Angle JS, Roseberg RJ (2004) The Effect of pH on Metal Accumulation in Two Alyssum Species. J Environ Qual 33 : 2090–2102.

Kumar, P.B.A.N., Dushenkov, V., Motto, H., & Raskin, I. (1995). Phytoextraction: The Use of Plant Store Move Heavy Metals from Soils. Environ. Sci. Technol., 29(5),1232–1238.

Kuo S, Jellum EJ, Baker AS (1985) Effects of Soil Type, Liming and Sludge Application on Zinc and Cadmium Availability to Swiss Chard. Soil Sci 139: 122–130.

Kyambadde, J., F. Kansiimme, L. Gumaelius and G. Dalhammar. (2004) A Comparative Study of Cyperus Papyrus and Miscant-hidium Violaceum-based Constructed Wetlands for Wastewater Treatment in a Tropical Climate. Water Res. 38: 475-485.

Lasat, M.M., Fuhrmann, M., Ebbs, S.D., Cornish, J.E., & Kochian, L.V. (1998). Phytoremediation of Aradiocesium Contaminated Soil: Evaluation of Cesium-137 Bioaccumulation in the Shoots of Three Plant Species. Journal of Environmental Quality, 27(1),165–168.

LeBot J, Kirkby EA, Beusichem ML (1990) Manganese Toxicity in Tomato Plants: Effects on Cation Uptake and Distribution. J Plant Nutri 13: 513–525.

Lenntech Water Treatment and Air Purification (2004) Water Treatment, Published by *Lenntech, Rotter dam seweg*, Netherlands.

Lewis S, Donkin ME, Depledge MH (2001) Hsp70 Expression in *Enteromorpha Intestinalis* (Chlorophyta) Exposed to Environmental Stressors. Aqu Toxicol 51: 277–291.

Lewis, B.G., Johnson, C.M., & Delwiche, C.C. (1966). Release of Volatile Selenium Compounds by Plants: Collection Procedure Sand Preliminary Observations. Journal of Agriculturaland Food Chemistry, 14, 638–640.

Li HF, Gray C, Mico C, Zhao FJ, McGrath S P (2009) Phytotoxicity and Bioavailability of Cobalt to Plants in a Range of Soils. Chemosphere 75: 979–986.

Li Z, McLaren RG, Metherell AK (2004) The Availability of Native and Applied Soil Cobalt to Ryegrass in Relation to Soil Cobalt and Manganese Status and Other Soil Properties. NZ J Agri Res 47 : 33–43.

Li, Y M., Chaney, R, Brewer, E, Roseberg, R, Angle, J S, Baker, A, Reeves, R, Nelkin, J.: Development of a Technology for Commercial Phytoextraction of Nickel: Economic and Technical Considerations, Plant Soil, 249, 107–115, 2003.

Lin, Q. and I. A. Mendelssohn (1998) The Combined Effects of Phytoremediation and Biostimulation in Enhancing Habitat Restoration and Oil Degradation of Petroleum Contaminated Wetlands. Ecol. Eng. 10: 263-274.

Lombi E, Zhao FJ, Dunham SJ, McGrath SP (2001b) Cadmium Accumulation in Populations of *Thlaspi caerulescens* and *Thlaspi geosingense*. New Phytol 145: 11–20.

Lombi, E, Zhao, F J, Dunham, S J, MacGrath, S P (2001a). Phytoremediation of Heavy Metal-contaminated Soils: Natural Hyperaccumulation versus Chemically Enhanced Phytoextraction. Journal of Environmental Quality, 30, 1919–1926.

Lombi, E., Zhao, F. J., Dunham, S.J., & Mac Grath, S.P. (2001a). Phytoremediation of Heavy Metal-contaminated Soils: Natural Hyperaccumulation versus Chemically Enhanced Phytoextraction. Journalof Environmental Quality, 30,1919–1926.

Lone MIHE, Zhen-li, Peter JS, Yang X (2008) Phytoremediation of Heavy Metal Polluted Soils and Water : Progresses and Perspectives. J Zhejiang Univ Sci B 9(3): 210-220.

Luo CL, Shen ZG, Li XD, Baker AJM (2006) Enhanced Phytoextraction of Pb and Other Metals Fromartificially Contaminated Soils Through the Combined Application of EDTA and EDDS. Chemosphere 63(10): 1773–1784.

Luo, C.L., Shen, Z.G., Li, X.D., & Baker, A.J.M.(2006). Enhanced Phytoextraction of Pb and Other Metals from Artificially Contaminated Soils Through the Combined Application of EDTA and EDDS. Chemosphere, 63(10),1773–1784.

Mains D, Craw D, Rufaut CG, Smith CMS (2006b) Phytostabilization of Gold Mine Tailings from New Zealand. Part 2: Experimental Evaluation of Arsenic Mobilization During Revegetation. Intern J Phyto 8(2) : 163–183.

Marschner H (1986) Mineral Nutrition of Higher Plants. Academic Press, London, 674.

Martin, S. and Griswold, W. (2009) Human Health Effects of Heavy Metals, *Environmental Science and Technology Briefs for Citizens*, 15, 1-6.

Mattigod SV, Page AL (1983) Assessment of Metal Pollution in Soil. Appl Environ Geochem. Academic Press, London, UK. pp. 355–394.

Maurya PK, Zaidi J, Pal Amit (2012) Physico-chemical Properties of Barua Sagar Lake, Jhansi Uttar Pradesh India. Elixir-Pollution l (42) : 6355-6359.

Mc Grath, S.P.(1998). Phytoextraction for Soil Remediation. In R. R. Brooks (Ed.), Plants that Hyperaccumulate Heavy Metals: Their Role in Phytoremediation, Microbiology, Archaeology, Mineral Exploration and Phytomining (pp. 261–288). New York: CAB International.

McLaren RG, Clucas LM, Taylor MD (2005) Leaching of Macronutrients and Metals from Undisturbed Soils Treated with Metal Spiked Sewage Sludge. 3. Distribution of Residual Metals. Aust J Soil Res 43(2) : 159–170.

McLaren RG, Clucas LM, Taylor MD, Hendry T (2004) Leaching of Macronutrients and Metals from Undisturbed Soils Treated with Metal Spiked Sewage Sludge. 2. Leaching of Metals. Aust J Soil Res 42(4) : 459–471.

McLaughlin MJ, Hamon RE, McLaren RG, Speir TW, Rogers SL (2000) Review: A Bioavailability Based Rationale for Controlling Metal and Metalloid Contamination of Agricultural Land in Australia and New Zealand. Aust J Soil Res 38(6) : 1037–1086.

Meharg AA (1994) Integrated Tolerance Mechanisms-constitutive and Adaptive Plant-Response to Elevated Metal Concentrations in the Environment. Plant Cell Environ 17 : 989–993.

Meharg AA, Macnair MR (1992) Suppression of the High Afûnity Phosphate Uptake System; a Mechanism of Arsenate Tolerance in *Holcus lanatus* L. J Exp Bot 43:519–524.

Messer RL, Lockwood PE, Tseng WY, Edwards K, Shaw M, Caughman GB, Lewis MP, Rana NK, Yadav SK (2007) Cadmium Induced Oxidative Stress Influence on Glutathione Metabolic Genes of *Camellia sinensis* (L.) O. Kuntze. Environ Toxicol 22 : 368–374.

Messer, R.L., Lockwood, P.E., Tseng, W.Y., Edwards, K., Shaw, M., Caughman, G.B., Lewis, J.B., Wataha, J.C., 2005. Mercury(II)alters Mitochondrial Activity of Monocytes at Sublethaldosesvia Oxidatives Tress Mechanisms. Journal of Biomedical Materials Research B75,257–263.

Mkandawire, M , Dudel, EG (2005). Accumulation of Arsenic in Lemna Gibba L. (duckweed) in Tailing Waters of Two Abandoned Uranium Mining Sites in Saxony, Germany. Science of the Total Environment, 336, 81-89.

Mo, S.C., Choi, D.S., & Robinson, J.W.(1989). Uptake of Mercury from Aqueous Solution by Duckweed: The Effect of pH, Copper, Andhumic Acid. Journal of Environmental Health, 24, 135–146.

Mohanpuria, P., Rana, N.K., Yadav, S.K., 2007. Cadmium Induce Doxidative Stress Influence on Glutathione Metabolicgenes of Camelliasinensis (L.) O. Kuntze. Environmental Toxicology 22, 368–374.

Morikawa, H. and Ö. C. Erkin (2003) Basic Processes in Phy-toremediation and Some Applications to Air Pollution Control. Chemosphere 52: 1553-1558.

Nriagu JO (1988) A Silent Epidemic of Environmental Metal Poisoning? Environ Pollut 50:139–161.

Nriagu JO (1989) A Global Assessment of Natural Sources of Atmospheric Trace Metals. Nature 338 : 47–49.

Nriagu JO, Pacyna J (1988) Quantitative Assessment of Worldwide Contamination of Air, Water and Soil by Trace Metals. Nature 333 : 134-139.

Nriagu, J.O., 1990. Human Influence on the Global Cycling of Trace Metals. Global and Planetary Change 2, 113–120

Odjegba, VJ , Fasidi, IO. (2004). Accumulation of Trace Elements by Pistia Stratiotes: Implications for Phytoremediation. Ecotoxicology, 13, 637–646.

Olette, R., M. Couderchet, S. Biagianti, and P. Eullaffroy (2008). Toxicity and Removal of Pesticides by Selected Aquatic Plants. Chemosphere 70: 1414-1421.

Olette, R., M. Couderchet, S. Biagianti and P. Eullaffroy (2008) Toxicity and Removal of Pesticides by Selected Aquatic Plants. Chemosphere 70: 1414-1421.

Pacyna JM (1986) Atmospheric Trace Elements from Natural and Anthropogenic Sources. In: Nriagu JO, Davidson CI (eds) Toxic Metals in the Atmosphere, Chap 2. Wiley, New York.

Palmroth, M. R. T., J. Pichtel and J. A. Puhakka (2002) Phytore-mediation of Subarctic Soil Contaminated with Diesel Fuel. Biore-sour. Technol. 84: 221-228.

Pandey N, Sharma CP (2002) Effect of Heavy Metals Co, Ni, and Cd on Growth and Metabolism of Cabbage. Plant Sci 163 : 753–758.

Pandolfini T, Gabbrielli R, Comparini C (1992) Nickel Toxicity and Peroxidase Activity in Seedlings of *Triticum aestivum* L. Plant Cell Environ, 15 : 719–725.

Parker, DR, Feist, LJ, Varvel, TW, Thomason, DN, Zhang, YQ (2003). Selenium Phytoremediation Potential of Stanleya Pinnata. Plant Soil, 249, 157–165.

Passariello B, Giuliano V, Quaresima S, Barbaro M, Caroli S, Forte G, Garelli G, Iavicoli I (2002) Evaluation of the Environmental Contamination at an Abandoned Mining Site. Microchem J 73 : 245–250.

Peng, R. H., R. R. Xu, X. Y. Fu, A. S. Xiong, W. Zhao, Y. S. Tian, B. Zhu, X. F. Jin, C. Chen, H. J. Han, and Q. H. Yao (2011) Microarray Analysis of the Phytoremediation and Phytosensing of Occupational Toxicant Naphthalene. J. Hazard. Mater. 189: 19-26.

Peplow D (1999) Environmental Impacts of Mining in Eastern Washington, Center for Water and Watershed Studies Fact Sheet, University of Washington, Seattle.

Phillips DJH (1990) Arsenic in Aquatic Organisms: A Review of Emphasizing Chemical Speciation. Aqua Toxicol 16:151–186.

Pilon-Smits EAH (2005) Phytoremediation. An Rev Plant Biol 56 : 15–39.

Pilon-Smits, E. A. H., Desouza, M. P., Hong, G., Amini, A., Bravo, R.C., Payabyab, S.T., *et al.*, (1999). Selenium Volatilization and Accumulation by Twenty Aquatic Plant Species. J. Environ. Qual., 28(3),1011–1017.

Porter EK, Peterson PJ (1975) Arsenic Accumulation by Plants on Mine Wastes (United Kingdom). Environ Pollut 4 : 365–371.

Porter JR, Cheridan RP (1981) Inhibition of Nitrogen ûxation in Alfalfa by Arsenate, Heavy Metals, ûuoride and Simulated Acid Rain. Plant Physiol 68 : 143–148.

Prasad, MNV and Freitas, H (2003). Metal Hyperaccumulation in Plants – Biodiversity Prospecting for Phytoremediation Technology. Electronic Journal of Biotechnology, 6, 275–321.

Rahman H, Sabreen S, Alam S, Kawai S (2005) Effects of Nickel on Growth and Composition of Metal Micronutrients in Barley Plants Grown in Nutrient Solution. J Plant Nutri 28 : 393–404.

Raskin I, Kumar PBAN, Dushenkov S, Salt D (1994) Bioconcentration of Heavy Metals by Plants. Curr Opin Biotechnol 5 : 285-290.

Raskin I, Smith RD, Salt D (1997) Phytoremediation of Metals: Using Plants to Remove Pollutants from the Environment. Curr Opin Biotechnol 8 : 221–26.

Raven PH, Berg LR, Johnson GB (1998) Environment. Saunders College Publishing, New York, NY, USA, 2nd edition.

Reddy AM, Kumar SG, Jyotsnakumari G, Thimmanayak S, Sudhakar C (2005) Lead Induced Changes in Antioxidant Metabolism of Horsegram (*Macrotyloma uniûorum* (Lam.) Verdc.) and Bengal-gram (*Cicer arietinum* L.). Chemosphere 60:97–104.

Reed S C, Crites RW and Middle Brooks EJ (1995) Nat, 2nd Editorial Systems for Waste Management and Treatment, *McGraw-Hill, New York, NY, USAion.*

Reeves RD, Baker AJM (2000) Metal-accumulating Plants. In: Raskin I, Ensley BD (eds) Phytoremediation of Toxic Metals: Using Plants to Clean up the Environment. Wiley, New York, pp 193–229.

Ros R, Cooke DT, Martínez-Cortina C, Picazo I (1992) Nickel and Cadmium-related Changes in Growth, Plasma Membrane Lipid Composition, ATPase Hydrolytic Activity and Proton Pumping of Rice (*Oryza sativa* L. cv. Bahia) Shoots. J Exp Bot 43 : 1475–1481.

Ross SM (1994) Toxic Metals in Soil–plant Systems. Wiley, *Chichester*, 469.

Rylott, E. L. and N. C. Bruce (2009) Plants Disarm Soil: Engineering Plants for Phytoremediation of Explosives. Trends Bio-technol. 29: 73-81.

Salt DE, Blaylock M, Kumar PBAN, Dushenkov V, Ensley BD, Chet L. (1995) Phyto-remediation: A Novel Strategy for the Rremoval of Toxic Metals from the Environment using Plants. Biogeochem 13 : 468–474.

Salt DE, Rauser WE (1995) MgATP-dependent Transport of Phytochelatins Across the Tonoplast of Oat Roots. Plant Physiol 107 : 1293–1301.

Salt, D. E., Blaylock, M., Kumar, P.B.A.N., Dushenkov, V., Ensley, B. D., Chet, L., *et al.*, (1995). Phyto-remediation : A Novel Strategy for the Removal of Toxic Metals from the Environment Using Plants. Biogeochemistry,13,468–474.

Salt, D. E., Blaylock, M., Kumar, P.B.A.N., Dushenkov, V., Ensley, B.D., Chet, L., *et al.*, (1995). Phyto-remediation: A Novel Strategy for the Removal of Toxic Metals from the Environment Using Plants. Biogeochemistry, 13,468–474.

Salt, DE., Smith, RD., & Raskin, I. (1998). Phytoremediation. Annual Review of Plant Physiology and Plant Molecular Biology, 49,643–668.

Samantaray S, Rout GR, Das P (1997) Tolerance of Rice to Nickel in Nutrient Solution. Biologia Planta 40 : 295–298.

Santos, F. S., Hernández-Allica, J., Becerril, J.M., Amaral-Sobrinho, N., Mazur, N., & Garbisu, C.(2006). Chelate-Induced Phytoextraction of Metal Polluted Soils with Brachiaria Decumbens. Chemosphere, 65(1), 43–50.

Schnoor JL (2000) Phytostabilization of Metals Using Hybrid Poplar Trees. In : Raskin I, Ensley BD (eds) Phytoremediation of Toxic Metals - Using Plants to Clean-up the Environment. John Wiley & Sons, Inc., New York. pp. 133-150.

Schnoor, J.L., L.A. Light, S. C. McCutcheon, N. L. Wolfe, and L.H. Car reira. 1995. Phytoremediation of Organic and Nutrient Contaminants. Environ. Sci. Technol. 29(7): 318A-323A.

Schwartz C, Gerard E, Perronnet K, Morel JL (2001) Measurement of in situ Phytoextraction of Zinc by Spontaneous Metallophytes Growing on a Former Smelter Site. Sci Total Environ 279 : 215–221.

Schwartz, C, Echevarria, G, Morel, J L (2003). Phytoex-traction of Cadmium with Thlaspi Caerulescens. Plant Soil, 24, 27-35.

Scoccianti V, Crinelli R, Tirillini B, Mancinelli V, Speranza A (2006) Uptake and toxicity of Cr (Cr^{3+}) in Celery Seedlings. Chemosphere 64 : 1695–1703.

SCOPE (1974) Saharan Duct. Scientiûc Committee on Problems of the Environment. Wiley, New York Seaward MRD, Richardson DHS (1990). Atmospheric Sources of Metal Pollution and Effects on Vegetation. In: Shaw AJ (ed) Heavy Metal Tolerance in Plants Evolutionary Aspects. CRC Press, Boca Raton, 75–94.

Sekhar KC, Kamala CT, Chary NS, Sastry ARK, Rao TN, Vairamani M (2004) Removal of Lead from Aqueous Solutions using An Immobilized Biomaterial Derived from a Plant Biomass. J Hazard Mat 108 : 111–117.

Shallari S, Schwartz C, Hasko A, Morel JL (1998) Heavy Metals in Soils and Plants of Serpentine and Industrial Sites of Albania. Sci Total Environ 19(209) : 133–142.

Shanker AK, Cervantes C, Loza-Tavera H, Avudainayagam S (2005) Chromium Toxicity in Plants. Environment International 31 : 739–753.

Sharma DC, Sharma CP, Tripathi RD (2003) Phytotoxic Lesions of Chromium in Maize. Chemosphere 51 : 63–68.

Sharma P, Dubey RS (2005) Lead Toxicity in Plants. Bra J Plant Physiol 17 : 35–52.

Sharma, NC., Gardea-Torresdey, JL., Parsons, J, Sahi, S V (2004). Chemical Speciation and Cellular Deposition of Lead in Sesbania Drummondii. Environmental Toxicology and Chemistry, 23, 2068–2073.

Sharples JM, Meharg AA, Chambers SM, Cairney JWG (2000) The Symbiotic Solution to Arsenic Contamination. Nature 404 : 951–952.

Shen, C., X. Tang, S. A. Cheema, C. Zhang, M. I. Khan, F. Liang, X. Chen, Y. Zhu, Q. Lin, and Y. Chen (2009) Enhanced Phytore-mediation Potential of Polychlorinated Biphenyl Contaminated Soil from e-waste Recycling Area in the Presence of Randomly methylated-ß-cyclodextrins. J. Hazard. Mater. 172: 1671-1676.

Skeffington RA, Shewry PR, Perterson PJ (1976) Chromium Uptake and Transport in Barley Seedlings (Hordeum vulgare L.). Planta 19 : 807–810.

Smith, R.A.H., & Bradshaw, A.D. (1992). Stabilization of Toxic Mine Wastes by the Use of Toleran Plant Populations. Transactions of the Institution of Mining and Metallurgy, 81, A230–A237.

Stadtman ER, Oliver CN (1991) Metal-catalyzed Oxidation of Proteins. J Biol Chem 266 : 2005–2008.

Stoltz E, Greger M (2002) Accumulation Properties of As, Cd, Cu, Pb and Zn by Four Wetland Plant Species Growing on Submerged Mine Tailings. Environ Exp Bot 47(3) : 271–280.

Sumner ME (2000) Beneficial Use of Effluents, Wastes and Biosolids. Soil Sci Plant Analysis 31(11–14) : 1701–1715.

Suszcynsky, E. M., & Shann, J.R. (1995). Phyto Toxicity and Accumulation of Mercury Subjected to Different Exposure Routes. Environmental Toxicology and Chemistry, 14, 61–67.

Suszcynsky, E.M., & Shann, J.R. (1995). Phytotoxicity and Accumulation Mercury Subjected to Different Exposure Routes. Environmental Toxicology and Chemistry, 14,61–67.

Tandy S, Schulin R, Nowack B (2006) The Influence of EDDS on the Uptake of Heavy Metals in Hydroponically Grown Sunflowers. Chemosphere 62(9) : 1454–1463.

Tandy, S., Schulin, R., Nowack, B. (2006). The Influence of EDD Son the Uptake of Heavy Metal Sinhy Droponically Grown Sun Flowers. Chemosphere, 62(9), 1454–1463. Terry, N., Carlson, C., Raab, T.K., & Zayed, A. (1992). Rates of Selenium Volatilization Among Crop Species. Journal of Environmental Quality, 21, 341–344.

Teamkao, P. Thiravetyan, P. (2010) Phytoremediation of Ethylene Glycol and Its Derivatives by the Burhead Plant (Echin-odorus cordifolius L.): Effect of Molecular Size. Chemosphere 81: 1069-1074.

Terry, N, Carlson, C, Raab, T K , Zayed, A M (1992). Rates of Selenium Volatilization Among Crop Species. J. Environ. Qual. 21: 341-344.

Thangavel P, Subhuram CV (2004) Phytoextraction – Role of Hyper Accumulators in Metal Contaminated Soils. Proc Indian National Sci Acad Part B 70(1) : 109–130.

Thomas F, Malick C, Endreszl EC, Davies KS (1998) Distinct Responses to Copper Stress in the Halophyte, Mesembryan-themum Crystallium. Physiologia Planta 102 : 360–368.

Tian, JL, Zhu, H T, Yang, YA, He, YK (2004). Organic Mercury Tolerance, Absorption and Transformation in Spartina Plants. Zhi Wu Sheng Li Yu Fen Zi Sheng Wu Xue Xue Bao (Journal of Plant Physiology and Molecular Biology), 30, 577–582.

Tordoff GM, Baker AJM, Willis AJ (2000) Current Approaches to the Revegetation and Reclamation of Metalliferous Mine Wastes. Chemosphere 41(1–2) : 219–228.

United Nations Environmental Protection/Global Program of Action (2004) Why the Marine Environment Needs Protection From Heavy Metals, Heavy Metals 2004, UNEP/GPA Coordination Office.

United States Department of Labor (2004) Occupational Safety and Health Administration (OSHA); Safety and Health Topics: Heavy Metals, USDOL Publication, Washington, DC.

USEPA Rep. 832/R-93/003, USEPA, Washington, DC, USA. USEPA. (1996). Report: Recent Developments for In Situ Treatment of Metals Contaminated Soils, U.S. Environmental Protection Agency, Office of Solid Waste and Emergency Response.

Vajpayee P, Tripathi RD, Rai UN, Ali MB, Singh SN (2000) Chromium Accumulation Reduces Chlorophyll Biosynthesis, Nitrate Reductase Activity and Protein Content in *Nympaea alba L. Chemosphere 41 : 1075–1082.*

Van den BK, Vandecasteele C, Geuns JMC (1998) Speciation by Liquid Chromatography-Inductively Coupled Plasma-mass Spectrometry of Arsenic in Mung Bean Seedlings Used as a Bio-indicator for Arsenic Contamination. Anal Chim Acta 361 : 101–111.

Verkleji JAS (1993) The Effects of Heavy Metals Stress on Higher Plants and their Use as Bio Monitors. In: Markert B (eds) Plant as Bioindicators: Indicators of Heavy Metals in the Terrestrial Environment. VCH, New York, pp. 415–424.

Vermette SJ, Bingham VG (1986) Trace Elements in Frobisher Bay Rain Water. Arctic 39:177–179.

Vymazal, J., 2002. The Use of Sub-surface Constructed Wetlands for Wastewater Treatment in the Czech Republic: 10 Years Experience. Ecol. Eng. 18, 633–646.

Warne MS, Heemsbergen D, Stevens D, McLaughlin M, Cozens G, Whatmuff M, Broos K, Barry G, Bell M, Nash D, Pritchard D, Penney N (2008) Modeling the Toxicity of Copper and Zinc Salts to Wheat in 14 Soils. Environ Toxicol Chem 27:786–792.

Wei, SH, Zhou, Q X, Wang, X, Cao, W, Ren, L P , Song, Y F (2004). Potential of Weed Species Applied to Remediation of Soils Contaminated with Heavy Metals. Journal of Environmental Science-China, 16, 868–873.

Williamson A, Johnson MS (1981) Reclamation of Metalliferous Mine Wastes. In Lepp NW (eds) Effect of Heavy Metal Pollution on Plants. Barking, Essex, UK: Applied Science Publishers. vol. 2 pp. 185–212.

Wójcik M, Tukiendorf A (2004) Phytochelatin Synthesis and Cadmium Localization in Wild Type of Arabidopsis Thaliana. Plant Growth Regu 44 : 71–80.

Wu S (1994) Effect of Manganese Excess on the Soybean Plant Cultivated under Various Growth Conditions. J Plant Nutri 17 : 993–1003.

Wu, J, Hsu, FC, Cuningham, SD (1999). Chelateassisted Pb Phytoextraction: Pb Availability, Uptake and Translocation Constraints. Environ. Sci. Technol., 33(11),1898–1904.

Xiong, YH, Yang, XE, Ye, ZQ, He, ZL (2004). Characteristics of Cadmium Uptake and Accumulation by Two Contrasting Ecotypes of Sedum Alfredii Hance. Journal of Environmental Science and Health. Part A, Toxic/Hazardous Substances & Environmental Engineering, 39, 2925–2940.

Yanqun Z, Yuan L, Jianjun C, Haiyan C, Li Q, Schratz C (2005) Hyperaccumulation of Pb, Zn and Cd in Herbaceous Grown on Lead zinc Mining Area in Yunnan, China. Environ Inter 31 : 755–762.

Yoon J, Cao X, Zhou Q, Ma LQ (2006). Accumulation of Pb, Cu, and Zn in Native Plants Growing on a Contaminated Florida site. Sci. Total Environ. 368:456464.

Zaidi J, Ganesh S, Pal Amit (2011) Assessment of Water Quality in River Betwa and Pahuj Around Jhansi City, Uttar Pradesh, India. Intern J Curr Res 33(5) : 27-31.

Zanthopolous N, Antoniou V, Nikolaidis E (1999) Copper, Zinc, Cadmium and Lead in Sheep Geazing in North Greece. Bull Environ Contam Toxicol 62 : 691–699.

Zhang WH, Tyerman SD (1999) Inhibition of Water Channels by HgCl2 in Intact Wheat Root Cells. Plant Physiol 120 : 849–857.

Zhou ZS, Huang SQ, Guo K, Mehta SK, Zhang PC, Yang Z M (2007) Metabolic Adaptations to Mercury-induced Oxidative Stress in Roots of Medicago Sativa L. J Inorg Biochem 101 : 1–9.

Zhu YL, Zayed AM, Quian JH, De Souza M, Terry N (1999) Phytoaccumulation of Trace Elements by Wetland Plants: II. Water Hyacinth. J Environ Qual 28 : 339–344.

Zornoza P, Robles S, Martin N (1999) Alleviation of Nickel Toxicity by Ammonium Supply to Sunflower Plants. Plant Soil 208 : 221–226.

Index